T0259006

GLOBAL HEALTHCARE DISASTERS

Predicting the Unpredictable with Emerging Technologies

GLOBAL HEALTHCARE DISASTERS

Predicting the Unpredictable with Emerging Technologies

Edited by
Adarsh Garg, PhD
D. P. Goyal, PhD

First edition published 2023

Apple Academic Press Inc.
1265 Goldenrod Circle, NE,
Palm Bay, FL 32905 USA

4164 Lakeshore Road, Burlington,
ON, L7L 1A4 Canada

CRC Press
6000 Broken Sound Parkway NW,
Suite 300, Boca Raton, FL 33487-2742 USA

2 Park Square, Milton Park,
Abingdon, Oxon, OX14 4RN UK

© 2023 by Apple Academic Press, Inc.

Apple Academic Press exclusively co-publishes with CRC Press, an imprint of Taylor & Francis Group, LLC

Reasonable efforts have been made to publish reliable data and information, but the authors, editors, and publisher cannot assume responsibility for the validity of all materials or the consequences of their use. The authors, editors, and publishers have attempted to trace the copyright holders of all material reproduced in this publication and apologize to copyright holders if permission to publish in this form has not been obtained. If any copyright material has not been acknowledged, please write and let us know so we may rectify in any future reprint.

Except as permitted under U.S. Copyright Law, no part of this book may be reprinted, reproduced, transmitted, or utilized in any form by any electronic, mechanical, or other means, now known or hereafter invented, including photocopying, microfilming, and recording, or in any information storage or retrieval system, without written permission from the publishers.

For permission to photocopy or use material electronically from this work, access www.copyright.com or contact the Copyright Clearance Center, Inc. (CCC), 222 Rosewood Drive, Danvers, MA 01923, 978-750-8400. For works that are not available on CCC please contact mpkbookspermissions@tandf.co.uk

Trademark notice: Product or corporate names may be trademarks or registered trademarks and are used only for identification and explanation without intent to infringe.

Library and Archives Canada Cataloguing in Publication

Title: Global healthcare disasters : predicting the unpredictable with emerging technologies / edited by Adarsh Garg, PhD, D.P. Goyal, PhD.
Names: Garg, Adarsh, editor. | Goyal, D. P., editor.
Description: First edition. | Includes bibliographical references and index.
Identifiers: Canadiana (print) 20220162980 | Canadiana (ebook) 2022016312X | ISBN 9781774910047 (hardcover) | ISBN 9781774910054 (softcover) | ISBN 9781003282020 (ebook)
Subjects: LCSH: Epidemiology—Forecasting—Data processing—Technological innovations. | LCSH: Emergency management—Data processing—Technological innovations. | LCSH: Health services administration—Data processing—Technological innovations.
Classification: LCC RA652.2.D38 G56 2022 | DDC 614.40285—dc23

Library of Congress Cataloging-in-Publication Data

Names: Garg, Adarsh, editor. | Goyal, D. P., editor.
Title: Global healthcare disasters : predicting the unpredictable with emerging technologies / edited by Adarsh Garg, D. P. Goyal.
Description: First edition. | Palm Bay, FL : Apple Academic Press, 2022. | Includes bibliographical references and index. | Summary: "The recent COVID-19 global pandemic exemplifies the need for efficient, reliable, and real-time tools and technology for forecasting and predicting healthcare disasters as well as for helping to restrict subsequent spread and fatality of deadly diseases. This new book discusses many of the innovative and state-of-the-art tools and technology that can help meet the challenges of predicting such disasters. The chapters offer a plethora of useful information for designing healthcare disaster management systems that can be dynamically configurable with implementation of today's modern technology, such as cloud computing, artificial intelligence, IoT, data analytics, and machine learning. These can increase effectiveness in remote sensing technologies, data analytics, data storage, communication networks, geographic information system (GIS), and global positioning System (GPS), to name a few. The book discusses mathematical models using graph-based approaches for analyzing dynamic, heterogeneous, and unstructured data for applications in epidemiology. The authors also address the use of mobile applications for communication efforts and remote monitoring for gauging health and the effectiveness of preventive healthcare measures. The chapters discuss influencing factors that directly or indirectly target public health infrastructure that can lead to or exacerbate global health crises, such as extreme climate changes, refugee health crises, terrorism and cyberterrorism, and technology-related incidents. The book further looks at efficient methods to analyze disasters and how to deliver healthcare in areas of conflict and crisis. This important volume, Global Healthcare Disasters: Predicting the Unpredictable with Emerging Technologies, provides a bounty of useful information for health professionals, academicians, researchers, governmental agencies, and policymakers across the world to predict, mitigate, and manage global health disaster with emerging technologies"-- Provided by publisher.
Identifiers: LCCN 2022004846 (print) | LCCN 2022004847 (ebook) | ISBN 9781774910047 (hardback) | ISBN 9781774910054 (paperback) | ISBN 9781003282020 (ebook)
Subjects: MESH: Medical Informatics | Disease Outbreaks | COVID-19 | Disasters | Models, Theoretical | Forecasting
Classification: LCC R859 (print) | LCC R859 (ebook) | NLM WA 105 | DDC 362.10285--dc23/eng/20220307
LC record available at https://lccn.loc.gov/2022004846
LC ebook record available at https://lccn.loc.gov/2022004847

ISBN: 978-1-77491-004-7 (hbk)
ISBN: 978-1-77491-005-4 (pbk)
ISBN: 978-1-00328-202-0 (ebk)

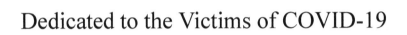

Dedicated to the Victims of COVID-19

—Editors

About the Editors

Adarsh Garg, PhD

Adarsh Garg, PhD, is currently Professor (IT and Analytics), GL Bajaj Institute of Management and Research, Greater Noida, India. She was formerly Professor at Galgotias University, Gautam Buddh Nagar, Greater Noida, India, and Visiting Professor at Delhi Technical University, Delhi, India. Prior to joining Galgotias University, she worked with organizations including WIPRO Tech, GE, IMT Ghaziabad, Punjabi University, and Patiala. She is currently supervising several PhD candidates. Dr. Garg has published over 50 research papers in refereed international/national journals and conference proceedings. She is a member of various professional bodies, including the Computer Society of India and the ACM-Computer Science Teachers' Association. She has 20 years of teaching, corporate, and research within the areas of her interest, which include business analytics, data mining, business intelligence, MIS, e-learning, and project management.

D. P. Goyal, PhD

D. P. Goyal, PhD, Director and Professor at the Indian Institute of Management, Shillong, India, and is also a Visiting Professor at Aarhus University, Denmark. Prior to joining IIM Shillong, he was Professor at MDI¸ Gurgaon, India.. He has more than 32 years of corporate, teaching, and research experience to his credit. His teaching and research interest areas include IS value, IS strategy, MIS, e-government, and business process management. He has published over 100 research papers in refereed international/national journals and conference proceedings. He is a member of various professional bodies and is associated with many business schools and universities in the capacity of member of board of governors, academic council, board of studies, academic advisory board, etc. He has been a consultant to the government of India for various assignments. He has authored almost 20 books, including textbooks on management information systems, IT project management, and enterprise resource planning.

Contents

Contributors

M. Bhuvana
ICSSR Post-Doctoral Research Scholar, School of Management Studies, Vels Institute of Science, Technology & Advanced Studies (VISTAS), Chennai, India

Adarsh Garg
GL Bajaj Institute of Management and Research, Greater Noida, India

Kapil Mohan Garg
Research Scholar, Galgotias University, Greater Noida, India

D. P. Goyal
Indian Institute of Management, Shillong, India

Sanjeev Kr. Jain
AVP, Data Science, 50 Hertz Ltd, New Delhi, India

Shahnawz Khan
Department of Information Technology, University College of Bahrain, Bahrain

Ruqaiya Khanam
Department of Computer Science and Engineering, Sharda University, India

Anthony Maina
School of Computer Science and IT, Dedan Kimathi University of Technology, Nyeri, Kenya

Akanksha Sehgal
Lotus Petal Foundation, Gurgaon

Sarika Sharma
Symbiosis Institute of Computer Studies and Research, Symbiosis International (Deemed) University, Pune, India

Deepika Sherawat
School of Computing Science and Engineering, Galgotias University, Greater Noida, Uttar Pradesh, India

Priyanka Shukla
School of Computing Science and Engineering, Galgotias University, Greater Noida, Uttar Pradesh, India

Archana Singh
Associate Professor, Faculty of Commerce & Management, Vishwakarma University, Pune, India

Sushmita Singh
Department of Computer Engineering, J.C. BOSE University of Science and Technology, YMCA, Faridabad, Haryana, India

Upasana Singh
School of Management, IT, and Governance, University of KwaZulu-Natal, Durban, South Africa

Sandeep Sinha
Head Healthcare Consulting, JLL MENA, Dubai, UAE

Manvi Siwach
Department of Computer Engineering, J.C. BOSE University of Science and Technology, YMCA, Faridabad, Haryana, India

Raju Shanmugam
USCI, Karnavati University, Gandhinagar, India

Sonia
School of Computing Science and Engineering, Galgotias University, Greater Noida, Uttar Pradesh, India

N. Thillaiarasu
School of Computing & Information Technology, Reva University, Bengaluru, India

K. Thirunavukkarasu
USCI, Karnavati University, Gandhinagar, India

S. Vasantha
Professor, School of Management Studies, Vels Institute of Science, Technology & Advanced Studies (VISTAS), Chennai, India

Abbreviations

ACF	autocorrelation function
ANFIS	adaptive neuro-fuzzy inference system
API	application programming interface
ARDS	acute respiratory distress syndrome
ARMA	auto-regression moving average
ARIMA	autoregression integrated moving average
ASV	average shared variance
AU	actual use
AVE	average variance explained
CAC	cumulative active cases
CDC	Centre for Disease Control
CFA	confirmatory factor analysis
CFI	comparative fit index
COVID-19	coronavirus disease 2019
CSI	channel state information
CR	construct reliability
DR	disaster
ECMO	extracorporeal membrane oxygenation
EM	emergency management
FAA	Federal Aviation Administration
FANGBM	fractional nonlinear grey Bernoulli model
FFT	fast Fourier transformation
FM	fire management
FPA	flower pollination algorithm
GDP	gross domestic product
GIS	geographical information systems
GM	Grey Model
GPS	global positioning systems
GROOMS	group of optimized and multisource selection
HIS	healthcare information systems
HFNC	high-flow nasal cannula
HMIS	health management information systems

IAMAI	Mobile Association of India
ICU	intensive care unit
ICMR	Indian Council of Medical Research
ICT	information and communication technology
ILI	influenza-like illness
IoT	internet of things
IUMA	intention to use mobile application
LDA	linear discriminant analysis
LR	linear regression
MLP	multilayer perceptron
MSV	maximum shared variance
MRE	minimum relative entropy
NGBM	nonlinear Grey Bernoulli model
NHC	National Hurricane Centre
NIC	National Informatics Centre
NIV	noninvasive ventilation
NOM	Novel Optimization Method
PACF	partial autocorrelation function
PCA	principal component analysis
PEoU	perceived ease of Use
PHEP	public health emergency preparedness
PPE	personal protective equipment
PU	perceived usefulness
RC	respiration curve
RD	respiratory distress
RF	respiratory functions
RF	random forest
RMSEA	Root Mean Square Error of Approximation
RNN	recurrent neural network
RoR	rate of respiration
RS	respiratory system
RSSI	radio signal strength indicator
SEIR	susceptible, exposed, infected, recovered
SEM	structural equation modeling
SIDR	Susceptible Infectious-Recovered-Dead
SQL	Structured Query Language
SSA	salp swarm algorithm

TAM	technology acceptance model
TLI	Tucker–Lewis index
VAR	vector autoregression
WHE	WHO's Health Emergencies Programme
WHO	World Health Organization

Acknowledgments

It is our pleasure to express with deep sense of gratitude to Apple Academic Press for providing us the opportunity to work on the project of editing this book, *Global Healthcare Disaster: Predicting the Unpredictable with Emerging Technologies.* We would like to express our sense of gratification and contentment to complete this project. We express our gratitude from the bottom of our heart to all those who facilitated us in both straight and unintended ways to accomplish the task. First of all, we would like to thank the authors who have contributed to this book. We acknowledge, with sincere appreciation, the benevolence of various authors at their respective institutions to carry out this research work. We take this exclusive opportunity to express our sincere appreciation to Sandra Jones Sickels, VP, Editorial and Marketing, Apple Academic Press Inc., for her sincere suggestions and kind patience during this project. We would like to thank our friends and faculty colleagues for the time they spared in helping us through the project. Special mention should be made of the timely help given by various reviewers during this project, those whose names cannot be mentioned here. The valuable suggestions they provided to the authors cannot be left unnoticed. We are enormously thankful to the reviewers for their backing during the process of evaluation. While writing, contributors have referenced several books and journals; we take this opportunity to thank all those authors and publishers. We thank the production team of Apple Academic Press Inc. for encouraging and extending their full cooperation to complete this book. Last but not least we are thankful the Almighty to show us the direction.

—*Editors*

Preface

Global health disasters are the merging of threats that strikes whole communities that are unable to survive the hostile impacts, especially when such disasters are unforeseeable. Having said this, this does not comply that it is completely possible to avoid such disasters, but efforts can be made to minimize their disastrous impact to the larger and global extent. The emerging technologies give a ray of hope to get real-time reflection on health disasters so as to generate timely cautionary signals. Remote sensing technologies, data analytics capabilities, communication networks, cloud computing, GIS, and GPS are a few emerging/emerged technologies that are covered here.

Healthcare disaster is one of the recent and significant topics of research. Considering the uncertain behavior of healthcare disasters, it is essential to design a new healthcare disaster management system that can be dynamically configurable with implementation in cloud computing, which helps to continue the saving and reformation activities of healthcare disaster situation.

IoT and sensing technology provide real-time monitoring and risk assessment of the probable onset of a healthcare disaster. With the real-time sensing of existing communicable diseases, we can predict new microorganisms that can have a disastrous impact on health and global spread by processing and analyzing of the gathered data. Reliable communication networks are vital to quickly detect emergency situations so as to mitigate and manage the healthcare disaster.

As the amount of data is quite gigantic and significant in healthcare, data storage has become an important concern in remote sensor networks, as a large amount of collected data needs to be archived for future information retrieval. If remote sensing is to be used to support early prediction of healthcare disasters, then it is equally important to store the data coming from sensors in distributed cloud computing for efficient quantitative analysis and help in forecasting.

This book on healthcare disaster is organized as follows:

Chapter 1 throws light on the use of knowledge graphs as a data analytics tool that can be used to handle a connection-rich type of dataset.

It is an arrangement of entities in the form of a network where these entities are linked to each other, making it an efficient choice for the representation and analysis of linked data of medical healthcare and epidemic outbreak data that is heavily interconnected and unstructured type of dataset. This chapter provides the benefits that can be derived from a graph-based approach for analyzing dynamic, heterogeneous, and unstructured data and its applications in epidemiology.

Chapter 2 describes the surge of the recent COVID-19 pandemic across India and its prevention, showing there is a strong need for forecasting the number of possible cases, which is vital to restricting subsequent spread and fatality. It focuses on the development of a methodology for forecasting the number of possible cases so that future healthcare requirements can be generated at the state level for the development of a better healthcare system using autoregressive Moving Average Models for each state in India based on daily frequency.

Chapter 3 emphasizes the need to develop AI-based models to enhance critical care of COVID-19 patients. It highlights the opportunities gained through the use of AI methods for diagnosis and prognosis. A three-staged model is used for detection and diagnosis of infectious disease. The model uses the heterogeneous data as input for processing using artificial intelligence.

Chapter 4 discusses various factors that directly or indirectly target public health infrastructure and leads to a global crisis, like extreme climate changes, refugee health crises, terrorism, and technology-related incidents. It analyzes various challenges during disasters that are related to the healthcare system and portrays how to deliver healthcare in areas of conflict and crisis

Chapter 5 talks about different IoT devices, data analytics, and machine learning algorithms that are used to predict disasters, which, in turn, affect the health of a population. Discussed are the tools that can give vision to the symptoms and can enable remote care of patients and equipment for real-time tracking of equipment, like wheelchairs, oxygen tanks, etc.

Chapter 6 proposes a hypothesized conceptual model based on a widely adopted technology acceptance model (TAM). The proposed model is then tested empirically by collecting data through a self-designed survey instrument. The data analysis is carried out using structural equation modeling (SEM).

Chapter 7 walks around the probability of monitoring the respiratory system (RS) of the patients (also non-patients) from inside as well as outside of homes to report to healthcare providers for quick action. A framework, CoReS, is proposed as a life-saving technology to monitor and manage the RS of patients to detect any sign of potential complication. This technology will support patient satisfaction and decrease the mortality rate in health disaster. The work given in the book will give some interesting insight to readers.

Chapter 8 accentuates on how IoT health and big data technologies are transforming healthcare. A much-needed exploration of the value of massive biomedical data sets, and novel technologies' capacity is carried out to improve individual and public health outcomes and drive health policy. By uncovering the policy landscape, the work provides a framework to understand and address the IoT-health and big data integration concerns in health systems. Moreover, it assimilates the often disjointed and isolated accounts of policy narratives

Chapter 9 is more oriented towards the impact of pandemic in rural areas, which covers 70 percent of total population in developing countries, such as India. The chapter is an endeavour to address the current situation of the pandemic infection of COVID-19 that impacts rural areas in India. The authors have developed a model called "Hierarchy of COVID-19 Disaster Healthcare Management System," based on the National Emergency Management System, to fight against coronavirus in rural areas.

Chapter 10 imbibes the role of sentiment analysis with the introduction of what it means and how it can help in health disaster outbreaks through the contribution of information in social media by general public worldwide. Various authors from different parts of the world have contributed toward the study on sentiment analysis used for social media comments through Facebook, Twitter, Pinterest, etc. during COVID-19. Two cases from India and UAE have been presented to provide better insight on the usage of sentiment analysis for sustainable healthcare.

Chapter 11 comes up with the belief model that can trigger the modelling of confidential and safe frameworks that are reliant on the belief-based cloud service providers for accomplishing executable modules within the framework. It pays attention to constructing enormous aggregated confidential and privacy offering framework with trouble-free access to the users.

CHAPTER 1

Role of Knowledge Graphs in Analyzing Epidemics and Health Disasters

SUSHMITA SINGH* and MANVI SIWACH

Department of Computer Engineering, J.C. BOSE University of Science and Technology, YMCA, Faridabad, Haryana, India

Corresponding author. E-mail: sushmi278@gmail.com

ABSTRACT

Medical healthcare and epidemic outbreak data are heavily interconnected and unstructured type of dataset. It is very difficult to represent and manage the large number of relationships between data items using traditional database management systems. Therefore, it is required to find a new framework to handle these datasets. A knowledge graph is a data analytics tool which can be used to handle a connection-rich type of dataset. It is an arrangement of entities (real-world objects or concepts) in the form of a network where these entities are linked to each other; therefore, knowledge graph is an efficient choice for the representation and analysis of linked data. This chapter provides the benefits that can be derived from a graph-based approach for analyzing dynamic, heterogeneous, and unstructured data applications in epidemiology.

1.1 INTRODUCTION

The term "health disasters" can be divided into two basic words "health" which means related to medical conditions of a human being and "disaster" which means a sudden event/happening that results in loss of life. Health disaster can be an outcome of multiple factors like—infectious or communicable disease that might lead to an epidemic outbreak; changes in climatic conditions due to increasing pollution; scarcity of one or more basic amenities like water, food, health facilities; natural or man-made disasters, etc.

Generally, the idea of incorporating data science in handling health disasters arises by the fact that the amount of health data in the form of medical records of hospitals, clinics, or emergency camps is huge and highly corelated. By analyzing this data at right time and in right manner, better decision strategies can be made. The first step in the processing of data is data acquisition and its representation, knowledge graph is a way to represent and analyze data. Therefore, knowledge graph can help in improving the efficiency and preciseness of decision-making systems. The main focus of this chapter is outbreak of an infectious disease and how a knowledge graph can help in anticipating the risk associated with the epidemic and also coping up with after effects of the disease's spread in order to take risk-management and disease-spread-controlling decisions. Therefore, before moving forward, firstly the terminologies and concepts related to this field are introduced in the rest of this section.

Disease is a condition of a living being in which the body behaves abnormally either structurally or functionally. There are four broad categories of diseases—infectious diseases, deficiency diseases, hereditary diseases, and physiological diseases. Infectious diseases are characterized by their contagious nature which means that the disease-causing agent can transfer from a suffering body to another body through a medium and can contaminate that body. When a disease starts spreading at large level rapidly it turns into an epidemic and if the disease transmission stretches at global level then it is known as pandemic.

Epidemiology is a branch of medical science that deals with the study of infectious diseases, epidemics, their outbreaks, and the aftermath. It comprises of four key aspects—frequency of disease, factor identification, risk analysis, and data modeling. It studies the existing health distribution, determinants of source of the infection, and the dynamics of health in human population.

The data associated with epidemics and outbreaks is called Epidemiological Data. It includes population census data, disease registries, patient data, birth rate, death rate, etc. is a heavily connected type of dataset, and normal relational database does not suffice and analyze the same using basic tools is also not possible and inefficient. To handle this highly unstructured and dynamic data, more efficient data analytics tools are required that deal with the logical analysis of raw data.

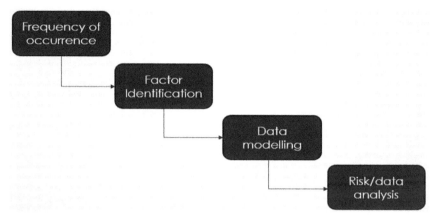

FIGURE 1.1   Key phases of epidemiology.

A knowledge graph is one of the best options to manage such kind of huge data which tends to be rich in links and connections. To process a knowledge graph, there exists a subdomain of data analytics called graph analytics.

The rest of the chapter is organized in the following manner: first it will give a brief idea of graph analytics and knowledge graphs alongside graph databases. Next in line, various use case applications of knowledge graphs in studying and analyzing health data are explored. Then the next sections give the idea of two important applications of knowledge graph in epidemic analytics. And finally, the future of knowledge graph and graph analytics in healthcare disasters and management is discussed.

1.2   GRAPH ANALYTICS

Graph analytics is an emerging form of data analytics that represents and analyses data in the form of graphs.

The data are stored in the form of entities, relationship between the entities, and the attributes of entities as well as relations; therefore, sometimes it is also called network analysis. These graphs that are used here in graph analytics for storing, analyzing, and visualizing data are called knowledge graphs. A knowledge graph is a network of entities with some attributes and the relationships between them. For example, Figure 1.2 represents diseases and their symptoms and pathogens.

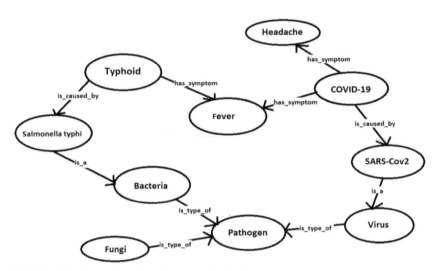

FIGURE 1.2 Example of knowledge graph for diseases, symptoms, and pathogens.

The use-case domain of graph analytics includes areas like disease and medical science, bioinformatics, social networking, fraud detection, route optimization, grid network failure detection, and many more. Now, the question is exactly how graphs are analyzed. To analyze and process a knowledge graph, there exist five approaches of graph analysis. Based on the need of the problem, either of these approaches is applied on the knowledge graph or sometimes they can be merged together.

Graph analytics comprises of following analyzing tasks:

- Community detection
- Centrality/importance
- Pathfinding and search
- Heuristic link prediction
- Node classification

1.2.1 COMMUNITY DETECTION

In a knowledge graph, multiple entities are connected with each other and the density of these connections is not even throughout the knowledge graph. Some areas in knowledge graph contain scattered entities which are loosely connected with each other while there exist some parts of knowledge graph which are densely populated and the entities in these areas are closely knit together. These opaquely-dense spots in a knowledge graph are called communities.

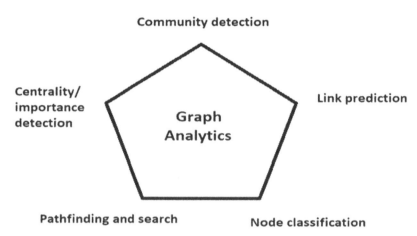

FIGURE 1.3   Approaches of graph analytics.

Community detection refers to the process of identifying community structures in a knowledge graph. A community structure is a set of densely interconnected nodes. It appears like a cluster of nodes. And these communities are very common in real-time graphs like social networks, biological knowledge graphs, business networking graphs, etc. The motive behind community detection is to analyze dense and heavy data and to derive useful information out of it. Community detection can be used for creating recommendation system, market analysis, detecting behavioral pattern, analyzing responses and opinions, and many other purposes. In outbreak analysis, community detection can be used to identify vulnerable groups and can even be used to determine the probability of community transmission (third stage of epidemic spread in which a whole community gets infected).

1.2.2   *CENTRALITY/IMPORTANCE*

Centrality detection is a process of identifying the supernodes (the nodes which are linked with billions of other nodes) or the center nodes of a community/cluster in a knowledge graph.

Centrality is defined as the aspect of being in center of something. Centrality detection is different from community detection; however, it can follow community detection. Community detection means to identify the clusters or groups. But, centrality/importance detection refers to the determination of important individual nodes in the graph. For example, in social media network analysis identifying the social influencers, detection of the origin of a viral video, or in epidemic outbreak analytics finding the source of disease spread, etc. There exist different measures for centrality detection like degree, closeness, betweenness, and many more. For example, degree of a node can tell how important it is in a knowledge graph like supernodes are identified based on their degree (no. of links connected). Some centrality detection approaches also require community detection as a prerequisite.

1.2.3   PATHFINDING AND SEARCH

A knowledge graph comprises of nodes and their connecting links. Searching in a knowledge graph generally resolves the queries that either requires a particular node or a link that connects two nodes. Pathfinding and searching are important tasks in graph theory. It is a process of determining sequential chain of links that form a path from one node to another node. Suppose in disease prediction, there is node representing a patient infected by a contagious disease the people he/she has met in near past can be tracked searching or tracking the nodes linked to the patient by the link name say, met or visited. Pathfinding means to find the optimal paths and evaluate route availability. Pathfinding and search can be used in different scenarios, for example, finding routes with minimum time in geographical maps, backtracking a data packet in networking, fraud detection, etc. In epidemiology, pathfinding can be used in tracing back the source of infection and sometimes tracing the forward links to identify the susceptible patients.

1.2.4   HEURISTIC LINK PREDICTION

The real-time graphs are dynamic in nature; the status of nodes and links is very likely to change; therefore, there arises a need to estimate the likelihood of nodes forming a new relationship. It means to check if there exists some probability of a node connecting with a new node or disconnecting with the previous one. The process of prediction of links involves forecasting the creation of probable links in future among some nodes that do not exist in the present time. This process generally requires heuristic intelligence. For example, in recommender system predicting what a purchaser may like or dislike, in social networking certainty of connecting with new people. In outbreak analysis, calculating vulnerability for an infectious disease in disease prediction systems, etc. In outbreak analytics, link prediction may serve as the core process for analyzing the risk associated with the disease spread, for example, the link of a person(node1) with the disease(node2) getting developed can be predicted based on the places node1 has visited or the people node1 has met.

1.2.5 NODE CLASSIFICATION

Classification generally means to divide the dataset into classes and label them. Node classification in knowledge graph means to classify the nodes into predefined classes. Classification is allocation of nodes into labeled classes; it means to classify new nodes into already existing clusters based on some criterion like common interest, similar behavior, similar types of links, etc. It means to label the nodes that are not already labeled based on the different nodes and their attributes, they are connected to. For example, in a social networking site classifying account profiles based on their opinion in public domain. In disease prediction, identifying disease on the basis of symptoms of the patient and in epidemiology classifying the patients as infected, vulnerable, and safe.

Graph analytics is a domain that requires knowledge graph as the foundation on which different techniques are applied to get some result. Hence, next section focuses on what is meant by the term "knowledge graph" and other information related to it.

1.3 KNOWLEDGE GRAPH

The discrete form of "data" is the input, when this discrete data is processed it gets converted into the "information". Now, furthermore this information goes through classification, summarization and attributes, properties are assigned to get "knowledge". When this knowledge is used to make decisions that are beyond the limits of the provided information and is based upon the inferences then it becomes "wisdom". Data graph is used to answer "when/where/who", information graph is used to answer "what", knowledge graph is used to answer "how," and wisdom graph is used to answer "why".

It is a computer understandable structure which is generally used to describe real-world scenarios in terms of simple entities and their connections with the other entities, in other words, how the physical world is connected with each other.

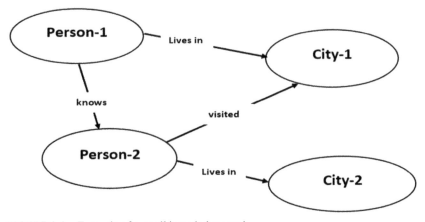

FIGURE 1.4   Example of a small knowledge graph.

The data are stored in the form of entities (real-world objects, concepts, processes), relationships between the entities, and the attributes of entities as well as relations. Figure 1.4 shows a small example of knowledge graph in which vertices of the graphs are used to represent entities and edges are used to represent the relation. Figure 1.4 represents following statements:

Statement 1: Person-1 lives in city-1.
Statement 2: Person-2 lives in city-2.
Statement 3: Person-2 visited city-1.

Now from the above information, the knowledge that can be derived, for example, there can be a possibility of person-2 visiting person-1. This is termed as knowledge graph processing, that is, to derive knowledge from the give information by analyzing the graph. Ehrlinger et al. defined knowledge graph as an RDF graph and precisely gives the following definition for the knowledge graph—"A knowledge graph acquires and integrates information into an ontology and applies a reasoner to derive new knowledge." So, one can say that a knowledge graph is a simple knowledge base, that is, ontology integrated with a reasoning engine.

To store the knowledge graph, there arises a requirement of a database that is efficient and more compatible with the graph data hence comes the concept of graph database. Knowledge graph is a representation of knowledge to which graph database serves as a backend for the knowledge graph. The relation between knowledge graph and graph analytics can be visualized as two layers, knowledge graph being the abstract top layer with graph database as bottom layer providing the physical storage.

1.4 GRAPH DATABASES

A graph database is a type of NoSQL database (a NoSQL database does not store data in the form of tables as in traditional relational databases). It stores data in the form of nodes and edges, nodes store the data items and edges store the relationships between these nodes. It preserves the structure of a connected or interlinked dataset in the form of entities, their properties, and the relationship among them. Graph database is recommended for a connection-based dataset, when one requires to track the links between the data items.

1.4.1 GRAPH MODELS

Graph databases use two types of graph models:

a) **Resource Description Framework (RDF) graph.**
   In an RDF graph, the data are stored in the form of the triples, that is, subject, object, and predicate. The subject and the object are represented using the nodes and predicate is represented using edge that connects the subject and the object. These elements (subject, object, and the predicate) are Uniform Resource Identifiers (URIs). There is no internal structure of vertices and edges.

b) **Label property graph**
   In a labeled property graph, nodes have a unique ID and a set of key-value pairs that characterize them. Similarly, edges or connections between nodes also have a unique ID and they also have a type and a

set of key-value pairs or properties that characterize the connections. Nodes and edges have their own internal structure.

1.4.2   GRAPH STORAGE STRUCTURE

Now, the graph database is divided into two categories on the basis of their storage structure:

a) **Native graph databases**
   Native graph databases are the databases that have underlying storage structure that is designed for processing of graph specifically. Graph data is kept in storage files which contain data for a specific part of the graph such as nodes, relationships, labels, and properties. For example, Neo4j.

b) **Non-native graph databases**
   In non-native graph database, the storage is not dedicatedly constructed for graph data but it is taken from other type of databases like relational database or other NoSQL databases. It requires an additional layer of mapping interface between the internal database storage and the knowledge graph representation.

1.5   USE CASE APPLICATIONS OF KNOWLEDGE GRAPH IN HEALTHCARE DATA

Healthcare industry offers to be a large application area for graph analytics. Healthcare industry comprises of medical institutions and organizations that include hospitals, pharmaceuticals, medical educational institutes, medical research institutes, clinics, etc.; medical tools and diagnostic devices; medicine industry. Knowledge graph can be used in multiple subdomains of healthcare to represent and process data. Therefore, this section discusses different possible use case applications of knowledge graphs in healthcare management.

1.5.1   DISEASE PREDICTION

Disease prediction is one of the major branches of the healthcare industry. Disease prediction systems aim to forecast probable disease and can even suggest precautions and cures that exist. A human doctor diagnoses several diseases based upon multiple sources of knowledge and general machine learning algorithms take into focus only the clinical data. Therefore, papers like Liu et al. suggest that multiple factors should be taken under consideration for the purpose of enhancing the precision, like medical history of the patient, rule book of the diseases, clinical health records of varied patients, experience of the experts, etc. disease prediction basically consists of three steps—collecting the data, data processing, and decision-making.

Knowledge graph can play an important role in handling healthcare data as healthcare data tends to be highly interconnected and complex. Disease prediction basically consists of three steps—collecting the data, data processing, and decision-making. The use of knowledge graph, therefore, comes in the first two steps, that is, data collection & representation and data processing. The data required to diagnose and predict a disease includes medical history of patient, clinical data, disease data, and expert advice. Generally, the knowledge graphs created for this purpose are:

a) Knowledge graph for diseases and symptoms (KG1),
b) Knowledge graph of health records from hospitals (KG2),
c) Knowledge graph for causes, diseases and cures (KG3),
d) Knowledge graph for medicine (KG4).

Decision-making in disease prediction is complicated as the outcomes of the cure may vary from person to person; therefore, it is hard to attain the accuracy. Integrating reasoning approach with graph analytics may provide efficient results. Hence, it is important to identify a suitable reasoning technique to make decisions that take the abovementioned criteria into their account and provide a precise output. The process of decision-making in disease prediction can be categorized under the task of node classification. It is a three-phase step, first phase consists of matching the symptoms of the patient with existing symptoms from the processed knowledge graphs, second phase is applying reasoning techniques on existing nodes and links, and third phase classifies the new node as part of one of the predefined clusters (i.e., predicts the disease of the patient node). For example, suppose there are four abovementioned knowledge graphs, now let's say a new patient arrives to the hospital with some symptoms (KG-2 gets updated); next the symptoms are matched with diseases form KG-1 and the patient is associated with that disease and based on reasoning technique cure and relevant medicines of that disease from KG-3 and KG-4 are mapped.

1.5.2   PREDICTION OF COMORBID DISEASES

Multi-morbidity is defined as the coexistence of more than one disease (chronic or acute) in a single human being. When more than one disease exists together in same human being then they are called comorbid diseases. Comorbidity increases the chances of failure of the treatment for single diseases and hence may lead to severe conditions of the patient. Generally, the knowledge graphs created for this purpose are:

- Knowledge graph of genes and phenotypes,
- Knowledge graph of diseases,
- Knowledge graph of cures and medicines.

Various researchers are working on comorbidities and their prediction. He et al. use multiscale data to predict the existing comorbidities in a patient; Biswas et al. create a knowledge graph using three ontologies about genes, humans, and diseases and then apply knowledge graph completion to predict multimorbidity. It is a process to identify the missing data and then to predict the missing parts. Other factors can be involved like gene-gene interaction, genetic mutations, etc.

1.5.3   EPIDEMIC AND OUTBREAK ANALYTICS

Epidemic and outbreak analytics is an emerging field of data analytics that is concerned with the collection and analysis of the data related to the epidemic outbreaks. Epidemic and outbreak analytics is an intersection of heterogeneous fields namely public health planning, epidemiology, methodological development, and information technology. Different measures are used to analyze the intensity of outbreak like number of susceptible humans, number of infected humans, number of recovered humans, transmissibility rate, disease growth rate, population size, sample size, etc.

In order to analyze the data and extract knowledge and insights for research and analyzing purpose, it is required to know and classify epidemic outbreak-related data.

Polonsky et al. coin a term for this epidemic outbreak related data called Outbreak data which can be classified into three subdivisions:

- Case data: This includes the case files of reported patients and is required to analyze the medical history as well as current details of patient.

- Background data: This includes the demographics of the population and epidemiological data and is required to find out the spreading pattern of disease, the control measures to analyze the data related to particular disease like its epicenter, its increase rate.
- Intervention data: This includes the data related to actions taken to control the outbreak and is necessary to predict the growth and to analyze the risk associated with the intervening actions.

Additionally,

- Clinical data so that previous data can be integrated with current experiences of doctors and the medical rule book to identify the severity of disease (fatal or nonfatal) and also other factors involved with disease fatality.
- Social data to analyze the social structure of the affected population.

Few systems have been proposed to study and analyze the spread of infectious diseases which use relational database instead of a graph database for storage and a knowledge graph for representation. Like a regression model is developed which uses twitter data and Influenza-like illness (ILI) data generated by Centre for Disease Control (CDC) to predict the spread of influenza and similarly in another paper matrix decomposition method is used to predict the seasonal spread of an infectious disease. But the outbreak data combined with clinical and social data is so dynamic and heterogeneous that it is needed to develop systems that can predict and analyze more efficiently.

However, in 2005, a paper came with the idea of combining graph (network) theory with epidemic model. Recently a US-based research came for analyzing epidemic data which depicts how a knowledge graph is employed in analyzing the growth pattern of opioid epidemic in the United States.

1.6 INFECTIOUS DISEASE TRANSMISSION DETECTION AND PREDICTION

A knowledge graph can be used to represent the distribution of the disease over the population and hence this approach can be used to identify the growth rate, transmission pattern, and can trace the links to identify the susceptible and affected people which is not possible if data are stored in linear tables. Growth rate of an infectious disease tells how fast the number of patients is increasing. Similarly, transmission pattern describes the way of disease spread.

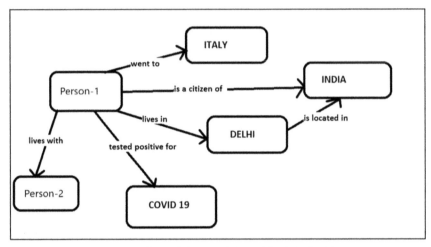

FIGURE 1.5   An example of knowledge graph for epidemiological data.

Infectious disease transmission detection and prediction requires:

- Knowledge graph of social networking
- Knowledge graph of diseases and symptoms

The main task is to predict the vulnerability of a person of getting infected. The outbreak controlling measures sometimes involve back-tracking of the contact list of the infected patient, that is, contact tracing. These contact-tracing applications either rely on Bluetooth or GPS to collect the information regarding the disease spread and create a database. This phase of data storage can be improvised by maintaining a knowledge graph of the collected data so that the network of infected and vulnerable people can be explored and analyzed efficiently. For example, Blue Trace—a Singapore government application for epidemic spread tracing involves an interview with the patient to get the information of patient's visitors and contacts he/she had in near past. The knowledge graph can help in logically retrieving the implicit knowledge and hence this can fasten and ease the process of tracing the contacts. Different other contact-tracing apps have been introduced by different governments such as NTK by Germany, ROBERT by France, Aarogya Setu by India, etc.

The diagram in Figure 1.5 is a very tiny example of a knowledge graph which represents case data of a patient Person-1 who recently went to Italy, lives with Person-2 in Delhi, belongs to India and has tested positive for COVID-19 (caused by SARS-COV-2)—a worldwide pandemic. Now, the insight that can be derived from this small piece of information is that Person-2 who lives with Person-1 is susceptible to the infection and can also be the medium of transmission to other people.

1.7 RISK ANALYSIS IN EPIDEMIC

Risk analysis in outbreak analytics refers to the assessment of risk involved with the epidemic, its outbreak, and its recovery process. The primary goals of this analysis are to calculate the severity of the disease and vulnerability of the population. The risks associated with an epidemic can be divided into two categories—personal level and public/general level.

- Personal level risks involve death risk, fatality risk, risk of developing another disease (comorbidities), risk of reinfection of disease, etc.
- Public/general level risks involve abnormal changes in death rate, risk of reoccurrence of epidemic, changes in social demographics of the population.

The risks involved can be computed by processing:

- Knowledge graph of diseases and symptoms,
- Knowledge graph of medical history,
- Knowledge graph of contacts and movement of the patients, etc.

1.8 PROCESS OF OUTBREAK ANALYSIS USING KNOWLEDGE GRAPH

The process of infectious disease transmission detection and risk analysis is divided into three phases:

i) Data collection: It involves selecting the datasets and integrating them. Multiple digital resources can be utilized appropriately in order to access the disease data and dynamic health information. The data collected are generally unstructured.

ii) Knowledge base creation: It refers to obtain a structured knowledge base from the unstructured data collected in previous phase and then to create a knowledge graph using a graph database management system (e.g., Neo4j).

iii) Designing a knowledge graph analysis system: It involves query processing and decision-making on the basis of the insights derived from the knowledge graph using a reasoning technique.

1.9 DISCUSSIONS

There exist a number of research studies that explore the domain healthcare and disease prediction and many researchers have even diversified their area by trying their hand in the field of epidemic and outbreak analytics.

In future, more and more knowledge bases based on genes and genetic mutation can be integrated to get precision. New ontologies can be introduced as well as reusing other ontologies related to genes, pathogens, pathogen mutation, proteins, etc. Other than development in ontological needs, data handling and processing needs can also be taken care of, for example, integrating knowledge graphs with cloud computing. Multiple benefits can be carved out of knowledge graphs, when incorporated in health and medical information systems for the purpose of medical knowledge representation and processing.

1.10 CONCLUSION

This chapter tries to highlight the impact data science has on the medical field and how cross integration of these two can help in coping up with various health hazards that occur naturally or due to some human interventions. Precisely the domain discussed in here is knowledge graph and graph analytics how it can be useful in health disaster management therefore this chapter focuses on how the approach of analyzing the health data of population can be modified and improved by using knowledge graph analytics.

Hence, it explains graph analytics, knowledge graph, graph database, and finally it explains three major use case applications of graph analytics in healthcare data, that is, disease prediction, prediction of comorbidities, and epidemic outbreaks. Also, the chapter puts some light on the process of risk analysis and outbreak (disease spread) analysis of epidemics

KEYWORDS

- **knowledge graph**
- **graph database**
- **healthcare data**
- **epidemic**
- **outbreak analytics**

REFERENCES

Biswas, S.; Mitra, P.; Rao, K. S. Relation Prediction of Co-morbid Diseases Using Knowledge Graph Completion. *IEEE/ACM Trans. Comput. Biol. Bioinform.* **2019**.

Ehrlinger, L.; Wöß, W. Towards a Definition of Knowledge Graphs. *Semant. Web J.* **2016**.

He, F.; Zhu, G.; Wang, Y. Y.; Zhao, X. M.; Huang, D. S. PCID: A Novel Approach for Predicting Disease Comorbidity by Integrating Multi-Scale Data. *IEEE/ACM Comput. Biol. Bioinform.* **2017**.

Hirose, H.; Wang, L. Prediction of Infectious Disease Spread Using Twitter: A Case of Influenza. In *2012 Fifth International Symposium on Parallel Architectures, Algorithms and Programming.*

Hirose, H.; Nakazono, T.; Tokunaga, M.; Sakumura, T.; Sumi, S.; Sulaiman, J. Seasonal Infectious Disease Spread Prediction Using Matrix Decomposition Method. In *2013 4th International Conference on Intelligent Systems, Modelling and Simulation.*

Hossein, M.; Samina, A.; William, W.; Syed, A: Investigating Plausible Reasoning over Knowledge Graphs for Semantics-Based Health Data Analytics. In *2018 IEEE 27th International Conference on Enabling Technologies: Infrastructure for Collaborative Enterprises.*

Jeyaraj, N. Conceptualizing the Knowledge Graph Construction Pipeline. *Towards Data Sci.* **2019**.

Kamdar, M.; Hamamsy, T.; Shelton, S.; Vala, A.; Eftimov, T.; Zou, J.; Tamang, S. A Knowledge Graph-Based Approach for Exploring the U.S. Opioid Epidemic. In *ICLR AI for Social Good Workshop 2019.*

Keeling, M. J.; Eames, K. T. D. Networks and Epidemic Models. *J. R. Soc. Interface* 2005.

Liu, P.; Wang, X.; Sun, X.; Shen, X.; Chen, X.; Sun, Y.; Pan, Y. A Hybrid Knowledge Graph Based Paediatric Disease Prediction System by Penghe Liu et al.; Springer International Publishing AG, 2017.

Polonsky, J.; Baidjoe, A.; Kamvar, Z.; Cori, A.; Durski, K.; Edmunds, J., Eggo, R.; Funk, S.; Kaiser, L.; Keating, P.; Waroux, Olivier le Polain de; Marks, M.; Moraga, P.; Morgan, O.; Nouvellet, P.; Ratnayake, R.; Roberts, C.; Whitworth, J.; Jombart, T. Outbreak Analytics: A Developing Data Science for Informing the Response to Emerging Pathogens. In *The Royal Society Publishing, 2018.*

Salathé, M.; Bengtsson, L.; Bodnar, T. J.; Brewer, D. D.; Brownstein, J. S.; Buckee, C.; Campbell, E. M.; Cattuto, C.; Khandelwal, S.; Mabry, P. L.; Vespignani, A. Digital Epidemiology. *PLoS Comput. Biol.* 2012, *8*(7), e1002616.

Villazon-Terrazas, B.; Garcia-Santa, N.; Ren, Y.; Faraotti, A.; Wu, H.; Zhao, Y.; Vetere, G.; Jeff, Z. *Pan: Knowledge Graph Foundations*; Springer International Publishing: Switzerland, 2017.

Woodward, M. *Epidemiology: Study Design and Data Analysis*, 3rd ed.

Yucong, D.; Zhangbing, Z.; Lixu, S.; Quan, Z, Gongzhu H, Zhaoxin L: Specifying Architecture of Knowledge Graph with Data Graph, Information Graph, Knowledge Graph and Wisdom Graph. In *IEEE SERA 2017, June 7–9*; London, UK, 2017.

CHAPTER 2

Forecasting of COVID-19 with the ARIMA Model in India as a Preventive Measure of Healthcare Catastrophe

SANJEEV KR. JAIN[1] and KAPIL MOHAN GARG[2*]

[1]*AVP, Data Science, 50 Hertz Ltd, New Delhi, India*

[2]*Research Scholar, Galgotia's University, Greater Noida, India*

Corresponding author. E-mail: kapilmohangarg@gmail.com

ABSTRACT

Across the world, researchers are busy developing analytics/procedures/ methods of forecasting to identify the likelihood of getting affected by coronavirus at the individual level as well as for the macro level to formulate national/state policies. The present study is an attempt to forecast the total number of COVID-19 cases across Indian states individually and cumulative for the country so that the resources could be sourced well advance in time to prevent healthcare failure and/or mismanagement of existing resources to minimize the impacts of the pandemic as well as to identify the need of mobilization of required healthcare support to appropriate places vis-à-vis to develop new facilities like isolation, quarantine centers, and medical facilities, etc. Key points are the surge of pandemic across India and to prevent the healthcare disaster. There is a strong need for forecasting number of possible cases which is vital to restrict subsequent spread and fatality. The main objective is to develop a methodology for forecasting the number of possible cases so that future healthcare requirements shall be generated at the state level for the development of a better healthcare system.

Employing autoregressive moving-average models for each state in India based on daily frequency. The impact of the epidemic is not uniform across the nation and estimating one model may generate erogenous results.

ARIMA model has been estimated, for India and major states of India. It is based on the Cumulative Active Cases (CAC) from April 01, 2020 to September 07, 2020 in a machine learning environment where short-term forecasting was the target to understand and determine new requirements, of the healthcare system and related measures, on daily basis. Although the rate of change in daily active cases is a small fraction of the rate of new cases confirmed daily, most of the states including India are showing stationarity on second order which is a clear sign of a nonlinear sharp upward trend. In such a situation, it seems that India is about to enter the third stage of the epidemic where spread will be maximum, and so the catastrophic conditions. In such circumstances, predictions may be the only way to procure the desired amount of facilities to avoid forthcoming health-related hazards. To avoid healthcare hazards, it is recommended to opt for a system to understand the futuristic need for requisite health and medical infrastructure, both for the short and long run.

2.1   INTRODUCTION

An epidemic is considered as a disease that may normally be absent or infrequent in a population but may be responsible for outbreaks of greatly amplified proportion and austerity. A pandemic is simply an epidemic on a widespread topographical gauge, worldwide or at least affecting a wider expanse of the world. On records, there are almost 50 significant epidemics and pandemics dated back from fifth century B.C.E to the end of the 20th century (Hays, 2005). About half of these pandemics occurred in the past 165 years. Among major inclusion are three plague pandemics in the 6th, 14th, and 19th century and the influenza pandemic of 1918–1919 (Hays, 2005). Influenza is a highly infectious airborne disease that affects a significant percentage of the world's population; local annual epidemics and pandemics have occurred since ancient times, causing tens of millions of deaths (Soema et al., 2015). Similarly, over the centuries, other pandemics were described that worldwide resulted in millions and millions of deaths.

Such outbreaks pose a significant threat to the healthy subsists and well-being of billions worldwide and share the facets of difficulty, ambiguity, and estimation that characterize grand challenges (George et al., 2016; Gümüsay and Haack, 2020). During such pandemics, multiple public health sections seek to advance and expand their capacity to respond to such large-scale events that affect millions of people as such pandemics affect people both directly and obliquely. Similar is the situation due to the outbreak of the novel coronavirus-caused infectious disease COVID-19.

In late December 2019, a group of patients was admitted to infirmaries, healthcare centers, and hospitals with an initial judgment of pneumonia of an unknown etiology. These patients were epidemiologically linked to the seafood and wet animal wholesale market in Wuhan, Hubei Province, China (Bogoch et al., 2020; Lu at al., 2020). On March 11, 2020, the World Health Organization (WHO) declared the COVID-19 outbreak a global pandemic and by June 22, COVID-19 had affected 213 countries, with more than 9,000,000 confirmed cases and more than 470,000 reported deaths globally. This resulted in the countries response embrace lockdowns to downsize the ill effects on the health of the mass population which further leads to an acute and drastic shortage of essential supplies, including personal protective equipment, diagnostics, and clinical management. It was just the start of economic disorder for almost all countries worldwide along with significant damage to human lives and livelihoods.

To fight out this pandemic, much Public Health Emergency Preparedness (PHEP) efforts come to life. PHEP requires both the capability to perform traditional public health purposes—including disease surveillance, monitoring patterns, rapid laboratory diagnosis, and contact tracing for people, public education and awareness, mobilization of community partnerships, and assurance of availability of medical care—and to accomplish execution and enactment of quarantine process and coordination with on spot responders, such as police departments (Nelson et al., 2007). Almost all countries, including India, follows the PHEP requirements, and probably India is the only country that employs 100% and most stringent lockdown process in the world history of pandemics.

As per the WHO guidelines, National Public Health Emergency management processes were stimulated, during the lockdown, with the engagement of relevant ministries such as health, education, travel and tourism, public works, environment, and agriculture, to provide coordinated management of COVID-19 preparedness and response (WHO, 2020).

Lockdown ensures a state of confusion and it continues when the administration prepares to open up from lockdowns and enters an unprecedented state of vulnerability, or what many have called "the new normal," it makes sense to reflect on what we have learned, revisit our fundamental assumptions, and start charting the way forward to contribute to building a sustainable world (Pan et al. 2020)

PHEP has always been challenging, whether 100 years back or in present, in part because of the lack of clarity about what constitutes preparedness and also because no one knows what amount of preparedness is required. This requires forecasting to identify a possible estimate of future situations in terms of medical and healthcare resource requirements. It depends on the possibility of the probable number of people that may get affected and the availability of time to prepare. In this study, an attempt has been made to forecasts the active cases of COVID-19 using a robust time series forecasting model to advance the futuristic requirements.

2.2   LITERATURE REVIEW

Forecasting is a prime concern for COVID-19 data as it determines the futuristic needs. Such projected scores may further guide the possible unwanted catastrophes or the related management of resources. Forecasting is the need of an hour as it will help in devising a better strategy to tackle this crucial hour, across the globe, that has arised due to COVID-19 infectious disease (Sujath et al., 2020). It is and was in the focus for various epidemic situations that had hit the World in the past, the most compared is 1918–1920 pandemic. The pandemic of influenza which swept over the world in 1918 was the most severe outbreak of this disease which has ever been known, and it takes an unpleasantly high rank in the roster of epidemics (Pearl, 1919). Numerous studies were conducted and published during the said span and lots of mathematical work was carried out especially for such epidemics, like susceptible infectious-recovered (SIR) model (Weisstein, 2020) developed in 1927. Similarly, another milestone in terms of the univariate prediction model was the development of the autoregression integrated moving average (ARIMA) model by Box and Jenkins (1970), and by Sims (1980), the subsequent development of vector autoregression (VAR) model in 1980 (Weisstein, 2020; Box and Jenkins, 1970; Sims, 1980).

The studies which were intended for the prediction task may be categorized as the models developed for epidemic forecasts/estimation only or adopted from the pre-developed models for forecasting. The same may be classified as Mathematical, Statistical, and Econometrical. The methodology or model employed like SIR model (Almeshal et al., 2020), susceptible infectious-recovered-dead (SIDR) model (Anastassopoulou et al., 2020), susceptible, exposed, infected, recovered (SEIR) model (Anastassopoulou et al., 2020; Wirawan and Januraga, 2020; Reno et al. 2020), Group of Optimized and Multisource Selection-GROOMS (Fong et al., 2020), Grey Model (GM(1,1)), nonlinear grey Bernoulli model (NGBM(1,1)) and fractional nonlinear grey Bernoulli model (FANGBM(1,1)) (Şahin and Şahin, 2020), Boltzmann Function and the Richards Function (Gao et al., 2020), improved adaptive neuro-fuzzy inference system (ANFIS) using an enhanced flower pollination algorithm (FPA) by using the salp swarm algorithm (SSA; Al-qaness et al., 2020), ANFIS model using a novel optimization method (NOM; Al-qaness et al., 2020), Guaging Model (Rizk-Allah and Hassanien, 2020; Elmousalami and Hassanie, 2020), Linguistic FMEA, fuzzy inference system and fuzzy data envelopment analysis model (Rezaee et al., 2020), minimum relative entropy (MRE) hypothesis (Cui and Singh, 2017), novel methodology called GSADenseNet121 (Ezzat and Ella, 2020) may classify as driven from mathematical and statistical methods.

Various models adopted from econometrics or regression-based methodology such as linear regression (LR), multilayer perceptron (MLP), and VAR model, logistic regression and growth models (Almeshal et al., 2020; Chen et al., 2020), lead–lag effect models (Stübinger and Schneider, 2020), exponential smoothing family models (Hyndman et al., 2002; Taylor, 2003; Makridakis, et. al., 1982; Makridakis et al., 2020; Martinez et al., 2020) and ARIMA Models (Kırbaş et al., 2020; Ribeiro et al., 2020; Sujath et al., 2020).

For short-term forecasting, ARIMA is predicting more accurately as compared to other univariate modeling procedures (Kırbaş et. al., 2020; Sujath et al., 2020), Hence to forecast, Simple Time Series Forecasting Approach namely ARIMA is evaluated in the task of time series forecasting with a short-term objective of 5 days, that is, "test set" ahead of the COVID-19 cumulative active cases (CAC) in 20 Indian states and India as a whole in the machine learning environment. The lag lengths of AR and MA along with the level of integration are decided as per methodology adopted since this method has shown good forecast accuracy over several forecasting methods, especially for short series and to predict for the short run.

2.3 RESEARCH METHODOLOGY

The Box and Jenkins (1970) method in Time Series Analysis popularly known as autoregression moving average (ARMA) with a generalization to ARIMA are either to better understand the data or to predict future points in a univariate setup (Box and Jenkins, 1970). The term is coined with three features namely autoregression (AR), I (order of integration), and moving average (MA). The seeds of AR are planted in Fisher (1925) Dynamic Model and subsequent transformation into Koyck (1954) Distributed Lag Model which later formed as Johnston (1960) AR process (Fisher, 1925; Koyck, 1954; Johnston, 1960). The AR indicates that the series or variable is regressed on its lags, that is, immediately prior values in the past. An AR process with one lag called AR (1), which is exemplified more easily as:

$$Y_t = \alpha_0 + \alpha_1 Y_{t-1} + e_t.$$

Similarly, an AR with "p" leg length or p^{th} order AR process indicated as AR(p), can be represented as:

$$Y_t = \alpha_0 + \sum_{i=1}^{p} \alpha_i Y_{t-i} + e_t.$$

The MA term is indicating that the error, that is, "e_t" generated from the AR process is a linear combination of its past values. MA with first lag is called MA(1) and is denoted as:

$$Y_t = \mu + \beta_0 e_t + \beta_1 e_{t-1} + \varepsilon_t.$$

MA(q) process may be formed in a similar manner where "q" is the lag length of MA term, which may be called as q^{th} order MA process, more generally presented as:

$$Y_t = \mu + \sum_{j=0}^{q} \beta_i e_{t-i} + \varepsilon_t.$$

Merging both the terms together forms an ARMA process, ARMA (1,1) can be written as:

$$Y_t = \theta + \alpha_1 Y_{t-1} + \beta_0 e_t + \beta_1 e_{t-1} + \varepsilon_t.$$

It is called ARMA (1, 1) because there is one lag for each term. A generalized version of ARMA (p, q) can be depicted as:

$$Y_t = \mu + \sum_{i=1}^{p} \alpha_i Y_{t-i} + \sum_{j=0}^{q} \beta_i e_{t-i} + \varepsilon_t.$$

The ARMA model is built on the basic assumption that the time series per se is weakly stationary but in the real world, most of the time series are nonstationary means they are integrated. If a time series is stationary, that is, the mean, variance, and covariance are constant over time is called integrated at the level and represented as I(0). A time series is integrated at order 1 or I(1) if its first difference is I(0), that is, stationary. Therefore, if we need to differentiate a time series "d" times to make it stationary it is called I(d) or integrated at order "d". Implying it with ARMA (p, q), it is converted to the ARIMA (p, d, q), which is the model used for the prediction purposes in this study. The equational display is similar except in later cases the time series is taken as stationary on the desired level of integration, that is, I(d) and represented as Y_{dt}.

In general, an ARIMA (p, d, q) is considered in a nonseasonal setup with "p," "d," and "q" non-negative integers which are defined as:

p: The number of lags included in the model, also called the lag order.

d: The number of times the time series are differenced to make it stationary also called the degree of difference.

q: The size of the moving average window or the lag length of error term taken in the model, also called the order of moving average.

To estimate an ARIMA model, a LR-based setup is constructed including the specified number and types of terms. Data are prepared by a degree of differencing to make it stationary, that is, remove trend and seasonal structures that negatively affect the regression model.

Configuring an ARIMA Model—the classical approach for fitting it is to follow the Box and Jenkins (1970) approach. It is the process to discover appropriate parameters to build a robust model for accurate predictions (Box and Jenkins, 1970). The steps and related procedures are as follows:

Model Identification—to find out the parameters, use of plots, and summary statistics to identify related aspects like the trend, seasonality, and autocorrelation elements to get an idea about the selected time series. Parameters-wise strategy adopted is as under.

'd' to find out the stationarity in time series: The Augmented Dickey and Fuller (1979) test, also called the ADF test, has been used to find out the order of stationarity in the series (Dickey and Fuller, 1979). The test statistics are following τ statistic under the null hypothesis that the time series is nonstationary. The ADF test can be estimated based on the following regression.

$$\Delta Y_t = \gamma_1 + \gamma_2 t + \delta Y_{t-1} + \sum_{i=1}^{m} \varphi_i \Delta Y_{t-i} + \epsilon_i.$$

Here, ϵi is the pure white noise error term. The lag length may be decided by any information criterion like AIC, BIC, and HQIC, etc. In ADF the value and level of significance of δ which is assumed as 0 under the null hypothesis are determining the stationarity in the time series.

'p' for AR process: to determine the lag length in an AR process the partial autocorrelation function (PACF) is used. It is the correlation between the 0th lag and k^{th} lag without considering the contribution of all lags in between them. So, PACF conveys the pure correlation which is used to determine the lag for the AR term. PACK of lag k of a series is the coefficient of that lag in the AR linear equation depicted as α_k

$$Y_t = \alpha_0 + \alpha_1 Y_{t-1} + \alpha_2 Y_{t-2} + \ldots + \alpha_k Y_{t-k} + e_t.$$

"q" for MA: The autocorrelation function (ACF) plot is employed to determine the order of the moving average. The ACF at lag k denoted by ρ_k is defined as:

$$\rho_k = \frac{\gamma_k}{\gamma_0},$$

where, γ represents the covariance at lag k.

Coefficients Estimation—after determination of the right parameters, the regression model builds to compute the desired coefficients. Along with coefficients individual significance level, a check on relevant information criteria along with the overall fit of the model is taken care and in case of any deficiency in the model, the lag lengths of AR and MA terms adjusted suitably to make the model the best fit.

Model Checking—after coefficient estimation, a check on residual to determine the amount and type of temporal structure not captured by the model is performed including normality and related aspects.

Accuracy Matrices for Forecasting—various accuracy matrices to determine the model validity and connected features to build a machine learning model for prediction are considered based on the following formulae—here "n" represents the number of forecast values.

Mean error (ME):

$$ME = \sum_{i=1}^{n} \frac{(forecast_i - actual_i)}{n}.$$

Mean percentage error (MPE):

$$MPE = \sum_{i=1}^{n} \frac{(forecast_i - actual_i) \big/ (actual_i)}{n}.$$

Root mean square error (RMSE):

$$RMSE = \sqrt[2]{\sum_{i=1}^{n} \frac{(forecast_i - actual_i)^2}{n}}.$$

Corr: correlation between forecasted and actual values.

ACF: Lag 1 Autocorrelation of error, that is, difference between forecast and actual values.

Python structure in machine learning setup—following specific function and libraries are employed for the estimation and predictions:

adfuller( ) from the statsmodels.tsa.stattools
plot_pacf( ) and plotacf( ) from the statsmodels.graphics.tsaplots
ARIMA( ) from the statsmodels.tsa.arima_model
Auto.arima( ) from the pmdarima
model.predict( ) from the pmdarima

2.4 DATA ANALYSIS AND INTERPRETATIONS

Daily frequency data are taken from https://www.covid19india.org/ from April 1, 2020 to 07 September to predict the futuristic requirement of medical and related facilities for best prevention from COVID-19. The variable of interest is the number of the active cases, is calculated as:

Cumulative Active Cases = Daily New Confirmed − Daily New Recovered − Daily New Deceased + Yesterday's Active Cases

Behind the consideration of active cases, it is found that recovery primarily depends on the medical facilities so the deceased but active cases are more prominent for future needs since the infrastructural need is driven by the number of active cases only, which includes new confirmed cases too. CAC will go up along with the growth of new confirmed cases. It will be higher than recovered and deceased cases, which is a crucial function of the management of preventive measures of healthcare and related catastrophe and is reflected in the CAC. The forthcoming CACs are the measures of expected medical facilities and requirements. Increasing CAC will be an indication of mismanagement or upheaval, the first difference of CAC (per day addition in active cases—AC) is the daily addition of active cases that requires new medical/infrastructural facilities. The forecasting is scheduled on gross variable, that is, CAC through ARIMA to identify the future need as a preventive measure or the same may be considered as directly proportion to disaster in management of COVID-19 and the related healthcare system. The first difference of predicted values may be taken for the calculation of AC as stated above.

Table 2.1 represents descriptive statistics of the CAC for India and selected states and each is containing a sample size of 160 days to understand the distribution.

It is visible from the above table that all the states are showing diverse mean and variances; hence, the ARIMA model for the prediction of CAC for each state has been employed to cater to the need to analyze the dearth of resources and their futuristic need at the country level vis-à-vis state to identify the local catastrophes for gross resources requirements being predicted figures of CAC, and daily additional resources requirements through a first difference of CAC, that is, AC.

Table 2.2 represents the order of integration, that is, "d," lag of AR, that is, "p" in AR or AR(p), and lag length of moving average or "q" in MA(q). The selection of "d" is based on ADF while PACF and ACF are used for the selection of "p" and "q," respectively. The situation of under differenced and over differenced has been adjusted by the increase/decrease in "p" and "q," respectively conditional to the individual significance level. The same strategy has also been adopted if all or any coefficient(s) of AR and MA process is/are not significant individually or jointly despite the order of integration, and the lag length is/are added if it increases the significance level of previously selected lag lengths based on PACF and ACFs to make the models more robust which is duly checked by the normality in residual terms. The classical determination to find out the right differencing, that is, order of "d" which is at the minimum differencing, is required to get near stationary, instead of a higher order of 'd,' that is, over differencing is considered through the ADF test. In the case, where it is really difficult to decide between two adjacent orders of differencing, the least variance differenced series is considered as the order of ",d". The Final selection of the ARIMA model to decide 'p', 'd', and 'q' is done based on AIC, where AIC is the minimum among all considered models. The following table is showing the model's parameters.

Except for five states which are showing stationarity at the first difference, all others are reaching on stationarity level in the second order. The lag lengths for AR and MA process are also ranging from 1 to 2 only except Jharkhand where the MA term is insignificant which is discarded from the model to minimize the MAPE—a measure for the forecasting error. The above table is an indication of the empirically verified and tested parameters so that the various measures related to

TABLE 2.1 Statistical Summary.

States	Mean	Std	Min	25%	50%	75%	Max
India	278,960.6	272,923.2	399	44,008	167,933	530,686.8	882,130
Maharashtra	77,931.76	66,338.11	30	17,343.25	56,614.5	145,731.8	237,040
Andhra Pradesh	27,544.06	37,504.44	66	925.75	4057	65,098.25	103,658
Karnataka	27,388.58	35,243.92	8	312.5	3167	67,921	100,134
Uttar Pradesh	16,586.28	20,038.4	11	1668.75	6035	30,573	62,057
Tamil Nadu	27,596.49	22,339.07	110	5606	24,051.5	52,178.25	57,851
Telangana	8984.2	9952.827	27	532.5	3092.5	14,830.25	32,407
Assam	6578.2	8514.065	7	29.75	2098.5	8707.5	28,694
Odisha	6096.85	8452.858	0	311	1356	10,133.5	27,881
West Bengal	9895.244	10,127.59	0	1325.5	5228.5	19,683	28,038
Kerala	5407.806	7428.616	-199	-4.5	1202	9954.25	23,508
Delhi	11,933.59	8383.173	32	4856.5	10,872.5	17,879	28,217
Madhya Pradesh	4822.869	4215.285	31	1934.75	2725	8318.5	16,899
Punjab	3693.806	5019.155	4	212	1478	4397.5	16,603
Gujarat	8004.156	4967.869	8	4845.25	6518	13,535.5	16,351
Haryana	3957.831	3754.167	-10	309.75	4071	6297.25	16,308
Bihar	7556.25	9529.747	2	375	2308	15,325.25	32,696
Rajasthan	5661.375	5123.517	27	1477	2946	10,782.25	14,906
Jharkhand	3140.35	4411.874	0	88.75	660	5829.5	15,523
Jammu and Kashmir	3447.725	3079.907	6	414.5	2522	6943.5	10,957
Uttarakhand	1541.875	1979.518	0	25	698.5	2921	8037
Others	8651.338	7798.26	4	273.25	8690.5	12,029.75	28,368

Source: Developed for this research work.

accuracy matrices can be optimized on its best to produce the best candidate model. The accuracy matrices are duly formed for the assessment of the particular model to a suitable selection for a machine learning environment. The said matrices are computed based on the machine learning module in Python with training and testing sets of data. The results are shown in Table 2.3 for the evaluation of the outcome of each candidate model.

TABLE 2.2   ARIMA Parameters.

ARIMA (p, d, q)	AR(p)	I(d)	MA(q)
State	PACF	ADF	ACF
India	1	2	1
Andhra Pradesh	1	2	1
Assam	1	2	1
Bihar	2	1	3
Delhi	1	2	2
Gujarat	1	1	1
Haryana	1	2	2
Jharkhand	1	2	0
Jammu and Kashmir	0	2	1
Karnataka	1	3	1
Kerala	1	1	2
Maharashtra	2	2	1
Madhya Pradesh	0	2	1
Odisha	1	2	1
Punjab	1	2	1
Rajasthan	1	2	1
Telangana	2	1	3
Tamil Nadu	1	2	1
Uttarakhand	2	2	1
Uttar Pradesh	1	2	2
West Bengal	2	1	3
Others	1	2	1

Source: Developed for this research work.

TABLE 2.3 Error Matrices.

State	ME	MPE	RMSE	Corr	ACF1
India	−10,641.867	−0.012	12,195.444	0.974	0.083
Andhra Pradesh	4551.258	0.046	6299.274	−0.760	0.597
Assam	−1515.193	−0.055	1633.450	0.939	0.308
Bihar	580.356	0.036	1082.784	−0.613	0.366
Delhi	−1279.234	−0.065	1373.262	0.933	0.099
Gujarat	14.683	0.001	45.802	0.988	0.006
Haryana	−675.975	−0.044	737.411	0.998	0.482
Jharkhand	−962.641	−0.064	996.457	0.783	−0.457
Jammu and Kashmir	−1401.218	−0.138	1652.287	0.992	0.456
Karnataka	2739.982	0.028	4123.934	0.250	0.319
Kerala	−972.660	−0.044	1290.207	−0.734	0.478
Maharashtra	−9550.902	−0.041	12,330.427	0.975	0.468
Madhya Pradesh	−639.260	−0.040	710.005	0.979	0.074
Odisha	−511.600	−0.019	690.053	0.964	0.272
Punjab	396.887	0.025	408.411	0.968	0.029
Rajasthan	−2347.046	−0.159	2457.320	−0.800	0.247
Telangana	1109.996	0.035	1420.543	−0.604	0.334
Tamil Nadu	623.680	0.012	654.087	0.949	0.056
Uttarakhand	−493.896	−0.065	522.449	0.987	0.203
Uttar Pradesh	−1376.068	−0.023	1537.685	0.990	0.486
West Bengal	20.176	0.001	114.319	0.959	0.081
Others	−654.468	−0.024	769.753	0.870	−0.020

Source: Developed for this research work.

A variety of outcomes in terms of Accuracy Matrices have been recorded where almost all the values of matrices showing the favorable results except for Jammu and Kashmir and Rajasthan where MPE is crossing the 5% target. The recommendation for the adoption of the ARIMA parameter needs to cater accordingly. The forecasting error in terms of MPE for India is a mere 1.2% with an insignificant Autocorrelation of the first-order (−0.083) in produced error term by ARIMA (1, 2, 1). A negative ME is indicating that the average of predicted to actual difference is negative implying that the forecasted values are smaller than actual, that is, −10,641. RMSE is measuring the root square average distances in a summative form between forecast and actual value showing a more scientific measure compare to ME which is 12,195 seems a bigger figure but well countered by the very high correlation between predicted and actual value of 0.974. The outcome of each state's model can infer accordingly.

2.5 FINDINGS AND CONCLUSIONS

It is visible by summary statistics that the average active cases in India are 278,960 with a rocketing standard deviation 272,923 indicating an alarming situation, as on the date of data collection, that is, 07/09/2020 the total active cases were recorded are 882,130 which is an all-time high till the date. Astounding, that is, around a lakh new case per day are indicating an alarming situation for healthcare measures and related arrangements. Although the rate of change of the daily active case is a small fraction of the rate of new cases confirmed daily, most of the states including India are showing stationarity on second order which is a clear sign of a nonlinear sharp upward trend. In such a situation it seems that India is about to enter the third stage of the epidemic where spread will be maximum so the catastrophic conditions. In such circumstances, predictions may be the only way to procure the desired amount of facilities to avoid forthcoming health-related hazards.

2.6 RECOMMENDATIONS

The recovery rate is very high and the death rate is small (in comparison to the world's average). But, both of these are a crucial function of medical facilities, which are not so sound as compared to the western world. India as the second largest populated country is having a health infrastructure where the availability of a bed and a doctor is a rare phenomenon for most of the rural and semi-urban populations. In such conditions and poor health infrastructure, the controlled active cases are the only hope which may be optimized for suitable medication and allied services. To avoid healthcare hazards, it is recommended to opt for a system to understand the futuristic needs for adequate health and medical infrastructure, both for the short and long run.

KEYWORDS

- **COVID-19**
- **ARIMA**
- **pandemic**
- **healthcare**
- **Corona**
- **forecasting**

REFERENCES

Almeshal, A. M.; Almazrouee, A. I.; Alenizi, M. R.; Alhajeri, S. N. Forecasting the Spread of COVID-19 in Kuwait Using Compartmental and Logistic Regression Models. *Appl. Sci.* **2020,** *10*(10), 3402. https://www.mdpi.com/2076-3417/10/10/34023

Al-qaness, M. A. A.; Ewees, A. A.; Fan, H.; Aziz, Mohamed Abd El. Optimization Method for Forecasting Confirmed Cases of COVID-19 in China. *J. Clin. Med.* **2020,** *9*(3), 674. https://doi.org/10.3390/jcm9030674

Al-qaness, M. A. A.; Ewees, A. A.; Fan, H.; Abualigah, L.; Aziz, Mohamed Abd El. Marine Predators Algorithm for Forecasting Confirmed Cases of COVID-19 in Italy, USA, Iran and Korea. *Int. J. Environ. Res. Public Health* **2020,** *17*(10), 3520. https://doi.org/10.3390/ijerph17103520

Anastassopoulou, C.; Russo, L.; Tsakris, A.; Siettos, C. Data-Based Analysis, Modelling and Forecasting of the COVID-19 Outbreak. *PLOS ONE* **2020.** https://doi.org/10.1371/journal.pone.0230405.

Bogoch, Watts, A.; Thomas-Bachli, A.; Huber, C.; Kraemer, M. U. G.; Khan, K. Pneumonia of Unknown Etiology in Wuhan, China: Potential for International Spread via Commercial Air Travel. *J. Trav. Med.* **2020,** *10.* 1093/jtm/taaa008

Box, G.; Jenkins, G. *Time Series Analysis: Forecasting and Control*; San Francisco: Holden-Day, 1970.

Chen, D.; Chen, X.; Chen, J. K. Reconstructing and Forecasting the COVID-19 Epidemic in the United States Using a 5-Parameter Logistic Growth Model. *Global Health Res. Policy* **2020,** *5*(25). https://doi.org/10.1186/s41256-020-00152-5

Cui, H.; Singh, V. P. Application of Minimum Relative Entropy Theory for Streamflow Forecasting. *Stoch. Env. Res. Risk Assess.* **2017,** *31*(3), 587–608.

Dickey, D. A.; Fuller, W A Distribution of the Estimators for Autoregressive Time Series with a Unit Root. *J. Am. Stat. Assoc.* **1979,** *74*, 427–471.

Elmousalami, H. H.; Hassanien, A. E. Day Level Forecasting for Coronavirus Disease (COVID-19) Spread: Analysis, Modeling, and Recommendations, 2020. arXiv preprint arXiv:2003.07778

Ezzat, D.; Ella, H. A. GSA-DenseNet121-COVID-19: A Hybrid Deep Learning Architecture for the Diagnosis of COVID-19 Disease Based on the Gravitational Search Optimization Algorithm, 2020. arXiv preprint arXiv:2004.05084

Fisher, R. A. *Statistical Methods for Research Workers*; Oliver and Boyd: Edinburg, 1925.

Fong, Simon J.; Li, G.; Dey, N.; Crespo, Rubén G.; Viedma, Enrique H. Finding an Accurate Early Forecasting Model from Small Dataset: A Case of 2019-nCoV Novel Coronavirus Outbreak. *Int. J. Interact. Multimedia Artif. Intel.* **2020**, *6*, 1.

Gao, Y.; Zhang, Z.; Yao, W.; Ying, Qi; Long, C.; Fu, X. Forecasting the Cumulative Number of COVID-19 Deaths in China: A Boltzmann Function-Based Modeling Study. *Infect. Control Hosp. Epidemiol.* **2020**, *41*, 841–843. https://doi.org/10.1017/ice.2020.101

George, G.; Howard-Grenville, J.; Joshi, A.; Tihanyi, L. Understanding and Tackling Societal Grand Challenges Through Management Research. *Acad. Manag. J.* **2016**, *59*(6), 1880–1895.

Gümüşay, A. A.; Haack, P. COVID-19 Insights: Tackling COVID-19 as a Grand Challenge. *Bus. Soc.* **2020**. http://businessandsociety.org/2020/06/11/COVID-19-as-a-grand-challenge/

Hays, J. N. *Epidemics and Pandemics: Their Impacts on Human History;* ABC-CLIO, Inc., 2005; pp 9–12,

Hyndman, R. J.; Koehler, A. B.; Snyder, R. D.; Grose, S. A. State-Space Framework for Automatic Forecasting Using Exponential Smoothing Methods. *Int. J. Forecast.* **2002**, *18*(3), 439–454.

Johnston, J. *Statistical Cost Analysis*; McGraw Hill: New York, 1960.

Kırbaş, I.; Sözen, A.; Tuncer, A. D.; Kazancıoğlu, F. S. Comparative Analysis and Forecasting of COVID-19 Cases in Various European Countries with ARIMA, NARNN and LSTM Approaches. *Chaos Solitons Fractals* **2020**, *138*, 110015. https://www.ncbi.nlm.nih.gov/pmc/articles/PMC7293493/

Koyck, L. M. *Distributed Lags and Investment Analysis*; North-Holland: Amsterdam, 1954.

Lu, H.; Stratton, C. W.; Tang, Y. W. Outbreak of Pneumonia of Unknown Etiology in Wuhan China: The Mystery and the Miracle. *J. Med. Virol.* **2020**, *92*(4), 401–402. 10.1002/jmv.25678

Makridakis, S.; Andersen, A.; Carbone, R.; Fildes, R.; Hibon, M.; Lewandowski, R.; Newton, J.; Parzen, E.; Winkler, R. The Accuracy of Extrapolation (time series) Methods: Results of a Forecasting Competition. *J. Forecast.* **1982**, *1*(2), 111–153. https://doi.org/10.1002/for.3980010202

Makridakis, S.; Spiliotis, E.; Assimakopoulos, V. The M4 Competition: 100,000-Time Series and 61 Forecasting Methods. *Int. J. Forecast.* **2020**, *36*(1), 54–74.

Martinez, E. Z.; Aragon, D. C.; Nunes, A. A. Short-Term Forecasting of Daily COVID-19 Cases in Brazil by Using the Holt's Model. *Trop. J. Brazilian Soc. Tropical Med.* **2020**, *53*, e20200283. https://www.ncbi.nlm.nih.gov/pmc/articles/PMC7269522/

Nelson, C.; Lurie, N.; Wasserman, J.; Zakowski, S. Conceptualizing and Defining Public Health Emergency Preparedness. *Am. J. Public Health* **2007**, *97*(1), S9–S11. DOI: 10.2105/AJPH.2007.114496

Pan, Shan L.; Zhang, S. From fighting COVID-19 Pandemic to Tackling Sustainable Development Goals: An Opportunity for Responsible Information Systems Research. *Int. J. Inform. Manag.* **2020**. https://doi.org/10.1016/j.ijinfomgt.2020.102196

Pearl, R. On Certain General Statistical Aspects of the 1918 Epidemic in American Cities. *Public Health Rep.* **1919,** *34*(32), 1743–1783.

Reno, C.; Lenzi, J.; Navarra, A.; Barelli, E.; Gori, D.; Lanza, A.; Valentini, R.; Tang, B.; Fantini, M. P. Forecasting COVID-19-Associated Hospitalizations under Different Levels of Social Distancing in Lombardy and Emilia-Romagna, Northern Italy, Results from an Extended SEIR Compartmental Model. *J. Clin. Med.* **2020,** *9*, 1492. DOI: 10.3390/jcm9051492. http://www.mdpi.com/journal/jcm

Rezaee, M. J.; Yousefi, S.; Eshkevari, M.; Valipour, M.; Saberi, M. Risk Analysis of Health, Safety, and the Environment in Chemical Industry Integrating Linguistic FMEA, fuzzy inference system and fuzzy DEA. *Stoch. Env. Res. Risk Assess.* **2020,** *34*(1), 201–218.

Ribeiro, M. H. D. M.; Silva, R. G. da; Mariani, V. C.; Coelho, L. D. S. Short-Term Forecasting COVID-19 Cumulative Confirmed Cases: Perspectives for Brazil, Chaos, Solitons and Fractals, *Nonlinear Sci. Nonequilibrium Complex Phenom.* **2020,** *135*, 109853. https://doi.org/10.1016/j.chaos.2020.109853

Rizk-Allah, R. M.; Hassanien, A. E. COVID-19 Forecasting Based on an Improved Interior Search Algorithm and Multi-Layer Feed Forward Neural Network, 2020, arXiv:2004.05960 [cs.NE]

Sims, C. A. "Macroeconomics and Reality," *Econometrica* **1980,** *48*, 1–48.

Soema, P. C.; Kompier, R.; Amorij, J. P.; Kersten, G. F. Current and Next-Generation Influenza Vaccines: Formulation and Production Strategies. *Eur. J. Pharm. Biopharm.* **2015,** *94*, 251–263.

Stübinger, J.; Schneider, L. Epidemiology of Coronavirus COVID-19: Forecasting Future Incidence in Different Countries. *Healthcare* **2020,** *8*(2), 99. https://doi.org/10.3390/healthcare8020099

Sujath, R.; Chatterjee, J. M.; Hassanien, A. E. A Machine Learning Forecasting Model for COVID-19 Pandemic in India. *Stoch. Environ. Res. Risk Assess.* **2020,** *34*, 959–972.

Taylor, J. W. Exponential Smoothing with a Damped Multiplicative Trend. *Int. J. Forecast.* **2003,** *19*(4), 715–725.

Utkucan, Ş.; Tezcan, Ş. Forecasting the Cumulative Number of Confirmed Cases of COVID-19 in Italy, UK, and the USA Using Fractional Nonlinear Grey Bernoulli Model. *Chaos Solitons Fractals.* **2020,** *138*. https://doi.org/10.1016/j.chaos.2020.109948

Weisstein, Eric W. SIR Model., *Math World* - A Wolfram Web Resource, August 12, 2020. https://mathworld.wolfram.com/SIRModel.html

WHO. COVID-19 Strategic Preparedness and Response Plan: Operational Planning Guidelines to Support Country Preparedness and Response, August 11, 2020. https://www.who.int/docs/default-source/coronaviruse/COVID-19-sprp-unct-guidelines.pdf?sfvrsn=81ff43d8_4

Wirawan, A. I. M.; Januraga, P. P. Forecasting COVID-19 Transmission and Healthcare Capacity in Bali, Indonesia. *J. Prev. Med. Public Health* **2020,** *53*, 158–163. https://doi.org/10.3961/jpmph.20.152

Yang, Z.; Zeng, Z.; Wang, K.; Wong, S. S.; Liang, W.; Zanin, M.; Liu, P.; Cao, X.; Gao, Z.; Mai, Z.; Liang, J. Modified SEIR and AI Prediction of the Epidemics Trend of COVID-19 in China Under Public Health Interventions. *J. Thorac. Dis.* **2020,** *12*(3), 165.

Role of Artificial Intelligence in the Era of COVID-19 to Improve Hospital Management

RUQAIYA KHANAM*

Department of Computer Science and Engineering, Sharda University, Uttar Pradesh, India

E-mail: dr.kruqaiya@gmail.com

ABSTRACT

The respiratory illness caused by the novel SARS-CoV-2 virus is known as COVID-19. It has become a pandemic and a challenge to the world. The most crucial challenge of this pandemic is the management of COVID-19 patients' urgency of critical respiratory care. Based on the need of this situation, an AI-based model was developed to enhance the critical care of COVID-19 patients. A broad review of literature was completed from all the published research available on PubMed, Google Scholar, Web of Science, and other databases. Most of the clinicians and engineers are rigorously working on a vaccine, testing facilities, and monitoring systems. This paper highlights the prospects of use of AI methods for diagnosis and prognosis system. Three stages-based model (input, processing, and output) is used for uncovering and finding the infectious disease. Heterogeneous data are considered as input, processing stage included artificial intelligence, and the output is a set of decision-making system with diagnosis, treatment for the patients, risk stratification based on patient's health status, prognosis, and clinical management. Major efforts of the healthcare system to fight COVID-19 using AI-based decision-making system would support managing the patients infected with COVID-19 more efficiently.

3.1 INTRODUCTION

The coronavirus (SARS-CoV-2) infection that spread rapidly in December 2019 (COVID-19) in Wuhan, China, has created an extraordinary challenge across the world (World Health Organization, 2020a, 2020b, 2020c). This critical problem has different and unknown features that people has never faced before.

COVID-19 infection increased significantly from December 2019 and has proved to be quite strenuous to global healthcare systems (World Health Organization, 2020c). Thus, this has put an urgent need for efficient early detection, diagnosis of suspected COVID-19 patients, and prognosis of those patients. Previous reports show that elderly patients, those with comorbidities, and patients with dyspnea are unsafe. They are more exposed to severe morbidity and mortality after experiencing of COVID-19 infection. Viral nucleic acid testing and chest-computed tomography are the most general methods for diagnosing COVID-19, but are more time-consuming process.

Figure 3.1 demonstrates the classification on different stages of COVID-19 and reveals the level of severity among patients. Mostly three stages are noticed, namely, early infection (mild) when fever is greater than 99.6°F and dry cough, pulmonary phase (moderate) with shortness of breath, and third phase is critical (systematic hyperinflamation).

Stage 1: Early Infection
Stage 2: Pulmonary Phase
Stage 3: Hyperinflammation Phase

3.1.1 LEVEL OF SEVERITY

Table 3.1 shows the level of severity of the COVID-19 disease such as mild, moderate, severe, and the failure of critical respiratory (Wang et al., 2020; Guan et al., 2020; Huang et al., 2020; Chen et al., 2020).

The mortality rate (MR) and fatality rate (FR) of COVID-19, depend on many important factors, but among these factors, the healthcare of patients in critical condition is a vital issue. Therefore, the management of COVID-19 patients is a serious challenge for critical respiratory care. There are the clinical challenges such as intensive care unit (ICU) with number of COVID-19 patients; patients are on noninvasive ventilation, intubated while clinical practitioner's challenges the virus in personal protection equipment (PPE) and a percentage of them exhausted. Depending on the current situation, there is a huge requirement of ICU beds and quality of care as well (Chen et al., 2020).

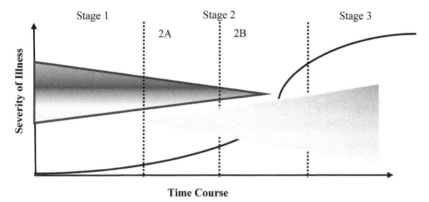

FIGURE 3.1 Stages of the infection in COVID-19.

TABLE 3.1 The Level of Severity of the COVID-19 Disease.

Severity	Definition
Mild	Signs of pneumonia on imaging not visible
Moderate	Heavy dyspnea, respiration ≥30/min, blood O_2 Saturation of O_2 ≤93%
Severe	Fever, symptoms with radiological findings of pneumonia PaO_2/FiO_2 ratio <300, and/or lung infiltrates >50% within 1–2 days
Critical respiratory failure	Septic shock and/or dysfunctioning of multiple organs or even failure

It is observed that the COVID-19 patients in the ICU were aged in comparison to the less critical patients and suffer a multiple organ failure problem such as cardiovascular disease, diabetes, high blood pressure, obstructive sleep apnea, chronic obstructive pulmonary disease, liver disease, and chronic kidney disease.

On admission, ICU patients had lower oxygen levels rather than non-ICU patients. Number of patients have high levels of troponin, indicating heart damage, "brain natriuretic peptide," "D-dimer (indicating blood clots)," "procalcitonin (indicating tissue damage)," and "high-sensitivity C-reaction protein" (indicating inflammation). In one cohort study, 44% of ICU patients were recorded by arrhythmia problem (Yang et al., 2020).

3.2 CHALLENGES IN CLINICAL MANAGEMENT (COVID-19)

Table 3.2 shows the summarized information of challenges in clinical management for COVID-19 patients.

3.2.1 DIAGNOSIS

Lot of challenges have to be faced by the hospitals to control this pandemic situation, by inpatients, and by the ICU patients (Yang et al., 2020; Arentz et al., 2020; Cao et al., 2020), such as slow testing, no systematic detection of COVID-19, less number of ICU beds, need highly expert intensive care physicians who can do fast analysis and respond to recently developed disease, increase multiple organ failure, and cytokine storm syndrome (CSS) caused of sudden exacerbations and death. The role artificial intelligence (AI) will play in a dynamic atmosphere needs to be an innovative effort, otherwise the process of patient care and clinical decision making would be noneffective. This model is to assess the role of AI in the management of inpatients and critically ill patients in ICU with COVID-19. AI-based model would improve the critical care of the COVID-19 patients and will also save the lives of patients.

As the COVID-19 outbreak spreads worldwide, ICU practitioners and/ or clinician, policymakers, hospital administrators and staff, governments, and researchers must be prepared for critically ill patients with COVID-19. Most of the patients are older and have comorbidities along with diabetes than noncritically sick patients. The nonspecific symptoms are high fever, dry cough, fatigue, and dyspnea (Chen et al., 2020; Al-Jarrah et al., 2015; Andreu-Perez et al., 2015; Jee and Kim, 2013; Martin-Sanchez and Verspoor, 2014; Liang and Kelemen, 2016). Developing pneumonia, median time from symptom onset is approximately 5 days and also median time from symptom onset to severe hypoxemia and admission in ICU is 7–12 days (Al-Jarrah et al., 2015; Jee and Kim, 2013; Yang et al., 2020; Arentz et al., 2020). Lot of patients have bilateral opacities on chest X-Ray and CT scan images. Around 60–70% of patients admitted to the ICU have

TABLE 3.2 Challenges in Clinical Management (COVID-19).

	Epidemiology and clinical features	Diagnosis	Management of acute respiratory failure	Intensive care management
Problems	• Prediction of disease is difficult in early stage	• Clinical features are non-specific • RT-PCR sensitivity • Assays for critically ill patients is unknown • Non available RT-PCR • Availability of assays in ICUs, assays will consume more time to complete	• Benefits of NIV and HFNC, risks of infection transfer through aero-solisation, which are unclear state • Intubation poses a risk of viral communicable to health-care staff or workers • ECMO is extremely resource-intensive	• Patients often develop myocardial dysfunction with acute respiratory failure • Bacterial and influenza pneumonia are arduous to distinguish from COVID-19 alone • Unclear the good and bad of systemic corticosteroids • Shifting from ICU for CT scans (risk of viral transmission) • Viral shedding approaches to the upper respiratory tract lasts for more than 10 days after catching its symptoms being onset in severe COVID-19
Suggestions	• Making tools for prognosis & biomarker	Taking low threshold for diagnostic testing Redo the sampling from lower respiratory tract, if needed Update a record which is high index suspicion to COVID-19	• With airborne precautions reserve for mild ARDS, should be in single room, and intubation with low threshold • Perform intubation drills regularly; and an expert to intubate with full PPE and mask ventilation • Equalize the essentials of a higher no. of patients with less severe disease COVID-19	• Administer fluids for hypovolaemia, first with valuations for pre-load responsiveness • An early detection of myocardial involvement with troponin and beta natriuretic peptide measurements and echocardiography • Empirical broad- spectrum of antibiotics and neuraminidase • Minimize shifting by using other methods, e.g., point-of-care ultrasound • Quarantine patients only post-recovery and two negative RT-PCR assays performed 1 day apart

ARDS, acute respiratory distress syndrome; COVID-19, coronavirus disease 2019; ECMO, extracorporeal membrane oxygenation; HFNC, high-flow nasal cannula; ICU, intensive care unit; NIV, noninvasive ventilation; PPE, personal protective equipment.

acute respiratory distress syndrome (ARDS), myocardial dysfunction (20–30%), and kidney failure (10–30%) (Huang et al., 2020; Al-Jarrah et al., 2015; Jee and Kim, 2013; Martin-Sanchez and Verspoor, 2014).

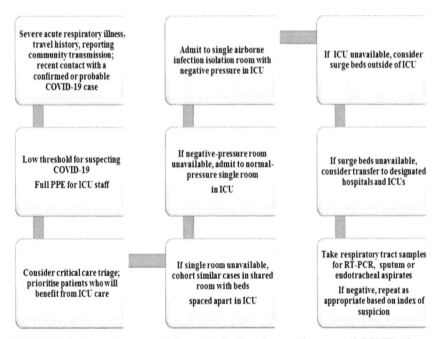

FIGURE 3.2   Inceptive approach for critically ill patients with suspected COVID-19.

3.3   BIG DATA IN HEALTHCARE

In the healthcare domain, Big data plays a vital role, which serves predictive analytic techniques and machine learning framework (Al-Jarrah et al., 2015) to provide a sustainable solutions such as treatment plans implementation and medical care (Andreu-Perez et al., 2015). Big data has three characteristics, namely, 3V—volume (hugeness of data availability), velocity (flow of data), and variety (data from different sources with diversified format) to find out their features from unstructured data (Jee and Kim, 2013). Data sources are broadly classified in three categories like structured data, semi-structured, and unstructured data. In the case of structured data, it includes data type, format, and structure. For instance, data in healthcare domain includes various diseases terminologies, their symptoms and diagnosis information, laboratory results, information of patient such as admission record, drug, and billing information. Semi-structured data is properly organized with minimal structure. Example for this data is generated from sensor devices for effective monitoring of patient's behavior. Unstructured data are those that have no standard structure, which could be included medical prescriptions in the text form, clinical letters, biomedical literature, discharge summaries, and so forth. Big data renders huge potential which would support a broad range of medical and healthcare functions mainly clinical decision support system, population health management, and disease surveillance. Increasing a number of electronic health records (EHR) of patients, social data, ICT-based mHealth omics and behavioral data, eHealth and telehealth devices have approached to develop a novel healthcare frameworks for improving precision medicine and patient care (Martin-Sanchez and Verspoor, 2014; Liang and Kelemen, 2016).

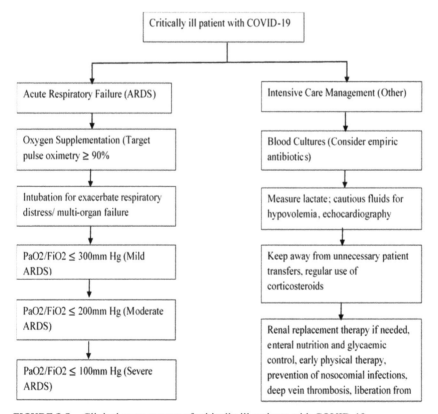

FIGURE 3.3 Clinical management of critically ill patients with COVID-19.

3.4 EXPERIMENTAL METHODS AND MATERIALS

In our Indian healthcare system, many difficulties are being encountered, including nonavailability of resources like hospital rooms, ICU beds, medicines, inefficient testing and shortage of clinical professionals, etc. In an AI-based model, the input data is heterogeneous input data in high volume, that is, from number of patients with diverse format, for example, genetic, medical, environmental, and routine information are gathered from individuals to big cohorts. Big data source comes from different sources, such as demographic, electronic healthcare records, patients' registries, their records, and medical imaging.

Electronic health records are a collection of one million or more patients' data including medical imaging. EHRs have many advantages for handling a huge and modern healthcare related data. An advantage of using EHRs is that complete medical history of patient can be accessed by healthcare professionals and it includes all information related to the medical diagnoses, prescriptions, allergies, demographics, and the results are carried out from various laboratory tests.

Two primary tests RT-PCR and CT are being used to diagnose COVID-19 disease. In this regard, many studies have utilized CT and RT-PCR to evaluate their diagnostic performances (Cao et al., 2020; Zhou et al., 2020; Wang et al., 2020). Figure 3.4 shows the CT scan image of infected COVID-19 patients from mild-to-critical stages. Figure 3.4a illustrates the result of an axial CT image of mild-type patient in this type of category, the patient symptom being onset within 5 days is reflected in the CT image. It shows the thickening of the lung texture.

Figure 3.4b demonstrates an axial CT image of common type patient (Li et al., 2020), after 6 days these symptom onset to CT scan, reflects in both lungs ground-glass opacities. Figure 3.4c shows an axial CT image of moderate ill patient, which illustrates high ground-glass opacities and pulmonary consolidation, enlargement of bronchi, and vessels. Figure 3.4d demonstrates an axial CT image of critically ill COVID-19 patient symptoms can be seen in 9 days. It illustrates extensive ground-glass opacities in several lobes and white lung.

The potential of artificial intelligence (Alimadadi et al., 2020) and machine learning will have to improve the patient care in terms of prediction and classification for real valued attributes. Advancement of machine learning and AI will make an efficient predictive model for large number of COVID-19 patients and will be helpful to all health practitioners.

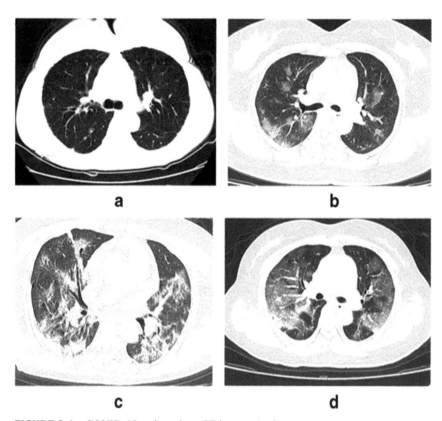

FIGURE 3.4   COVID-19 patient chest CT images (a–d).

Source: Reprinted with permission from Bernheim et al. ©2010 Radiological Society of North America, Inc. (RSNA).

3.5   RESULTS AND DISCUSSION

The application of AI plays a dynamic role in patients who are severely affected by COVID-19. In real sense, AI is able to control and optimize the complex data sets that are in complex system. Caring for hospital and ICU patients (Yang et al., 2020; Arentz et al., 2020; Cao et al., 2020) requires many steps for controlling data with its variation and every data is dependent on or are connected with other multiple steps. Hence, this three-stage model is designed for COVID-19 patients in the form of input, process, and output. The main objective of designing the model is to improve early detection and serious healthcare of patients with COVID-19. Input data are taking from various patients with different format like demographic, epidemiological data, clinical, cellular/molecular, imaging (X-Ray and CT scan), and others. Lot of patients' data will be handled using Big data technique. AI is used for diagnosis and prognosis for patients' disease and decision-making system is also used in making a correct and accurate result to support clinical practitioners in this panic situation.

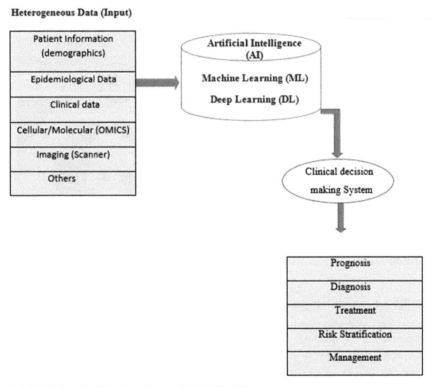

FIGURE 3.5   Artificial intelligence in COVID-19.

3.6   CONCLUSION

The respiratory illness caused by the novel SARS-CoV-2 virus known as COVID-19. It has become pandemic and is a challenge all over the world. The most crucial challenge of this pandemic is the management of COVID-19 patients' urgency of critical respiratory care. Based on the need of this situation, an AI-based model was developed to enhance the critical care of COVID-19 patients. A review of available literature was carried out like PubMed, Google Scholar, Web of Science, etc. More and more clinicians and engineers are working rigorously on a vaccine, testing facilities, and monitoring systems. This chapter highlights the opportunities gained through the use of AI methods for diagnosis and prognosis system. Major efforts of the healthcare system to fight COVID-19 using AI-based decision-making system would support in management of the critically ill patients with COVID-19 more efficiently. By gathering, categorizing, and studying of clinical information from the large number of patients are approaching to diagnosis and decide toward treatment process.

KEYWORDS

- **clinical management**
- **COVID-19**
- **artificial intelligence**
- **diagnosis**
- **prognosis**

REFERENCES

Alimadadi, A.; Aryal, S.; Manandhar, I.; Munroe, P. B.; Joe, B.; Cheng, X. Artificial Intelligence and Machine Learning to Fight COVID-19. *Physiol. Genomics.* **2020**. doi:10.1152/physiolgenomics.00029.2020

Al-Jarrah, O. Y.; Yoo, P. D.; Muhaidat, S.; Karagiannidis, G. K.; Taha, K. Efficient Machine Learning for Big Data: A Review. *Big Data Res.* **2015**, *2*, 87–93. DOI: https://doi.org/10.1016/j.bdr.2015.04.001.

Andreu-Perez, J.; Poon, C. C. Y.; Merrifield, R. D.; Wong, S. T. C.; Yang, G. Z. Big Data for Health. *IEEE J. Biomed. Heal. Inform.* **2015,** *19*, 1193–1208. DOI: https://doi.org/10.1109/JBHI.2015.2450362.

Arentz, M.; Yim, E.; Klaff, L.; et al. Characteristics and Outcomes of 21 Critically Ill Patients with COVID-19 in Washington State. *JAMA* [Online] Mar 19, **2020**. DOI: 10.1001/jama.2020.4326.

Bernheim, X.; Mei, M.; Huang, Y.; et al. Chest CT Findings in Coronavirus Disease-19 (COVID-19): Relationship to Duration of Infection. *Radiology* 0200463. DOI: doi: 10.1148/radiol.2020200463.

Cao, J.; Hu, X.; Cheng, W.; Yu, L.; Tu, W. J.; Liu, Q. Clinical Features and Short-term Outcomes of 18 Patients with Corona Virus Disease 2019 in Intensive Care Unit. *Intensive Care Med.* [Online] Mar 2, **2020**. DOI: 10.1007/s00134-020-05987-7.

Chen, N.; Zhou, M.; Dong, X.; et al. Epidemiological and Clinical Characteristics of 99 Cases of 2019 Novel Coronavirus Pneumonia in Wuhan, China: A Descriptive Study. *Lancet* **2020**, *395*, 507–513.

Guan, W. J.; Ni, Z. Y.; Hu, Y.; et al. Clinical Characteristics of Coronavirus Disease 2019 in China. *N. Engl. J. Med.* [Online] Feb 28, **2020**. DOI: 10.1056/NEJMoa2002032.

Huang, C.; Wang, Y.; Li, X.; et al. Clinical Features of Patients Infected with 2019 Novel Coronavirus in Wuhan, China. *Lancet* **2020**, *395*, 497–506.

Jee, K.; Kim, G. H. Potentiality of Big Data in the Medical Sector: Focus on How To Reshape the Healthcare System. *Healthc. Inform. Res.* **2013**, *19*, 79–85. DOI: https://doi.org/10.4258/hir.2013.19.2.79.

Li, X.; Zeng, X.; Liu, B.; Yu, Y. COVID-19 Infection Presenting with CT Halo Sign. *Radiol. Cardiothoracic. Imaging.* **2020**. DOI: https://doi.org/10.1148/ryct.2020200026.

Liang, Y.; Kelemen, A. Big Data Science and Its Applications in Health and Medical Research: Challenges and Opportunities. *J. Biom. Biostat.* **2016**, *7*, 1–9. DOI: https://doi.org/10.4172/2155-6180.1000307.

Martin-Sanchez, F.; Verspoor, K. Big Data in Medicine Is Driving Big Changes. *Yearb. Med. Inform.* **2014**, *9*, 14–20. DOI: https://doi.org/10.15265/IY-2014-0020.

Phua, J.; Weng, L.; Ling, L.; et al. Intensive Care Management of Coronavirus Disease 2019 (COVID-19): Challenges and Recommendations. *Lancet Respir. Med.* **2020**, *8*, 506–517. DOI: https://doi.org/10.1016/S2213-2600(20)30161-2.

Wang, D.; Hu, B.; Hu, C.; et al. Clinical Characteristics of 138 Hospitalized Patients with 2019 Novel Coronavirus-infected Pneumonia in Wuhan, China. *JAMA* [Online] Feb 7, **2020**. DOI: 10.1001/jama.2020.1585.

World Health Organization. *Clinical Management of Severe Acute Respiratory Infection When Novel Coronavirus (nCoV) Infection Is Suspected*; 2020a. https ://who.int/public cations-detail/clinical-management -of-sever e-acute -respirator y-infection-when-novel -coronavirus(nCov)-infections suspected.

World Health Organization. *Coronavirus Disease (COVID-2019) Situation Reports*; 2020b. https ://www.who.int/emergencies/diseases/novel –coronavirus s-2019/situation-reports.

World Health Organization. *Global Surveillance for Human Infection with Coronavirus Disease (COVID-19)*; 2020c. https ://www.who.int/publications-detai l/global-surveillance for human infection-with-novel -coronavirus-(2019-ncov).

Yang, W.; Cao, Q.; Qin, L.; et al. Clinical Characteristics and Imaging Manifestations of the 2019 Novel Coronavirus Disease (COVID-19): A Multi-center Study in Wenzhou City, Zhejiang, China. *J. Infect.* **2020**, *80*, 388–393.

Yang, X.; Yu, Y.; Xu, J.; et al. Clinical Course and Outcomes of Critically Ill Patients with SARS-CoV-2 Pneumonia in Wuhan, China: A Single Centered, Retrospective, Observational Study. *Lancet Respir. Med.* [Online] Feb 24, **2020**. DOI: https://doi.org/10.1016/S2213-2600(20)30079-5.

Zhou, F.; Yu, T.; Du, R.; et al. Clinical Course and Risk Factors for Mortality of Adult Inpatients with COVID-19 in Wuhan, China: A Retrospective Cohort Study. *Lancet* **2020**, *395*, 1054–1062.

CHAPTER 4

Challenges of Global Healthcare Disasters

DEEPIKA SHERAWAT*, SONIA, and PRIYANKA SHUKLA

*1*School of Computing Science and Engineering, Galgotias University, Greater Noida, Uttar Pradesh, India*

Corresponding author. E-mail: sehrawatdeepika18@gmail.com

ABSTRACT

Human health is rising under the fear of an emerging international health crisis where public health can be easily compromised. In this chapter, various factors that directly or indirectly target public health infrastructure and lead to global crisis like extreme climate changes, refugee health crisis, terrorism and technologyrelated incidents, are discussed. On analysis of the factors that may lead to such disasters, various challenges faced during the disasters are listed specifically pertaining to the healthcare system. The greater risk of disaster can be seen there, where there is a lack of basic amenities, limited access to healthcare, and lack of resources required to cope up from disease. In such situations, it becomes an utmost priority to contain infectious disease and prepare for epidemics, protecting adolescents, elevating health in the climate debate, and delivering healthcare in areas of conflict and crisis. Some of the challenges that are acknowledged by the WHO experts from around the world are issues like healthcare equality, access to medicine, preparedness for epidemics, preventing use of dangerous products, developing new technology and most important clean water, sanitation and hygiene.

4.1 INTRODUCTION

In 2020, the whole world faced a global human crisis which was a big challenge for the medical professionals. Human life is wealth for the nation. When the adverse impact comes upon public health such as threat or natural hazard which exceeds the ability to recover the impacted population is known as public health disaster. In general language "Disaster can be defined as which is growing at a very fast rate and it disrupts its day to day or routine functioning and results in losses of life, environment and economy." Basically, there are two types of disasters.

a)   Natural disaster
b)   Technological disaster

Natural disaster is a kind of disaster which is not in the control of human beings and which is spreading at a very fast rate. And this public health disaster is very dangerous for the whole world as well as for the nation's growth. Whether the world will cope up from the pandemic depends upon the affected population and simultaneously the number of available resources to recover from that including medical, health, human, and financial resources. Disaster can be communicable as well as noncommunicable but it has a great impact on mental health as well as on long term disability. Due to the pandemic situation, most of the people are going into depression because this kind of environment is new to everyone. Disasters are mostly defined as the events which have a sudden onset, but the term does not include all the terrible consequential events that nations and the global community face today. The crisis increases rapidly with the global public health issues taken into consideration as no one is able to find out the solution at first and it takes months or sometimes years to study about the virus and to understand the causes and impact of that particular virus which is a big challenge. Once medical professionals get to know the causes, the World Health Organization can warn the people to take further precautions to prevent it. It is important to understand the challenges that the healthcare industry faces in the face of disastrous situations and it is equally crucial to identify the reasons for the same.

Now everyone is rethinking the policies, practice, research and priority of each disastrous event. Human health is basically defined as a "framework and structure essential to acknowledge urban settings, communities and public states to provide personal well-being and social care to their community" (Institute of Medicine, 1997). Human health is rising under the fear of an emerging international health crisis where public health can be easily compromised. Public health emergencies are emergencies that adversely affect the public health system. The protective framework such as shelter, water, food, sanitization, energy, and health have resulted in remarkable explicit and implicit fatality and distress which is increasing besides the competence of traditional disaster management and its distributors (De Haen and Hemrich, 2007). The greater risk of disaster can be seen there, where there is a lack of basic amenities, limited access to healthcare, and lack of resources required to cope up from disease.

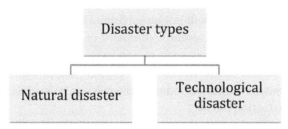

FIGURE 4.1 Types of disaster.

Various gaps can be understood by analyzing the previous disaster situations. To study these gaps is very essential because without this to come up with a solution is almost impossible. By studying such cases, it has been found that certain factors contribute toward the problems faced by the healthcare industry in case of disastrous situations. In most of the cases, it was observed that the training, education, or the operational competencies that are provided to deal with the disastrous situations no longer apply because education, training, and all the operational competencies are not capable of this new era of disaster which comes up abruptly with no parameters. In situations like crisis, it needs to bring together multidisciplinary and transdisciplinary skill sets of multiple facets of experts and knowledge. Some disaster cycle framework should be developed which would help in creating strategic, educational, and operational pathways in the wake of crisis. Such a framework would also help in developing decision-making skills. Global threats and risks to global public health protections, in particular, have become a "unique phenomenon" in the field of disaster medicine. Because of such issues, it has been recommended to add "crisis health" as an independent specialty of medicine. Along with that the training for crisis in the previous decades mostly consisted of content that was very narrow. Despite times where only direct consequences for crisis were considered important, all crises today must measure, define, and manage both direct and indirect consequences. Only in the last decade have recovery and rehabilitation medicine specialists become an integral part of the phase-related cycle, but have primarily focused on sudden-onset disasters and their consequences.

The interdisciplinary understanding of how and what are the human health crisis that can be translated into practical participation of predominant events during, before and after. At the same time various disastrous events have started to reach these challenges. Extraction of a list of natural and human-made disasters can be helpful to understand traditional disaster classification although this methodology will not be useful toward increasing the limit of events. Main focus of the disaster community of healthcare depends upon the public health emergencies such as pandemic and epidemic or sudden onset natural disasters or war and conflict. A systemic approach to reduce the factors or parameters of disaster reducing the risk can be expressed as a work in practice of reduction of risk.

In this chapter, we will discuss about various factors that directly or indirectly target public health infrastructure and lead to global crisis like extreme climate changes, refugee health crisis, terrorism and technology-related incidents. After analyzing the factors that may lead to such disasters, we will try to analyze the challenges during disasters that are related to the healthcare system. In such situations, it becomes an utmost priority to contain infectious disease and prepare for epidemics, protecting adolescents, elevating health in the climate debate, and delivering healthcare in areas of conflict and crisis. Some of the challenges that are acknowledged by the WHO experts from around the world are issues like healthcare equality, access to medicine, preparedness for epidemics, preventing use of dangerous products, developing new technology and most important clean water, sanitation and hygiene.

4.2   IMPACT OF DISASTERS ON HEALTHCARE

Impacts can be direct or indirect. Direct impacts are those which are visible or can be measured, for example, injuries to persons and deaths but indirect impacts are those which are not directly visible. The impact on the economy is not directly visible by a normal human being because an individual person will first work on its own requirements but in the long run it is going to affect the economy as well (Davis et al. 2010). Various kinds of impacts can be shown on humans, healthcare, society, finance, and economy. To categorize this, it can be broadly divided into five categories:

- Impact on human life
- Impact on health care professionals
- Impact on health care resources

- Impact on economy
- Psychological impact on society

Impact of disasters on healthcare	Impact on Human life
	Impact on Health care professionals
	Impact on Health care resources
	Impact on Economy
	Psychological impact on society

FIGURE 4.2   Impact of disasters on healthcare.

These different terms will be explained in detail to understand what can be more harmful. Disaster poses great threats to those areas which have a lack of resources. In this way rural places always lag behind healthcare services and many more. Whenever one is going to study about the various impacts, one must ensure that health and healthcare discrepancies should be addressed.

4.2.1   IMPACT ON HUMAN LIFE

Human life is an asset for the nation. Without healthy humans, a nation cannot be wealthy. When a disaster occurs whether it is natural or technological, it first impacts the people who are directly associated with it. Disaster demands different needs at different locations at different times. When any kind of disaster happens like a terrorist attack or flood, it results in injuries and deaths of human life (Jonkman, 2005).

Sometimes the ratio of recovery rate is less than the ratio of loss of human life. And this recovery rate depends upon how well-trained healthcare professionals are available at a particular place, no matter if the medical professionals are trained but they don't have the required equipment or resources. And it becomes more difficult in the rural areas to recover from these disasters or any kind of disasters.

Conditions change according to time. Just the same way as now, a big challenge is that a new virus attacks the world and no one is aware of the causes, impacts, and how long will it take to recover. Beyond this, it seems a very big problem to the medical professionals and researchers because the reason is unknown and they are doing research on symptoms basis and symptoms vary from person to person. A virus can impact the people with different breakdowns and in different ratios whereas it becomes more serious for those who are already having a prior disease, for example, in case of coronavirus (Khaitan et al., 2020). This deadly virus started from a city in China and started spreading very fast all over the world and even after constant efforts from the researchers, vaccine is not available yet. New symptoms are showing with every new affected person. Some of the symptoms are general but some are very new. Problem starts when an asymptomatic person also becomes the carrier. This deadly virus has taken hold of a lot of people. The consequences of a pandemic are not limited to acute illness or physical injuries but these disasters result in adverse impact on patients of chronic illness such as heart patients.

4.2.2 IMPACT ON HEALTHCARE PROFESSIONALS

Everyone believes that when a disaster takes place it is either a terrorist attack, flood, or something else; the basic and main role is of the public healthcare professionals in how to control the situation. While it is true that it is very tough to control it in the beginning because sometimes conditions are worse and new to everyone and researchers are doing research on it. And by the time something is concluded, it starts spreading at a very fast rate.

The more risk of any disaster is to elderly people, children, and the persons who have underlying prior medical diseases. So, in this condition healthcare professionals play a key role in saving the people and eventually saving the nation and world. Because they are the only people who directly deal with this kind of disaster but sometimes it becomes very difficult for medical professionals also. If a problem arises due to diseases which are noncommunicable then the healthcare professionals can do the treatment and help the patients to recover but in cases when the disease is communicable it becomes very difficult for the healthcare professionals to handle. Some diseases or viruses are highly contagious and spread through the air. In this condition, it becomes a threat for medical professionals also because first they have to save themselves only then they can serve the affected people.

Another big challenge is to reach remote locations with required equipment to deal with these disasters. In a natural disaster like flood it becomes very difficult to supply basic services to survivors and bring people to a safe place. The medical professionals serving people should have good immunization in order to better withstand the need of a disaster.

4.2.3 IMPACT ON HEALTHCARE RESOURCES

A big challenge of any disaster is to make all the resources available required to recover from that particular crisis. Damage to the healthcare system or healthcare resources due to natural disaster or calamity can have a significant impact on the people in the affected area. In fact, making baseline resources available in this area becomes a typical task. If these primarily healthcare resources will not be available it will adversely impact the population of the affected area. Prenatal care, immunization, and management of chronic medical conditions like cardiac, hypertension, and diabetes as well as other basic healthcare services need to be prepared or maintained and make it available to the affected area. Sometimes it becomes a challenge to do so because natural calamity destroys the roads and it becomes impossible to work for the transportation system to make available all the resources. And to provide all the resources via air becomes difficult because of terrain constraints or practical feasibility.

And when disasters like a pandemic happens it becomes quite difficult to fight that even with the available resources if the cause is unknown. Some viruses are so strong that they spread at an alarming rate, and in the process resources required to fight the virus become scarce like in the current pandemic; coronavirus, various emergency resources are required and it has become quite difficult to arrange them on a large scale due to ever increasing demand. Even to provide the basic things such as masks, gloves, and PPE kits became tough at the very beginning due to its contagious nature and high demand. First these basic things are mandatory for healthcare professionals because they have to take care of the patients and after that the person who is affected becomes a priority. All such factors adversely impact the health of people. Lack of resources is directly proportional to the loss of human life. A country with a high level of healthcare resources should be considered as a safe and powerful country. Those who depend upon outside assistance will find that the process of recovery is more difficult and takes quite a long time.

4.2.4 IMPACT ON ECONOMY

When a pandemic, crisis, or disaster happens it directly or indirectly impacts the economy. Economic growth is the base of country growth. When a natural calamity happens or one can say a terrorist attack has takes place on the medical facility or any other thing which is the base of the country, the government needs to take action to establish it again and it directly impacts the economy (Hallegatte and Przyluski, 2010). Due to such crisis, sometimes the government has to take strict actions for the well-being of the natives of the nation, for example, in the wake of COVID-19 most of the nations opted for complete lockdown in order to curb the fast rate of spreading virus which impacted the economy of most of the nations around the world. This impacts the gross domestic product (GDP) and becomes difficult to stabilize the condition. In these conditions survival of the poor people or the labor class becomes very difficult and the government is bound to provide all the basic resources for their survival. These funds are withdrawn from the amount which has been kept for the nation's growth and it directly impacts the economy.

If external infrastructure of army base camps, hospitals, or any other basic things gets damaged because of any natural calamity then also to establish it again funds will be withdrawn from government funds which will affect the economy.

4.2.5 PSYCHOLOGICAL IMPACT ON SOCIETY

People always look for the physical effects on humans because it is visible but a natural disaster affects more on the mental state of a person. One can say that natural disasters change the mental state of a person, how to think in certain conditions, how to react in certain conditions. Sometimes it becomes the cause of the depression. Most of the people are getting into depression because of a sudden impact of disaster on their lives.

Fear in the people increases when the nature of disaster is a highly contagious disease and it becomes a more prominent factor for mental tension or depression. Emotional distress level of these disasters tends to range from minor emotional distress to counseling sessions and further-more to psychological pathology (Hall et al., 2004). It all depends upon the extent and severity of the psychological effects. In this pandemic, mental tension becomes the basic cause of suicide. People take severe steps due to depression because some of them don't have money to eat because several people lose their jobs.

4.3 GLOBAL CRISIS

A crisis is a situation in which something or someone is impacted by one or more serious problems and when this happens on a global scale then this kind of crisis is defined as a global crisis (Benatar et al., 2011). When any crisis is reaching people globally can be termed as a global crisis. Global crisis can be global health crisis, global financial crisis, global economic crisis, and many more.

The current crisis, that is, corona is a global health crisis which is affecting people not only of Asia but of the whole world. And when this kind of health crisis occurs this is defined as a pandemic. This pandemic situation is creating fear in everyone. Because corona is communicable through air and airborne diseases, it spreads at a very fast rate. And to find out the solution for this newly discovered virus is time consuming because every other day new symptoms are coming for different locations and with a different human being. And this global health crisis is not environmental, it is social because millions of people are affected by it, it is economical because the world's economy is getting affected by it.

4.3.1 IMPACT OF GLOBAL CRISIS ON HEALTHCARE SYSTEM

The world is in a mess and most of this mess is created by us only. Our healthcare system was not designed to deal with this unpredictable large-scale health challenge and this happened for the first time in history that a health crisis pulled down the complete global economy. It painfully describes that healthcare and economy have become inseparable and this is because developed markets are actually affected this time. This financial crisis let the markets down, GDP down, and many more, etc (Bialynicki-Birula, 2014). And Government is saying that people are the reason for this mess because this coronavirus like situation is spreading because of communication, as this disease is communicable. Educated people are sitting at home and taking most of the precautions but some people are acting as a coronavirus carrier due to many reasons.

When any natural disaster happens like earthquake, flood, or cyclone, the infrastructure of the hospitals is impacted. Even people do not get treatment for injuries because the damage caused by these natural disasters is so high that medical professionals are unable to get the medical resources. In the same way, banks also got affected by this type of damage and financial crisis can also be seen in this situation which is directly proportional to the economy. And if the economy goes down then the government also feels that to provide medical resources required for better conditions is getting difficult. So, one can say that any kind of global crisis whether it is a financial, terrorist attack, or anything else is going to badly affect the healthcare system, and a good healthcare system and better medical resources are the foundation of a well-developed and stable country (Bialynicki-Birula, 2014). Any kind of global crisis is going to have an adverse impact on the country in every term.

4.3.2   TYPES OF GLOBAL CRISIS THAT IMPACT HEALTHCARE

Global crisis that can impact the healthcare can be divided as:

- Natural disaster
- Pandemic
- Terrorist attack
- Food crisis
- Health and medical practice

4.3.2.1   NATURAL DISASTER

When any kind of natural disaster happens whether it is a flood, earthquake, cyclone, or terrorist attack (Severin and Phillip, 2020), it always impacts healthcare because healthcare services are required to handle its effects. And it becomes a tough challenge to arrange all these resources in such situations.

4.3.2.2   PANDEMIC

Any pandemic like situation like coronavirus spreads at a large rate, which affects the whole world. Medical professionals are searching for the vaccine based upon the symptoms and every time new symptoms are showing in different persons which are making it more difficult to invent.

4.3.2.3   TERRORIST ATTACK

Whenever any terrorist attack happens it leaves the people of that country or that particular place in a nonhealing situation because it creates a feeling of fear in the mind of people, in this way it is going to impact in a psychological way. People take time to recover and heal from such situations.

4.3.2.4   FOOD CRISIS

When any kind of natural disaster happens like an earthquake, terrorist attack, or cyclone, it directly impacts the transport services which are the source to deliver basic essentials like basic food items and products of daily life use. So in this way people usually face food crises.

4.3.2.5   HEALTH AND MEDICAL PRACTICE

These natural disasters directly impact the services provided by health professionals. If a terrorist attack happens in a hospital or in a medical facility then it becomes questionable how medical professionals are going to help the people when they themselves are under attack. Another side of this attack is to make available the medical resources which are a big task in these situations. So when any disaster occurs it affects the demand and supply of medical services depending on the severity and area of impact.

4.4   CHALLENGES IN HEALTHCARE DURING DISASTER

In the previous topic, it was discussed how crises at global level impact the health services and various types of such global crises. Some of the crises that impact the public health infrastructure are natural calamities due to climate change, terrorism, and accidents that are a byproduct of scientific advancements. All these factors have an impact on the healthcare services either directly or indirectly. As the factors affecting the healthcare services at such a large scale cannot be contained, so keeping in mind such situations some strategies are developed. According to WHO experts, the world faces problems like infectious diseases, epidemics, protecting adolescents, improving health due to change in climate, and providing help in areas of crisis and conflict. Such broad issues must be taken into account while preparing healthcare facilities for disaster.

The WHO Director-General stated that "most of the countries are unable to invest into good resources in core health priorities and systems which is a thing of concern." The concern expressed by Mr. Tedro Adhanom Ghebreyesus is very much valid because most of the developing and developed nations have not paid much attention to the development of healthcare facilities. This in turn puts lives, livelihoods, and economies in jeopardy. He also adds that "such issues are not as simple to address, but they are within reach" (WHO, 2020) All such issues are not only related to healthcare but are related to various other fields and sectors. Therefore, there is a need of response from more than just the healthcare sector. All the nations are at the shared risk for which it's a shared responsibility to act in the direction. Most of the top health challenges are listed by WHO and these challenges are not independent of each other; some of the issues are urgent and are interlinked. The challenges listed by WHO are:

- Climate crisis
- Delivering health in conflict and crisis
- Healthcare equality
- Expanding access to medicines
- Infectious diseases
- Preparing for epidemics
- Dangerous products
- Investing in people who defend our health

- Harnessing new technologies
- Clean water, sanitation, hygiene

4.4.1 CLIMATE CRISIS

According to WHO, climate crisis implies a health crisis. Climate change leads to extreme weather events, escalates malnutrition, and contributes to the spread of infectious diseases like malaria. Pollution is a major cause of climate change. The pollution emissions contaminate the air and cause global warming. Pollution is responsible for more than 25% of deaths from heart attack, lung cancer, stroke, and chronic respiratory disease.

The change in climate has adversely affected various aspects of human life with respect to extreme weather, loss of biodiversity, emergencies of insufficiency in food, energy and in particular water. When these issues are left unattended then they worsen and lead to crisis situations like disasters which eventually lead to public health emergencies and conflicts; in such cases preventive measures should be taken as well as preparations must be done for crisis management. Balkan Peninsula is a geographic area in southeastern Europe which is known for occurrences of territorial, religious, and ethnic conflict is at present suffering from climate change-induced water shortages (Cooke, 2019). A quarter of the world's population across 17 countries lives in "regions of extremely high water stress, a measure of the level of competition over water resources." Regions like Qatar, Israel, and Lebanon are the ones with supreme water-stressed while enlightening a more complex and demanding global water crisis that requires "better information, planning, and water management" emphasizing the strategic level of concern that these crises provoke (Holden and Doshi, 2019).

The health crisis managers need to identify the populations at risk, the health education, and public consciousness priorities of diverse groups, broad public health information promotions, financial support for the health crisis managers and their programs, and assurance that no adaptation approaches will exacerbate further health and social differences such as age, preexisting medical conditions, and social deprivations that along with exposure to heat and cold, air pollution, pollen, food safety risks, disruptions of both access to and functioning of health services and facilities, and both emerging infections and flooding in making people more vulnerable to adverse health outcomes (Burkle, 2019).

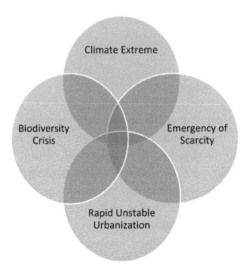

FIGURE 4.3   Conflict confluence of climate extremes, rapid unsustainable urbanization, emergencies of scarcity, and biodiversity crisis (Adapted from Burkle, 2019a).

The governments should work in collaboration with giant companies and NGOs to eradicate the issues of air pollution and eventually mitigate the related health issues. In 2019, over 80 cities in more than 50 countries committed to the WHO's air quality guidelines, agreeing to align their air pollution and climate policies.

4.4.2   DELIVERING HEALTH IN CONFLICT AND CRISIS

In situations of conflict among groups or any situation of crisis has a significant impact on healthcare. It is also observed that most of the places that need support from organizations like WHO are those which are more prone to conflict and at such places the possibility of disease outbreak is increased suggestively. And so is the trend to target the healthcare facilities and providers is quite disturbing. In the last year, approximately 193 people lost their lives due to attacks on healthcare facilities. There were 978 recorded attacks by WHO on the healthcare facilities in 11 countries in the previous year. Such attacks on the healthcare facilities not only disrupt the services but also deprive people of healthcare for years. In some areas people have been forced to move out of their homes and even travel to safer places in lieu of conflicts.

The WHO is working toward strengthening the healthcare system, availability of long-term financing and improving preparedness for complex healthcare emergencies in coordination with the countries and partners. There is a need for contributions from political organizations as well as nongovernment organizations to work in the direction to resolve conflicts. In addition to that significant work needs to be done in strengthening weak healthcare systems and in protecting workers and facilities from attacks.

4.4.3 HEALTHCARE EQUALITY

Most of the developing countries where there are issues like socioeconomic gaps face discrepancies in terms of quality of healthcare facilities. The most depressing scenario is that these situations are nowhere improving with the growth of the country's economy. The population from necessitous backgrounds is always lacking the healthcare facilities that are a right to all. And on the other hand, the affluent have access to all the top class facilities because they can afford it. According to WHO, there is not only an 18 year gap in the life expectancy of the dwellers of rich and poor nations but also the gap is significant in the rural areas and cities.

There are various categories in which WHO is working to bring equality like child and maternal care, nutrition, mental health, gender equality, and most important of all access to safe drinking water and adequate sanitization. It is a dire need to work in collaboration with nations that need support to fill in the gap in terms of equality for health. The WHO has also instructed countries to look in on these issues and to allocate 1% or more of their GDP to primary healthcare so that people can have access to essential services.

4.4.4 EXPANDING ACCESS TO MEDICINES

One third of the world population does not have access to proper diagnostic tools, medicines, vaccines, and essential health products. These situations lead to problems like loss of life and degradation of health. High cost of drugs, lack of generic medication, commercialization of healthcare facilities are the factors because of which most of the not-so well-off people do not have access to proper medical facilities. Lack of access to essential health facilities has an adverse effect on health and lives and eventually causes drug resistance. The WHO has been working in coordination with nations to improve access to medication, fake medical products, or drugs so as to increase the capability of low-income group countries to have good quality medical facilities and be capable of sufficient diagnostic machines and products for treating specifically noncommunicable diseases.

4.4.5   INFECTIOUS DISEASES

Every year millions of people die due to transmission of infectious diseases like HIV, malaria, tuberculosis, tropical diseases, viral hepatitis, and several others. Most of the people infected by such diseases are poor. Even there are certain diseases which can be prevented by vaccines but due to negligence and lack of proper diagnosis diseases like measles continue to take 140,000 lives almost every year. Another disease is dengue that sickens 50–100 million people every year according to WHO. Polio is a rearising concern, which once was eradicated but its cases are still on a rise since 2014. For some viral diseases, vaccines and antiviral drugs have allowed us to keep infections from spreading widely, and have helped sick people recover. In recent decades, several viruses have jumped from animals to humans and triggered sizable outbreaks, claiming thousands of lives. Some of such diseases are Hantavirus was first found in the United States in 1993, Marburg virus in 1967 in Germany which was caused due to import of infected monkeys from Uganda, Ebola outbreak in 2014 in West Africa that killed 90% of the infected people and the most recent one is SARS-CoV-2 also called COVID-19 which was first identified in December 2019 in a Chinese city in Wuhan.

There is a need for input from various sectors like political organizations, scientific and research laboratories, funding sources that can help in finding medication timely to treat such infectious diseases and prevent loss of lives and in strengthening immunization routine along with improving essential health services.

4.4.6   PREPARING FOR EPIDEMICS AND PANDEMICS

An epidemic is a disease that affects a large number of people within a community, population, or region, and a pandemic is an epidemic that is spread over multiple countries and continents. Pandemics and large-scale epidemics that can claim loss of lives of masses, disrupt civilizations, and shatter economies. WHO's Health Emergencies Programme (WHE) is working with member states to help countries to prepare for large-scale outbreaks and pandemics. Countries are also encouraged to involve the whole of society for effective pandemic preparedness and response. The pandemics are new and highly infectious airborne viruses that have an impact on the population that lack immunity. Some of the most infectious viruses that have infected masses are influenza. Some of the diseases are spread by blood-feeding anthropoids like mosquitoes, fleas, and ticks. Such diseases are called vector-borne diseases. The vector-borne diseases are Nile virus, dengue fever, malaria, Zika, and chikungunya to name a few. Most of these diseases are fanned by climate change.

Countries make huge investments in developing technologies, preparing for different kinds of attacks from terrorist organizations but preparing for protection against virus attacks that can be far more deadly than all others has always been ignored. Such attacks by the virus cannot just have an impact on the health of the natives of a country but also disrupts socioeconomic growth. Taking example from the current scenario of COVID-19, the world economy has been brought to its knees as an impact of this pandemic. Much needed efforts need to be put up by the nations to be prepared for facing such emergency situations by strengthening the healthcare system in accordance with it.

4.4.7 DANGEROUS PRODUCTS

During such scenarios, one of the most impacted supplies is the food. Problems like lack of food and unsafe food are the ones that are mostly faced by the nations in times of natural and man-made emergency situations. Another factor that can be held responsible for low immunity and people being more prone to diseases and infections is low-nutrition diets. Eliminating trans fats from dietary elements is a way by which many of such diseases can be prevented up to a great extent. The WHO is working in coordination with the countries to develop evidence-based policies, investments, and sustainable diets. One more significant factor that leads to lack of health is consumption of drugs and tobacco. The consumption of tobacco and other narcotic drugs results in degradation of health of the one who is consuming as well as of those who they live with. Strict control policies need to be implemented by the nations in order to keep a check on the availability of tobacco-based drugs.

4.4.8   INVESTING IN PEOPLE WHO DEFEND OUR HEALTH

The world is facing a shortage of healthcare workers. It was predicted that there will be a need of more than 18 million healthcare workers in low-income and middle-income group countries by 2030. It is being observed that most of the healthcare workers suffer in terms of good training according to the situations of disaster and lack of good salaries. Most of the healthcare workers face negligence in times of emergency situations.

4.4.9   HARNESSING NEW TECHNOLOGIES

Technological advancements need to be promoted in order to fight against the continuously evolving virus. Technologies like genome editing and using artificial intelligence can revolutionaries the ability to prevent disease, timely diagnoses, and treat different diseases. The WHO issued guidelines in 2019 on editing human genome and digitizing health by bringing together experts to review evidence and in guiding the policies. The organization is also working to help countries in planning, adopting, and benefiting from new tools that provide clinical and public health solutions.

4.4.10   CLEAN WATER, SANITATION, HYGIENE

Facilities like clean water, proper sanitation, and hygiene are one of the elementary requirements in which one of the four health facilities lack. Organizations lacking these factors lead to poor health and eventually increase the chances of infection for patients and health workers. These services are also termed as WASH. The WHO has been working with more than 35 countries to improve WASH services in healthcare facilities. International agencies should work along with governments and communities to achieve proper facilities in these aspects.

4.5 PHASE-RELATED HEALTH CRISIS MANAGEMENT

The role of the health professionals is not only confined to the time of event of crisis or in the process of mitigation of such situations but, the healthcare professionals are required to have multiple skill sets that can be applicable to all the phases of crisis management. The healthcare professionals are not only expected to work as a team with other healthcare professionals but also with the professionals from different other domains (Center for Disaster Philanthropy, 2019). The complete process of health crisis management can be categorized into three phases which are as follows:

- Prevention and preparedness phase
- Response phase
- Recovery and rehabilitation phase

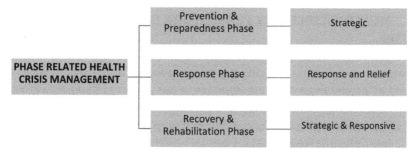

FIGURE 4.4   Phase-related health crisis management (Burkle, 2019b).

4.5.1 PREVENTION AND PREPAREDNESS PHASE

This phase works on the strategic level to take preventive measures in order to prevent a health crisis and to be prepared from all aspects in case of any such outbreak. The phase mostly concentrates on developing an integrated mitigation program that includes building strategies which can help in reducing the chances of risk.

4.5.2 RESPONSE PHASE

In the times of crisis and emergency situations, it becomes very crucial to have a well-prepared response team that is capable and trained to act according to the need of time. This phase focuses on the response and relief programs and emphasizes on providing skill-based requirements. It is also responsible for monitoring and mitigating direct and indirect mortality and morbidity.

4.5.3   *RECOVERY AND REHABILITATION PHASE*

After an epidemic or disaster, a lot of efforts need to be put-in in order to recover from that situation. There is a need to reconstruct the societies as well as make efforts to help the population recover. This is the main priority of this phase to work in accordance to the requirements of people to rehabilitate after any disaster.

4.6   MULTIDISCIPLINARY FRAMEWORK FOR GLOBAL HEALTH CRISIS

Whenever an epidemic or a disaster affects a nation or the world, there is a need of people from different domains to put in efforts to emerge out of such situations. Various researchers working in this area have proposed that there needs to be a common program that focuses on the core concepts from multiple disciplines (MacLachlan, 2009). The effectiveness of a group of people working as a response team is believed to increase if it consists of team members having multidisciplinary and interdisciplinary knowledge (MacLachlan, 2009). Interdisciplinary means combining subjects in a new way by working between different disciplines (Adams et al., 2013). By combining different streams, there is a need to create such teams that have knowledge of multiple streams and they shall be capable of performing a range of tasks in the time of need. In the same way careful planning, team member selection, procedure and protocol writing, training and practice will yield a similar success level.

Situations of the health crisis must be handled by multidisciplinary design methods like collaboration of natural and social science is crucial in solving various challenges that humanity is facing today (Van Noorden, 2015). On the one hand such things need to be implemented and are deemed essential for phase-related health crisis management but it still is unclear to what extent it can be actually implemented.

KEYWORDS

- **disaster**
- **healthcare**
- **COVID-19**
- **global crisis**
- **pandemic**

REFERENCES

Adams, L. M.; Smith, L.; Weeks, S. Multidisciplinary Team Response to Support Survivors of Mass Casualty Disasters: A Systematic Review Protocol. *JBI Database Syst. Rev. Implement. Rep.* **2013,** *11*, 8–20.

Benatar, S. R.; Gill, S.; Bakker, I. Global Health and the Global Economic Crisis. *Am. J. Public Health* **2011,** *101*(4), 646–653. https://doi.org/10.2105/AJPH.2009.188458

Bialynicki-Birula, P. Impact of Global Financial Crisis on Healthcare Expenditures in Developed Countries. In *Proceedings of Economics and Finance Conferences*, no. 0401539. International Institute of Social and Economic Sciences, 2014.

Burkle, F. Challenges of Global Public Health Emergencies: Development of a Health-Crisis Management Framework. *Tohoku J. Exp. Med.* **2019a,** *249*. 10.1620/tjem.249.33.

Burkle, F. Development of a Health-Crisis Management Framework Challenges of Global Public Health Emergencies: Development of a Health-Crisis Management Framework, 2019b.

Center for Disaster Philanthropy. The Disaster Life Cycle, Overview, 2019. https://disasterphilanthropy.org/issue-insight/the-disaster-lifecycle/

Cooke, K. Balkan Water Reserves May Soon Run Short. https://climatenewsnetwork.net/balkan-water-reserves-maysoon-run-short/ (accessed Aug 8, 2019).

Davis, J. R.; Wilson, S.; Brock-Martin, A.; Glover, S.; Svendsen, E. R.. The Impact of Disasters on Populations with Health and Health Care Disparities. *Disaster Med. Public Health Prep.* **2010,** *4*(1), 30.

De Haen, H.; Hemrich, G. The Economics of Natural Disasters: Implications and Challenges for Food Security. *Agric. Econ.* **2007,** *37*, 31–45.

Hall, Molly J., Anthony Ng, Robert J. Ursano, Harry Holloway, Carol Fullerton, and Jacob Casper. Psychological Impact of the Animal-Human Bond in Disaster Preparedness and Response. *J. Psychiatr. Pract.* **2004,** *10*(6), 368–374.

Hallegatte, S.; Przyluski, V., *The Economics of Natural Disasters*. In *CESifo Forum*, Vol. 11(2); ifoInstitutfürWirtschaftsforschung an der Universität München: München, 2010; pp 14–24.

Holden, E.; Doshi, V. Extreme Water Stress Affects a Quarter of the World's Population, say Experts. https://www.theguardian.com/global-development/2019/aug/06/extreme-water-stress-affects-a-quarter-of-the-worldspopulation-say-experts (accessed Aug 6, 2019).

Institute of Medicine (US) Committee on Using Performance Monitoring to Improve Community Health. *Improving Health in the Community: A Role for Performance Monitoring. Understanding Health and Its Determinants*; Durch, J. S., Bailey, L. A., Stoto, M. A., Eds.; National Academies Press (US): Washington (DC), 1997, 2. https://www.ncbi.nlm.nih.gov/books/NBK233009/

Jonkman, S. N. Global Perspectives on Loss of Human Life Caused by Floods. *Nat. Hazards* **2005,** *34,* (2), 151–175.

Khaitan, S.; Mitra, A.; Shukla, P.; Chakraborty, S. Statistical Investigation of Novel Corona Virus COVID-1. *Int. J. Control Autom.* **2020,** *13*(2s), 1–6.

MacLachlan, M. Rethinking Global Health Research: Towards Integrative Expertise. *Global Health* **2009,** *5*, 6.

Noji, Eric K. Disaster Epidemiology: Challenges for Public Health Action. *J. Public Health Policy* **1992,** *13*(3), 332–340.

Severin, P. N.; Phillip A. Jacobson. Types of Disasters. In *Nursing Management of Pediatric Disaster*, Springer: Cham, 2020; pp 85–197.

Van Noorden, R. Interdisciplinary Research by the Numbers. *Nature* **2015,** *525,* 306–307.

WHO Names Top 13 Global Health Challenges for the New Decade - Medscape - Jan 14, 2020.

CHAPTER 5

Healthcare Disaster Prediction with IoT, Data Analytics, and Machine Learning

PRIYANKA SHUKLA[1*], AKANKSHA SEHGAL[2], SONIA[1], and DEEPIKA SHERAWAT[1]

[1]Galgotias University, Greater Noida, India

[2]Lotus Petal Foundation, Gurgaon, India

*Corresponding author. E-mail: engpriyanka.8@gmail.com

ABSTRACT

Disaster may be natural or man-made, for example, terrorist attack, earthquakes, landslides, cyclones and storms/wave surges, floods or disease epidemics, and insect/animal plagues like COVID-19. Due to disaster, normal patterns of life get disturbed affecting the physical and psychological health. It is challenging to predict the likelihood of occurrence of disaster but people should have the aim to handle this acute and long term. Any type of disaster affecting the health stresses for healthcare. Due to this pandemic situation, the health of the person is affected. In the current scenario, so much has been impacted due to COVID-19. People are affected because they didn't get proper help, timely and admissible solutions for the same. When no one is prepared for this type of situation like disasters, people face issues like availability of hospitals and medicine, loss of their family, etc. To handle this problem, the Internet of things (IoT) is playing an important role in healthcare. There are so many android apps and IoT devices for health monitoring. To minimize the impact of this disaster or to predict it early, technical and medical innovations are necessary. One such example is Aarogya Setu app that is making use of GPS and Bluetooth to track coronavirus-infected people. IoT devices generate a huge amount of data that needs to be analyzed.

This chapter will discuss different IoT devices, data analytics, and machine learning (ML) algorithms that are used to predict disasters, thus, affecting the health.

5.1 INTRODUCTION

Unnatural disaster or man-made disaster are hard to predict but can be prevented. With a little vigilance, they shouldn't occur in the first place. Events such as gas leaks, oil spills, nuclear meltdowns, and industrial fires transpire through human error and carry grave consequences.

The Internet of things (IoT) is a vital field; it has been one of the major research areas in recent years. The quality for well-being of life remains the major concern while using a smart system. The demand of smart product has increased manifolds in healthcare domain. Healthcare makes an enormous environment including personal care, smart pills, smart beds, glucose meters, etc. IoT has predisposed and probable medical opportunities especially for the old. Its role is not only restricted to physical but mental well-being as well. The healthcare industry with pocket friendly and associable devices has a great potential going forward.

IoT-based medical devices primarily gather massive data for identifying the symptoms for giving further care to the patients remotely. It can use it for real-time tracking of equipment like wheelchair, oxygen tanks, etc. These data have tremendous power for the healthcare organizations raising the quality of healthcare given to the patients, for possible forecast of prolonged diseases. It can help to tackle the serious conditions more systematically. However, it is accompanied with the demerit, since the bulk of data has the personal information of the patients which poses a security and privacy threat. But this era has a significant rise in awareness of healthcare. This can help to predict disease so that the precautions can be taken.

Data analytics and machine learning (ML) can play a vital role in customer service, stock market, student performance prediction as well as in healthcare to predict the disease. On the basis of history dataset, the forecasting can be done. Like in case of floods, wind speed, rainfall intensity, central pressure of the hurricane, and precipitation, weather factors can be used for forecasting. Temperature, etc. is to be taken for learning the dataset then prediction can be done using ML algorithms. This will be a good effort, if an occurrence of disaster can be forecast. This will help in saving numerous lives and also help in maintaining the economy. In the current scenario, pandemic data related to health are being generated like positive cases, recovered case. As cases are increasing exponentially, so the requirement of availability of hospitals, beds, and medicine is also increasing. Prediction will be done with help of ML algorithms.

5.1.1 TYPES OF DISASTER

There are two types of disasters that are natural disaster and human made disaster. Natural disaster may be due to flood, earthquake, landslide, etc and man-made disasters like hazardous material incidents, terrorism, oil spill, industrial fires, gas leak (Severin, 2020).

TABLE 5.1 Types of Disaster.

Natural disaster	Man-made disaster
Earthquake	Nuclear
Flood	Biological
Landslide	Chemical
Cyclone	
Tsunamis	
Heat wave	

5.2 IMPACT OF DISASTER ON HEALTH

Every year huge populations get affected by natural disasters or man-made disasters all over the world. Many of the people get homeless, or injured due to disaster. Disaster directly or indirectly affects the health of the population. People need extra care during the disaster or after the disaster. After the disaster, the population gets so many health issues like, mental health issues, communicable diseases spread after natural disasters, safety risks, and various others. Because of the disaster, so many people die. This gives mental tension to the people. If the disaster has happened due to any communicable disease, then it will affect the people who come in contact with many others. Like in 2020, a pandemic due to COVID-19 has occurred (Khaitan et al., 2020). Coronavirus is a communicable disease that spreads due to contact with a person, from sneezing, coughing. So as to prevent community spread of the disease restrictions were put by the governments. Not just life, so many people have lost their jobs because of its impact on the economy of nations. There are so many types of health issues that are caused by disaster which have direct impact on health like injury, communicable disease, acute illness, chronic illness, psychological effects, and some indirect impact on people due to disaster are loss of primary healthcare and impact on normal living conditions. Various types of health issues that are impacted by disaster are:

Direct influence on health due to disaster may cause injury, communicable disease, acute illness, chronic illness, psychological effects. Injury may occur due to any natural disaster like earthquake, flood, etc. Communicable disease may be due to any man-made disaster like any chemical disaster, flu, etc. As in 2020, due to coronavirus people's mental health got affected and also got psychological effects.

a.　Direct influence on the healthcare system may affect hospitals, healthcare centers. This also damages the infrastructure, loss of family members. Like during the spread of COVID-19, shortage of medical equipment like ventilator, masks, sanitizer has happened all over the world and has been increased exponentially.

b.　The indirect effect on people's health may affect normal living conditions. Due to any disaster people who are not capable of taking service may suffer more. And people who are from outside assistance find the recovery process longer.

Indirect impact on the healthcare system may damage external infrastructure. This may impact business just like in COVID-19 lockdown has happened in India and various other nations because of which all the shops, industries, factories, etc. were totally closed, which indirectly impacted the economy. Healthcare systems depend on transportation of equipment and for medicine, and we talk about natural disasters that may destroy roads, infrastructure and due to infrastructure, shortage of medical care, water, food as a backup system does not always work systematically.

5.3　TYPES OF IoT DEVICES FOR HEALTHCARE

As we are living in the era in which experts and researchers are starting to utilize smart technology for securing life, the technologies have the capabilities to prepare for the risk during natural disasters. One such technology is LoRa devices. The wireless technology offers wider range with low power and is short for long range spread spectrum modulation technique. These devices enable smart IoT applications which solve major challenges like natural resource reduction, pollution control, and energy management.

5.3.1   DRONE

A drone is an IoT device which helps in monitoring the damage caused during disaster, analyzing healthcare needs, etc. Initially drones were made to keep an eye on particular areas by capturing photos, making videos, but nowadays its use is extended to give service to healthcare or to deliver the food essentials and medical supplies to the disaster-prone areas. It helps in the healthcare domain to deliver the vaccines, medicines, etc. Drone becomes an important IoT device during any epidemic situation where the cause is communicable disease causing virus.

In future, drones may be extended to work for small areas in homes to give healthcare services and can provide blood that is drawn from someone to the provider who asked for the same.

Mobile technology is being installed in healthcare organizations to solve the issues in today's world. Like some other wearable remote monitoring, telemedicine and information sharing platforms are altering healthcare. Robots, artificial intelligence (AI), and drones will help in healthcare to reduce the cost and error by humans.

According to the author, the advantage of drones is that it saves the travelling time for treatment and diagnosis. It also helps in difficult areas to get medical help like mountains, snow-covered, or valley areas. The disadvantage of it is while using the drone many people tend to lose their jobs as the requirement of staff will get affected. Another disadvantage of it is that it requires trained staff and it cannot cover long distances as well as not be able to load heavy things. Drone is designed to reach safely at a particular location but when the battery gets low then it may lose the communication (https://www.kaggle.com/).

A big obstacle in the use of medical drones is the legal permission from Aviation authorities. For instance, in India use of drones for commercial purposes is not allowed and in the United States under some rules of the Federal Aviation Administration (FAA) licenses are granted but the weight of the drone must not be greater than 25 kg and must be within the visual line-of-site where the maximum ground speed should be of 100 miles per hour and a maximum altitude of 400 ft above ground level (https://www. kaggle.com/).

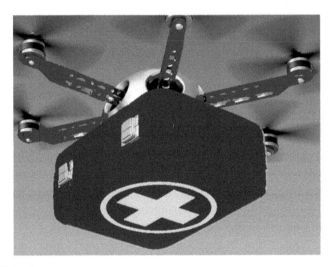

FIGURE 5.1   Drone.

5.3.2   ROBOTICS

Robotics helps health workers to measure the temperature, taking the blood pressure of patients remotely which in turn has the least chance of infection to health workers during the pandemic situation due to infections like coronavirus. Robots can also be used to provide food to patients who are isolated to prevent the viral spread. Robots are operating through mobile applications or remote control devices for doing monotonous tasks that require least human communication, which facilitates the healthcare workers to make use of their skills like emotional availability to patients which robots lack.

Using robots during disasters may help a lot in pandemic situations like COVID-19 robots are used to serve food and medicine in hospitals to reduce chances of spreading infection in many countries. However, the major disadvantage of robots is cost as developing these machines and training them to work efficiently is very expensive. Extensive use of robots also leads to the staff getting jobless and they work according to the restricted programming fed into it which may fail due to some technical issue.

FIGURE 5.2 Robot.

5.3.3 TELEMEDICINE

In telemedicine, electronic communication devices are used to exchange medical information from multiple places which improves the patient's health and care. During this pandemic due to COVID-19 telemedicine became an emerging technology. Because of COVID-19 people cannot go outside due to lockdown they need to maintain physical and social distance, travel constraints are also there. So for the treatment of chronic pain, it can be done at home. One of the good things about telemedicine is that can be used for supply and demand balance. We can virtually deploy doctors even in the remotest corner of the country and, at the same time, survey and treat the patients at their home," says Dr. Moorthy. The World Health Organization (WHO) has also recognized telemedicine (Mosavi et al., 2018) as important phase in the process of firming up the Health System Retort to COVID-19. The optimization of service delivery decisions and the clinical performance can be enhanced taking telemedicine as a substitute method, as recommended by WHO.

5.4 DISASTER PREDICTION USING IOT DEVICES

IoT devices are helping to predict disaster with great efficiency. One cannot prevent natural disasters but can detect it or predict it buy using sensors to monitor. Some of the sensors that have been deployed for predicting natural disasters are:

Seismic sensors (seismometers) and vibration sensors (seismoscopes) are used to monitor earthquakes (and downstream tsunamis).

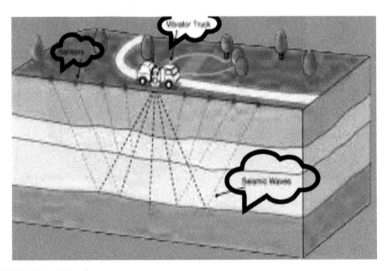

FIGURE 5.3   Seismic sensor.

Source: Adapted from http://www.innoseis.com/seismic-surveying/

Use of radar maps for sensing the signature "hook echo" of a tornado (i.e., a hook that extends from the radar echo).

Moisture levels are measured by the flood sensors. Monitoring of the height of water along a river, stream, etc is done by water level sensors.

Though at a nascent stage, but wildfire sensors hopefully will be able to sense trace amounts of smoke and fire.

IoT technology is not able to stop disaster or any pandemic; however, it can help to predict or prepare an early warning system to recover from disaster. IoT devices also help in as a relief system during or after disaster. We can take an example of it; if the tree sensors are installed, which can help to sense fire nearby measuring the parameters like moisture, temperature, carbon dioxide level, etc. Sensors connected with any android device through an app will get the alarm or message about location so that the population near to this kind of disaster can be saved. Other sensors: microwave sensor and infrared sensor which sense about the Earth movement and measure the flood and people's movement. Technology has been used to help communities predict natural disasters by using Semtech's LoRa technology.

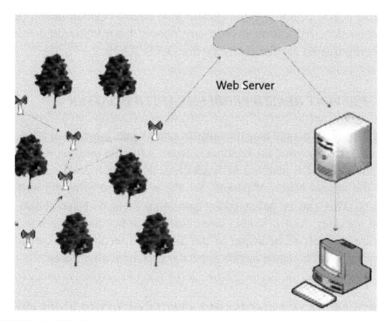

FIGURE 5.4   Wildfire sensor.

Phases of outbreak; the WHO's pandemic alert system moves from stage 1 (a low risk) to stage 6 (a full pandemic):

- Stage 1: In this phase, virus is caused in animals not in humans.
- Stage 2: Humans get infected from animal viruses.
- Stage 3: Infection starts spreading form human to human, but not at large scale.
- Stage 4: In this stage, disease starts spreading to people which leads to community level.
- Stage 5: In this stage, now the disease is spreading from one country to other through a person
- Stage 6: At least one more country, in a different region from Phase 5, has community-level outbreaks.

5.4.1 CLASSIFICATION OF INFECTIOUS DISEASE

The natural Disaster population may suffer from these infectious diseases including diarrheal diseases, upper respiratory infections, malaria, leptospirosis, measles, dengue fever, viral hepatitis, typhoid fever, meningitis, etc. And after human made disaster there is a possibility of people getting injured or death; communicable disease also leads to mental health issues like depression, frustration even many people have committed suicide while being treated or after recovery from COVID-19.

5.4.2 PREVENT HEALTH PROBLEMS AFTER DISASTER

After the disaster, people face the infrastructure issue, job-related issue, and economic issues beyond the healthcare issue. After the disaster, it has been found an unexpected increase in death cases as occurrence of such events affects the mental health of people. So, the prevention of health issues is necessary. This can be achieved by providing them with healthcare and medical supplies. And it is also important that policymakers, public, and healthcare officials to be aware of the disaster, infectious disease so that proper steps shall be taken to safeguard the society in all aspects.

5.5 ADVANTAGES AND DISADVANTAGES OF IOT DEVICES IN HEALTHCARE

The benefits of IoT application in healthcare:

a. Remote monitoring: Illness can be diagnosed and treated with the help of real-time monitoring remotely through interconnected IoT devices with smart alerts. This is helpful in saving lives in medical emergencies.

b. Prevention: Smart sensors investigate lifestyle choices, the environment, and health conditions and suggest preventative measures that will help to minimize the occurrence of acute states and diseases.

c. Reduction of healthcare costs: IoT makes testing more affordable because it minimizes the expense of hospital and the doctor.

d. Medical data accessibility: IoT made the accessibility of electronic medical records very easy and in a fast manner. It helps doctors to make the right decision in minimal time and restrict complications.

e. Improved treatment management: With the help of IoT devices, records are maintained electronically so as to track the direction of drugs and the response which we got from the treatment can be stored easily and by accessing these records helps in reducing medical error.

f. Improved healthcare management: Using IoT devices, management can get valuable information about equipment and get to know how effectively staff is using that device and how these devices can help in further research.

g. Research: Because IoT devices provide accurate results and in a quick manner, so these devices can be used in advance level of research. These devices help in collection and analysis of gigantic data. These devices can play a vital role in medical research purposes.

The disadvantages and threats of using interconnected devices in healthcare are as follows:

a. Risk of failure: One can't trust the electronic devices completely because it can be failed anytime due to power failure or entry of a virus or bugs in the hardware Sometimes power failure can make the healthcare operations at risk because sudden power failure can make the changes in the data by placing healthcare operations at risk. Many upgrades come from time to time to update the system and if it can't be done at that time then these devices can produce wrong results.

b. Security and privacy: These have the highest priority when we talk about medical data. But sometimes it becomes difficult to keep it secret as healthcare monitoring solutions can hack the data. If any kind of hacking happens for any purpose, it has many consequences due to which we cannot take all the benefits of IoT devices.

c. Integration: No agreement is made related to IoT standards and protocols, so it may be possible that the devices produced by various manufacturers fail to work when combined. The deficiency of consistency prevents full-scale integration of IoT, which results in ineffectiveness.

d. Cost: Although the use of IoT devices helps the staff very well but it increases the cost because to train the staff for a particular machine takes extra cost. Implementation and maintenance cost is also very high.

5.6   MACHINE LEARNING FOR PREDICTING DISASTER

ML is an application of AI which has the ability to learn a system automatically to perform some task from the experience. A subset of AI, which helps in discovery of knowledge for intelligent decision-making. ML algorithms work as supervised, unsupervised, and semi-supervised manner. The existing datasets are used to learn and can apply the trained machine on new dataset. That can help in predicting natural disasters which helps in saving many lives by giving prior information about disasters? ML helps us in multiple applications, that is, customer care, share market, e-commerce, healthcare, etc. Natural disasters that can be predicted using ML is as follows:

Earthquake: Millions of lives can be saved by using trained AI systems. They use the seismic data for analysis of magnitude and pattern of earthquakes; thus, helping in prediction of the location of possible earthquakes and aftershocks. Different ML algorithms are used to predict the earthquake that is support vector machine, random forest (RF), XGBoost, CatBoost Regressor.

Floods: An application can be developed to simulate the floods by recording and using the previous year's rainfall data. Level of water is to be monitored on the basis of these parameters like (Mosavi et al., 2018) water level, groundwater level, river flood, soil moisture, stream flow, rainfall discharge, precipitation, river inflow, peak flow, river flow, extreme flow, rainfall-runoff, flash flood, rainfall, seasonal stream flow, flood peak discharge, urban flood, plain flood, rainfall stage, flood frequency analysis, flood quantiles, surge level, storm surge, typhoon rainfall, and daily flows prediction of flood can be done (Zehra) using the support vector machine and NARX to predict the flood in which NATX gave the promising results. In this chapter (Zehra), literature of algorithms is given that are used to predict the flood which algorithms are SVM, MLP, ANN (Zehra). This study, presents several sorts of ML algorithms to sense flood severity then classification into three classes of floods as normal, abnormal, and high-risk. And generally neural network architectures show significant results in many applications; however, in this study RF classifiers perform well.

Hurricanes or cyclones: In this (Khalaf et al., 2018) study, algorithms decision trees, support vector machine, RF, and a model based on linear discriminant analysis (LDA) is used to detect tropical cyclones by using satellite data. Property worth millions is damaged in hurricanes almost every year. Data can be collected for analysis and prediction of future incidents of hurricane. Data can be of wind speed, rainfall, temperature, moisture (Alemany at al., 2019). Proposed recurrent neural network (RNN) in modeling hurricane behavior to forecast the route of hurricanes. In this author took latitude, longitude, wind speed, and pressure publicly provided by the National Hurricane Center (NHC) to forecast the route of a hurricane at 6-h intervals. And the result of this proposed approach shows that about 120 h of hurricane route can be predicted and is implemented by the NHC currently.

ML is supportive in emergency and disaster management. Forecasting will not only help in saving life but mitigate money and infrastructure loss as well. Real-time satellite images could be fed to the model for better response and relief to the impacted areas. Researchers are working on different ML algorithms for the prediction. The major work is to find better accuracy in prediction.

5.6.1 BROAD CATEGORY OF TASKS WITH RESPECT TO NATURAL DISASTERS

Following three major categories:

Prediction: In this category, the different attributes are taken, and learning is done on an existing dataset with some attribute and then prediction like time, place, and magnitude of disaster is done using ML algorithm. Future trends can be predicted from the past data with predictive data analytics which has powerful algorithm models. With correct application, predictive analytics helps improving disaster relief efforts leading to reduced economic impact of natural calamities. For example, warning times of thunderstorms are improved in the US by combining satellite imagery with predictive analytics. The key element for modern rescue operations is mapping data. However, effective data interpretation is essential for timely help of the rescue workers. Rescue workers can calculate the potential risks of the natural disaster with predictive analytics for developing better disaster management plans.

Detection: In this task, detection of disaster is done after it occurs. It is important to detect disaster location time so that extra precautions can be taken care.

Disaster management strategies: This task deals with identification of different entities that are taking part in fighting a disaster so that communication is boosted, suitable concern of the affected people is recognized, and supply of relief items is optimized. Every technology has pros and cons of using it as with ML.

5.7 DATA ANALYSIS IN HEALTHCARE

Data analysis is to collect the data and then analyze that data to get into sites of which give some hidden pattern. Data analysis helps medical professionals to improve the health system management, patient engagement, spending, and diagnosis. Data analysis in healthcare merges the real-time and past data analysis to predict the future trend. The quality of the clinical care is enhanced by the data analysis; thus, expanding healthcare organization which gives access to patient data and allows the health system to reveal trends and patterns around analysis, treatment, and continued care. Data analysis helps to identify the risk of prolonged disease, can track population health. This information helps to give better care to patients, and can also efficiently allocate the resources to increase revenue.

Data analysis is the field which helps to analyze the existing data and give the facts during the disaster or after the disasterthat can be visualization with the help of different tools. Researchers analyze and represent it so that the population gets the information from time to time. Like due to disaster what is the count of death, injured recovery with their geographical location as in this time from December 2019.

Steps to analyze healthcare data and the skills required are as follows:

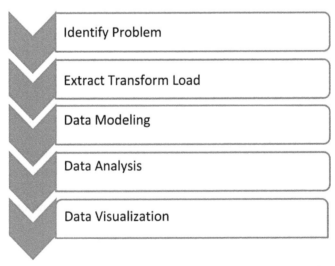

First step is to formulate the query. One should have the knowledge of Structured Query Language (SQL). There are some tools like Tableau having a drag and drop facility.

Second step is extract transform and load. In this step, collect healthcare data. Data should be extracted from an authentic source, transforming its format as required followed by the loading. Pulling the data from different systems like EMR system, cost system, and patient satisfaction system, then make a copy of this data and load it into the warehouse. Storage can be done in data warehouse, NoSQL, and in memory database.

Data modeling is used in healthcare to model the real-world procedure and workflow. If we take an example of hospital admission for that what information is needed: Name of patient, age, DOB, gender, address, etc. If we want to see clinical history in the same hospital, what was the reason? Does the patient come from emergency? and many more. A good data model will cover all the possible queries. Methods to prepare modeling are data mining, ML, statistical analysis, analytical tools.

Data analysis will give more information after analyzing the existing data and visualization is the pictorial representation. Data visualization helps to understand the result of analysis effectively; one of the tools which are used for visualization is Tableau.

Data analysis on the US natural disaster dataset is explained in figures. Data are taken from kaggle.com which consist of data updated till 2020. Figure 5.5 shows the year in which the incident occurred and the count of it is also shown. In this figure different incident type like storm, flood, hurricane, biological, severe storms etc. are shown. It shows that the year 2020 has the highest count for biological incident type.

There are a huge amount of incident types in the dataset. Figure 5.6 shows the top 10 incident types with its frequency and it shows that storms have the highest frequency. Flood and hurricane have near to each other, but the second highest is the hurricane.

Figure 5.7 shows the top 10 states vs their count with respect to incident type Texas (TX) is having highest frequency. Figure 5.8 shows the top five incident types with their count and states. Five incidents that top the list are severe storm, hurricane, flood, snow, and biological. In severe storms, Missouri (MO) is having the highest count and Guam (GU) is with lowest count and snow is lowest one among five. Figure 5.9 shows the declaration type with their number of records. Declarations of three types in given datasets are major disaster (DR), emergency management (EM), fire management (FM). In figure, major disaster is having the highest number of records and emergency management having the lowest number of records.

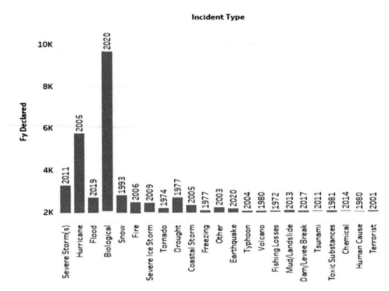

FIGURE 5.5   Year-wise incident type with count.

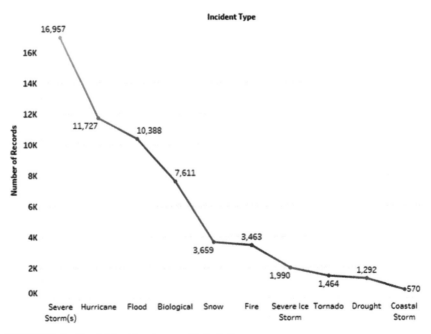

FIGURE 5.6   Top 10 incident types with their frequency.

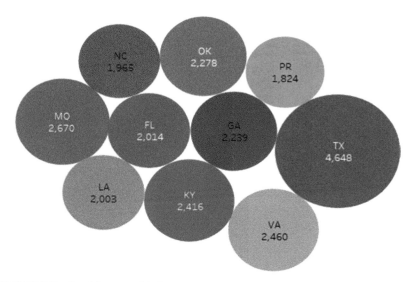

FIGURE 5.7   Top 10 states with frequency.

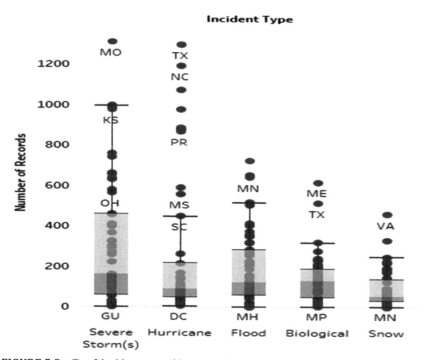

FIGURE 5.8   Top 5 incident type with state and count.

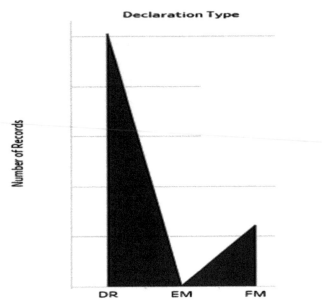

FIGURE 5.9   Declare type with their count.

The major element in modern rescue operations is the mapping data. For data to be useful in rescue operations, it has to be interpreted effectively. The potential risks of any natural disaster can be predicted by the rescue workers with the help of predictive analytics, and this would help in better planning of disaster management.

Predictive analytics uses data from multiple sources including geographical data, real images, data related to evidences, and the knowledge of rescue workers. The analyzed data show the dangers/risks which have probable association with the calamity. This reflects the multilayered approach of data mapping which is adopted by predictive analytics to deliver timely information to the rescue workers.

There are many critical elements which are considered for multilayered analysis; thus, making it more complex. Any negligence in selection of elements would lead to a disaster. For example, heat and smoke are important elements of data analytics to stop the fire workers to enter or exit the crucial points of burning land in US land fires. This otherwise would have been quite tough to achieve without using data analytics.

Similarly, finding "hotspots" for population detection depends on time element. At a given point of time, the rescue works must know the population base before they start the rescue operation timely. Any delay in the rescue operation may have further devastating effects on vast population resulting in a humanitarian crisis. It is this valuable feature of predictive analytics which plays an important role in disaster management. Different data sources like geographic information help to locate the concentration of the population and thus to identify the priority group which is closest to the disaster point and needs immediate operation.

Further, it is not only the civilians in general but data analytics also reveals much more useful information about civilians. For example, data analytics can reveal the location of elderly and handicapped who need the care on priority among other civilians. This information is quite helpful to the rescue workers to identify the location of the vulnerable groups. This identification, further, is used by the rescue team to prioritize and schedule the rescue operations in timely manner so as to be most effective.

For on-ground activity, the forecasting is improved to suggest the movement of the civilians during disaster but where? A few cities can work on predefined emergency protocol but it may appear difficult for everyone to follow at the time of disaster. In an attempt to answer the possibility of anticipating the likelihood of movement of the people during disaster so that rescue workers meet them halfway, the answer is optimistic by using the predictive analytics.

The major source of data primarily comes from the phone calls through the functioning towers. Such data are procured and provided data analysts. The data analysts track the pattern of movement of people at the time of disaster. Once such data are analyzed, it become easier for the rescue team to plan and develop effective rescue operations and procedures to evacuate people from the site of natural disasters.

Big data generated from geo-informatics and remote sensing platforms becomes the major contributor toward early warning systems. Geographical Information Systems (GIS), Global Positioning Systems (GPS), and environmental monitoring sensors over cloud show a potential to predict natural calamities such as snowmelt floods (Fang et al., 2015) and earthquakes (Fang, 2015). Geo-informatics information alongside transportation network data throw useful light to analyze the mobility patterns of the people during such calamities (Grolinger et al., 2013) whereas, social media (e.g., Twitter) offers awareness of distribution of disaster awareness (Song et al., 2015) and can provide very realistic and online information on the occurrence of disasters (Choi and Byunggul, 2015). There is smooth integration of multiple data streams with the processing, along with the processing models such as Hadoop ecosystem to upkeep he processing and storage for effective disaster preparedness. A multisourced social media data is another source to trajectory of hurricanes.

The potential effects of disasters can be minimized by plotting various geospatial maps for developing more active strategies. A study (Chen et al., 2014) reveals the application of Hadoop architecture for collecting data and an observation system for disaster retort and prevention. Efforts are not restricted to big data processing and storage but minimizing the execution time to query for faster decision-making.

In addition, research envisions creating large-scale events venue 3D simulation scenarios for simulation of emergency situations like fire and blasts. The large-scale events cover larger venues. The venues have many people gathered and traffic facilitates big datasets to develop interactive 3D models. These models are used for simulating disaster situations. Moreover, (Yusoff et al., 2015) the researchers emphasize on the significance of big data analytics. This helps to predict occurrences of the floods. However, it has limited datasets. But it can be made efficient warning system by incorporating more datasets and variables. However, integration of datasets with access to information is essential to implement a fully integrated disaster information management system and making it available to disaster managing companies for effective decision-making.

5.8 FUTURE SCOPE

In this chapter, different IoT devices have been discussed that are used to predict the disaster. IoT devices are also used in healthcare where sensors are used to generate data which is stored in a warehouse and discussed about ML algorithms which are used for predictive analysis. This chapter will help readers to know about data analysis and related ML algorithms along with different types of health issues that can be caused due to disaster. IoT devices used in healthcare in the wake of disaster with their pros and cons are also discussed.

KEYWORDS

- **COVID-19**
- **IOT**
- **disaster**
- **machine learning**
- **health care**

REFERENCE

Alemany, S.; Jonathan, B.; Adrian, P.; Sam, G. Predicting Hurricane Trajectories Using a Recurrent Neural Network. *Proc. AAAI Conf. Artif. Intell.* **2019,** *33*, 468–475.

Chen, J.; Huajun, C.; Guozhou, Z., Jeff, Z. P.; Honghan, W.; Ningyu, Z. Big Smog Meets Web Science: Smog Disaster Analysis Based on Social Media and Device Data on the Web. In *Proceedings of the 23rd international Conference on World Wide Web*, 2014, pp 505–510.

Choi, S.; Byunggul, B. The Real-Time Monitoring System of Social Big Data for Disaster Management. In *Computer Science and its Applications*; Springer: Berlin, Heidelberg, 2015; pp 809–815.

Fang, S.; Lida, X.; Yunqiang, Z.; Yongqiang, L.; Zhihui, L.; Huan, P.; Jianwu, Y.; Huifang, Z. An Integrated Information System for Snowmelt Flood Early-Warning Based on Internet of Things. *Inform. Syst. Front.* **2015,** *17*(2), 321–335.

Grolinger, K.; Miriam AM, C.; Emna, M.; Ernesto, E. Knowledge as a Service Framework for Disaster Data Management. In *2013 Workshops on Enabling Technologies: Infrastructure for Collaborative Enterprises*; IEEE, 2013; pp 313–318.

Karthik, B. L. Unmanned Aerial Vehicle (Drones) in Public Health: A SWOT Analysis. DOI: 10.4103/jfmpc.jfmpc_413_18 PMCID: PMC6436288PMID: 30984635 8(2), 342–346, 2019 Feb.

Khaitan, S.; Mitra, A.; Shukla, P.; Chakraborty, S. Statistical Investigation of Novel Corona Virus COVID-19. *Int. J. Control Automation* **2020,** *13*(2s), 1–6.

Khalaf, M.; Hussain, A. J.; Al-Jumeily, D.; Baker, T.; Keight, R.; Lisboa, P.; Fergus, P.; Ala, S. A. K. A Data Science Methodology Based on Machine Learning Algorithms for Flood Severity Prediction. In *the 2018 IEEE Congress on Evolutionary Computation (CEC)*; IEEE, 2018; pp 1–8.

Loridan, T.; Crompton, R. P.; Dubossarsky, E. A Machine Learning Approach to Modeling Tropical Cyclone Wind Field Uncertainty. *Monthly Weather Rev.* **2017,** *145*(8), 3203–3221.

Mosavi, A.; Pinar, O.; Kwok-Wing, C. Flood Prediction Using Machine Learning Models: Literature Review. *Water* **2018,** *10*(11), 1536.

Severin, Paul N.; Phillip, A. J. Types of Disasters. In *Nursing Management of Pediatric Disaster*; Springer: Cham, 2020; pp 85–197.

Song, X.; Quanshi, Z.; Yoshihide, S.; Ryosuke, S.; Nicholas, J. Y.; Xing, X. A Simulator of Human Emergency Mobility Following Disasters: Knowledge Transfer from Big Disaster Data. In *Twenty-Ninth AAAI Conference on Artificial Intelligence*, 2015.

Yusoff, A.; Norashidah Md, D.; Salman, Y.; Khan, S. U. Big Data Analytics for Flood Information Management in Kelantan, Malaysia. In *2015 IEEE Student Conference on Research and Development (SCOReD)*; IEEE, 2015; pp 311–316.

Zehra, N. Prediction Analysis of Floods Using Machine Learning Algorithms (NARX & SVM).

Zhang, T.; Lin, W.; Lin, Y.; Zhang, M.; Yu, H.; Cao, K.; Xue, W. Prediction of Tropical Cyclone Genesis from Mesoscale Convective Systems Using Machine Learning. *Weather Forecast.* **2019,** *34,* 1035–1049. https://doi.org/10.1175/WAF-D-18-0201.1.

https://www.kaggle.com/

Effectiveness of Aarogya Setu Mobile Application During COVID-19 Healthcare Management: A Technology Acceptance Model-Based Approach

SARIKA SHARMA[1*] and D. P. GOYAL[2]

[1]*Symbiosis Institute of Computer Studies and Research, Symbiosis International (Deemed) University Model Colony, Pune, India*

[2]*Indian Institute of Management, Mayurbhanj Complex, Nongthymmai, Shillong, India*

Corresponding author. E-mail: sarika4@gmail.com

ABSTRACT

The pandemic of COVID-19 had adverse impact on most of the sectors across the globe. It has shown its impact in India first in March 2020 and the government had taken various efforts to keep track of the individuals affected from this virus. The launch of Aarogya Setu mobile application for contact tracing is one such initiative. It gives a holistic view to the individuals as well as to the authorities involved. The effectiveness of this depends upon the user acceptance and usability. The chapter aims to study this by proposing a hypothesized conceptual model based on widely adopted technology acceptance model (TAM). The proposed model and four hypotheses are then tested empirically by collecting data through a self-designed survey instrument. The data analysis is done using approach structural equation modeling (SEM) in a two-step process. First, CFA is carried out and then path analysis of the proposed model is carried out. The results reveal that perceived usefulness (PU) has impact on intention to adopt the said mobile application and also ease of use impacts the PU of application. The researchers suggest theoretical as well as the practical implications of the study and future directions are presented at the end.

6.1 INTRODUCTION

The use of technology in health care management has witnessed exponential growth in recent years. In the present scenario, health care sector is facing challenges because of COVID-19 crisis, which is declared as pandemic by world health organization (WHO). The coronavirus pandemic has badly affected the lives of the people around the globe. Health management information systems (HMIS) are measured as significant as these are considered amongst the essential building blocks of health care management sector. HMIS comprises of data collection, storage and manipulation using information technology, which supports decisions, planning, and management of health care facilities to people and organizations.

Developments in information technology and system have facilitated immensely toward the health care industry. It has not only helped practitioners, health care leaders, and government health care agencies, but also contributed in improvement of health care delivery services and health care economics. Use of information systems in for of health care information systems (HIS) can be seen as a key enabler for effective implementation of facilities and improving health care quality along with the cost management. HIS are being used for various applications including, patient management, medical research, decision support, predictive analysis, etc.

Contact tracing, then isolation and initial treatment are key actions to fight communicable diseases (Eames and Keeling, 2003). The launch of mobile application (m-health app) Aarogya Setu by government of India is once such step taken to trace the contacts with respect to COVID-19 virus amongst people of India and has been significantly contributing pertinent to contact tracing and management of illness during COVID-19 (Kodali et al., 2020). Inefficiency of the manual contact tracing method and its longer time period lead to limited control over monitoring of the infection. Thus, vast numbers of nations have embraced information and communication technology (ICT)-enabled tracing facilities as a major strategy for containing the disease easily with quicker tracing. Mobile-based application helps users to be aware them about themselves and surrounding people for possible infection (Vaithianathan et al., 2020).

6.1.1 THE AAROGYA SETU MOBILE APPLICATION: AN OVERVIEW

Government of India decided to launch the mobile application also termed as app named Aarogya Setu to manage COVID-19 pandemic in India through community-driven contact tracing. The meaning of app is to be disease free and launched with punch line of "your shield for a safer India." The app works in a simple and systematic manner. The working is quite simple as whenever someone comes in contact with a COVID-19 affected person, the Aarogya Setu not just alerts you but also guides and assists in getting medical help. There is a facility of self-assessment which is carried by a person and possibilities of infection can be identified. It categorizes as high, medium, or low risk and potential of infection risk to you and others can be known in advance. It acts like a virtual shield for a person. Apart from the citizens, the app also helps the government to identify the COVID-19 hotspots and the timely action can be taken to counter the spread of virus. The government is asking more and more number of people to download and use it to chain down the spread.

The Aarogya Setu application can be an impactful technological solution to facilitate the contact tracing of persons infected or having the risk of COVID-19 infection. The application informs the user about the risk level, that is, high, medium, or low. The precautions which should be taken are also suggested. The application becomes a central repository about the data of all the persons using it, and helps the fast tracing of the cases. These data lead the central and the state level governments in mitigating the spread of COVID-19 virus and enhances their preparedness. This technological and data management solution has played a vital role during the pandemic in India. The data provided by the user are stored following the security and privacy provisions.

6.1.2 RATIONALE OF THE STUDY AND RESEARCH QUESTIONS

With the rapid spread of COVID-19 during March 2020 and thereafter, it was the dire need to know the affected cases and to take action by tracing these cases to avoid its further spread. Technological solutions are sustainable and adoptable. Therefore, government came up with Aarogya Setu mobile application making it mandatory for each smartphone user to install. The Aarogya Setu m-health app is developed by National

Informatics Centre (NIC) with a purpose to tackle COVID-19 crisis. It is used with smartphones having android or iOS operating systems. The databases comprising of individuals' data are shared with the Indian Council of Medical Research (ICMR).

India being the second largest population and sixth largest economy in the world is keen on adopting the internet-based technological solutions. With the internet users crossing 560 million, India is among the top three for online market in the world, which may rise up to 600 million by 2021 (Statista, 2020). As per IAMAI, in 2018 internet penetration in India was 829 million (Jena, 2019), social network users in year 2019 were 376.1 million (Diwanji, 2020). Therefore, using technology and information systems to provide a feasible solution is a viable idea.

According to the official government website (https://aarogyasetu.gov.in/), there are more than 110 million authorized users as on December 2020. With government making so much of efforts to make this mobile application available toward its maximum reach to the citizens, there is a need to know its usability and effectiveness. There is lack of quality research aiming at the user acceptance, citizen response, and effectiveness of the mobile application shows a research gap. The present study is an attempt to fill this gap by addressing this issue and posit three research questions, which are considered for further study.

RQ1: What factors influence the decision to use a health care mobile application adoption?

RQ2: Can a theoretical model be constructed based on literature review for the effectiveness and satisfaction of mobile application?

RQ3: What is the effectiveness of mobile application Aarogya Setu?

The aim of study is to analyze effectiveness of Aarogya Setu mobile application launched by government of India for providing a technology-based solution for tracing of the COVID-19 affected people. The chapter is arranged as follows: It starts with introduction to the subject, briefing about the Aarogya Setu mobile application, and the research questions are posited. The conceptual hypothesized model is developed through a rigorous literature review. The research methodology section deals with the research design for empirically testing the model through data collection using a survey instrument. The same section includes the data analysis using structural equation modeling (SEM). Results and discussion section presents the theoretical and practical inclinations of the study undertaken and lastly concludes with proposal of future research directions.

6.2 LITERATURE REVIEW

6.2.1 TECHNOLOGY ACCEPTANCE MODEL (TAM)

For last two decades various theoretical models are being proposed in literature to know the acceptance intent of technology and systems and acceptance behavior of the users. Though there are many competing models in information system domain which help in studying user's acceptance, TAM is often considered as the most popular and dominant model in the field of digital technologies and the most widely used too. According to Davis et al. (1989) observed usefulness and ease of use are the antecedents for deciding on the recognition and usage of system (Lu et al., 2003). It assert on concept that, if users find a certain technology useful and easy to use, it leads to the development of a positive attitude toward this technology. Various researchers proposed to use TAM as the basis for their conceptual model because of the reason that, TAM was adopted and tested empirically for a number of studies for health care information systems (Pai and Huang, 2011; Rahimi et al., 2018). Hu et al. (1999) applied TAM for predicting and explaining response of users toward HIS.

6.2.2 PERCEIVED USEFULNESS (PU)

According to Davis, 1989, PU is considered as an extent to which person believes to have enhanced the ability to perform a task with the use of some technology or a specific system. PU has a vital impact on the inclination of using the m-health apps (Mohamed et al., 2011). It was studied by Lim et al. (2011) while doing a study on Singaporean women. It reflected a significantly positive prediction of inclination to use mobile phones for health information by PU. The usage intention of health care mobile devices like mobile phones, tablets, etc. among the health care professionals is significantly and positively influenced by the PU of the devices (Rasmi et al., 2018). The PU significantly impacted on intention to use m-health apps by senior citizens in Iraq (Saree et al., 2019). With this background, a hypothesis can be formulated as:

> **H1: Perceived usefulness significantly affects the intention to use the m-health app *Aarogya Setu.***

6.2.3   PERCEIVED EASE OF USE (PEOU)

It refers to the perception of the user to take technology usage an effortless task where effort is considered as a kind of resource required to complete a task (Davis, 1989). Wu et al. (2007) in their research on the medical professionals established that PEoU impacts significantly on intention to use m-health care systems. Intention to use health care informatics via m-health app, designed for health care advice for women well-being, among the ageing women determined by the PEoU of the health care informatics (Xue et al., 2012). PEoU was taken as a major factor for intention to use m-health care services in a study conducted by Zhao et al. (2018). The study focused on analysis of influence of 8 factors toward attitude and behavior. According to Davis (1989), PEoU significantly impacts the PU. Following hypotheses are posit from this discussion:

H2: **Perceived ease of use positively influences intention to use the m-health app** *Aarogya Setu.*

H3: **Perceived ease of use positively influences perceived usefulness to use the m-health app** *Aarogya Setu.*

6.2.4   INTENTION TO USE MOBILE APPLICATION (IUMA)

Behavioral intention according to Davis (1989) is "An individual's motivation or willingness to exert effort to perform the target behavior". This study is about intention to use the information system with respect explained to m-health app Aarogya Setu. Rawstorne et al. (2000) explained behavioral intention has influence on acceptance of technology by the end users. In context, the adoption of radio frequency identification technologies by the medical teams, Chen et al. (2007) stated that intention to adopt the technology affects its actual use (AU). A study by Holdel and Karsh (2010) establishes a significant relationship between PU with the intention to use, and real health information systems usage.

H4: **Intention to use the m-health app** *Aarogya Setu* **positively influences AU.**

Based on the above discussions of this section, a theoretical conceptual model is suggested by the researchers as presented in Figure 6.1. The relationships of variables (both independent and dependents) in the model are present here. The details about the constructs/measures are as given below:

- *Dependent variable:* AU and IUMA are the dependent variables.
- *Independent variables:* Two independent variables namely PU and PEoU are included in the proposed conceptual model. The aim of the present research is to analyze the impact of independent variables identified above on intentions to use mobile application. PU is a dependent as well as an independent variable.

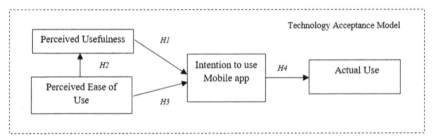

FIGURE 6.1   Conceptual hypothesized model.

6.3   RESEARCH METHODOLOGY

6.3.1   SAMPLING

Research method used in the study is a quantitative method. A survey is conducted to collect the data using a questionnaire (survey instrument) designed by researchers. The selected survey tool has its base in earlier similar studies (Davis, 1989; Hu et al., 1999; Rawstorne, 2000) and questions were reframed as per the present study. Questionnaire was used to record demographic information of the respondents in first part and in the second part responses were captured for 17 items of the four constructs of the hypothesized model proposed in the study. The questions for all constructs are designed based on the Likert's five-point scale (1: Strongly disagree to 5: Strongly agree), except for the construct AU, where a different scale is used (see Appendix I). The designed questionnaire was tested on 30 respondents and modifications were done based on the responses. Two experts were contacted to get it validated before the final use. The instrument is presented in Appendix I. Respondent's demographic data are presented in Table 6.1.

TABLE 6.1   Demographics.

Item	Type	Frequency	Percent
Gender	Female	211	41.05
	Male	303	58.9
Location	Pune city	376	73.1
	Pune Suburbs	138	26.8
Education	UG	259	50.38
	PG	172	33.46
	Other	83	16.14
	Total	514	

The study is about users' perspective toward the mobile application Aarogya Setu; therefore, researchers decided to include respondents from all spheres of life, who are using smart phones. The data were collected during October 2020 to November 2020 from the users of this particular mobile application in Pune city, India. Random sampling method was adopted. The questionnaires were filled mainly through online forms. A total of 514 completely and correctly filled questionnaires were included for the data analysis.

6.3.2   DATA ANALYSIS

For analyzing the data and testing the model, SEM approach is applied. Two-step process is adopted. In the first step, confirmatory factor analysis (CFA) is applied on the four constructed and model fitness was tested. The model fit indices suggested by Hair et al. (2010) were considered as benchmark. The goodness of fit of model is estimated using Chi square/degree of freedom (CMIN/df), comparative fit index (CFI), and Tucker–Lewis index (TLI). Badness of fit of model is estimated using Root Mean Square Error of Approximation (RMSEA). The results are given in Table 6.2 can be analyzed that all the values are in range and hence model is a good fit.

The CFA is conducted using IBM Amos 20.0 presented in Figure 6.2. Cronbach's Alpha was calculated to check the internal consistency of model, which is suggested to be more than 0.8 (Sekaran, 2003). This is achieved for all the constructs. Table 6.3 exhibits the values of individual items loadings. The calculated values of construct reliability (CR) should be more than 0.7, which is achieved for all constructs of the model. Average variance explained (AVE) should be more than 0.5, which is achieved for all the constructs. Also CR> average shared variance (ASV) for all the constructs; hence, it can be concluded that the convergent validity of the model is confirmed (Table 6.3).

TABLE 6.2 Indices for Fitness of Model.

Model fit measure	Acceptable value	Results value
CMIN/df	<5.0	1.299
CFI	>0.9	0.944
TLI	>0.9	0.958
RMSEA	<0.1	0.054

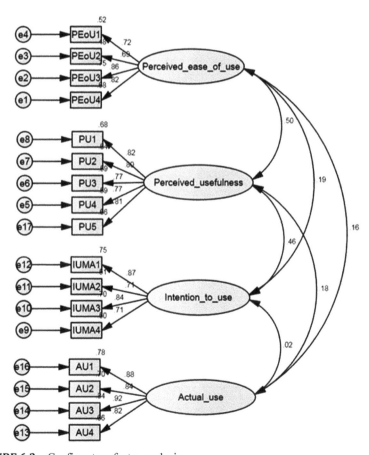

FIGURE 6.2 Confirmatory factor analysis.

TABLE 6.3 Measurement Model Characteristics.

Construct	Construct code	Items loadings (k)	AVE	CR	ASV
Perceived ease of use (PEoU)	PEoU1	0.72	0.602	0.857	0.080
	PEoU2	0.69			
	PEoU3	0.86			
	PEoU4	0.82			
Perceived usefulness (PU)	PU1	0.82	0.631	0.895	0.144
	PU2	0.80			
	PU3	0.77			
	PU4	0.77			
	PU5	0.81			
Intention to use mobile application (IUMA)	IUMA1	0.87	0.618	0.865	0.050
	IUMA2	0.71			
	IUMA3	0.84			
	IUMA4	0.71			
Actual use (AU)	AU1	0.88	0.750	0.923	0.014
	AU2	0.84			
	AU3	0.92			
	AU4	0.82			

Table 6.4 represents discriminant validity of the model with the correlation matrix and roots of AVEs. For all constructs, the values of AVE are greater than values of ASV. AVE is more in comparison to maximum shared variance (MSV) for all constructs; therefore, it can be stated that the discriminant validity seems to be satisfactory at construct level.

TABLE 6.4 Roots of AVEs and Correlation Matrix.

	CR	AVE	MSV	MaxR(H)	AU	PEoU	PU	IUMA
AU	0.921	0.745	0.033	0.929	0.863			
PEoU	0.858	0.604	0.245	0.875	0.162	**0.777**		
PU	0.895	0.631	0.245	0.897	0.182	0.495	**0.794**	
IUMA	0.863	0.614	0.210	0.880	0.025	0.192	0.458	**0.783**

6.3.3 PATH ANALYSIS USING SEM

The proposed conceptual model was entered in software IBM Amos and path analysis was carried out using SEM. Use of SEM is quite prevalent amongst the researchers (Kline, 2011). Figure 6.3 exhibits the path analysis carried out for the proposed model and the results are presented in Table 6.5.

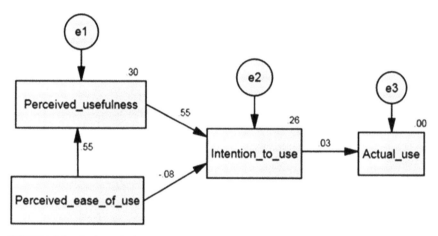

FIGURE 6.3 Path analysis.

From Table 6.5, it can be interpreted that PU of the mobile application impacts positively on intention to adopt it, and therefore hypothesis H1 can be accepted. PEoU doesn't significantly impact the intention to adopt Aarogya Setu mobile application and therefore hypothesis H2 is rejected. PEoU affects the PU and hence hypothesis H3 is also accepted. Hypothesis H4 which talks about the impact of intention to adopt mobile application is rejected as it has no significant impact on AU.

6.4 RESULTS AND DISCUSSIONS

This section presents the theoretical and practical implications of the study undertaken. The study is unique in the sense that it addresses the use and effectiveness of information systems in form of the mobile application Aarogya Setu. The application was launched specifically to keep track of COVID-19 cases during the pandemic in India. Theoretically, the study proposes the conceptual model based on the literature review and test it empirically by collecting data from respondents from India. Practically, it provides the meaningful insights on the use and effectiveness of Aarogya Setu, which is helpful in deciding the response to the mobile application. The study also presents the user's perspective for the same.

TABLE 6.5   Hypothesis Testing.

Hypothesis	R^2 (path coefficient)	Sig.(p-value)	Accepted/ rejected
H1: Perceived usefulness —>intention to adopt mobile application	0.55	$p<0.001$	Accepted
H2: Perceived Ease of use —> intention to adopt mobile application	-0.08	$p>0.05$	Rejected
H3: Perceived ease of use —>perceived usefulness	0.55	$p<0.001$	Accepted
H4: Intention to adopt mobile application—>actual use	0.03	$p>0.05$	Rejected

6.5   LIMITATIONS AND FUTURE SCOPE

The researchers tried to provide a holistic approach to the study undertaken, in no way it claims to be a complete, posing a limitations. First of all, the study is based on TAM which has two independent variables that affect the intention to adopt the mobile application. There can be some more variable which can influence the decision to adopt. These factors can be further explored by undertaking another similar study. Second limitation is that the sample is collected form Pune city of India, which is an urban city. Most of the respondents possessed smartphones. Therefore, results of the study cannot be generalized and another extended study for pan India sample can be conducted to generalize the results. The study on the health care information systems is taking a fast pace and some future areas of the research can be on the user acceptance of other mobile application which are developed specifically for the purpose of COVID-19 pandemic.

KEYWORDS

- **Aarogya Setu**
- **m-Health App**
- **technology acceptance model**
- **COVID-19 pandemic**
- **health care information systems**

REFERENCES

Ajzen, I.; Fishbein, M. *Understanding Attitudes and Predicting Social Behavior*; Prentice-Hall: Michigan, 1980.

Chen, C. C.; Wu, J.; Crandall, R. E. Obstacles to the Adoption of Radio Frequency Identification Technology in the Emergency Rooms of Hospitals. *Int. J. Electron. Healthcare* **2007**, *3*(2), 193–207.

Davis, F. D. Perceived Usefulness, Perceived Ease of Use, and User Acceptance of Information Technology. *MIS Quart.* **1989**, *13*(3), 319–340.

Diwanji, S. Number of Social Media Users in India 2015–2023. [Online] 2020. https://www.statista.com/statistics/278407/number-of-social-network-users-in-india/ (accessed Oct 2, 2020).

Eames, K. T. D.; Keeling, M. J. *Contact Tracing and Disease Control*, Proceedings of the Royal Society B: Biological Sciences, 2003, Vol. 270, pp 2565–2571.

Hair, J. F.; Black, W. C.; Babin, B. J.; Anderson, R. E. *Multivariate Data Analysis*, 7th ed.; Prentice Hall: Upper Saddle River, New Jersey, 2010.

Holden, R. J.; Karsh, B. T. The Technology Acceptance Model: Its Past and its Future in Health Care. *J. Biomed. Inform.* **2010**, *43*(1), 159–72.

Hu, P. J. H.; Chau, P. Y. K.; Sheng, O. R. L.; Tam, K. Y. Examining the Technology Acceptance Model Using Physician Acceptance of Telemedicine Technology. *J. Manag. Inform. Syst.* **1999**, *16*, 91–112.

Jena, R. The Power of Internet: Internet Penetration in India. [Online] 2019. https://www.emarketeducation.in/power-internet-penetration-online-india/ (accessed Nov 2020).

Kline, R. B. *Principles and Practice of Structural Equation Modelling*; Guilford Press: New York, 2011.

Kodali, P. B.; Hense, S.; Kopparty, S.; Kalapala, G. R.; Haloi, B. How Indians Responded to the Arogya Setu App? *Indian J. Public Health* **2020**, *64*(6), 228–230.

Lim, S.; Xue, L.; Yen, C. C.; Chang, L.; Chan, H. C.; Tai, B. C.; Choolani, M. A Study on Singaporean Women's Acceptance of Using Mobile Phones to Seek Health Information. *Int. J. Med. Inform.* **2011**, *80*(12) 189–202.

Lu, J.; Yu, C. S.; Liu, C.; Yao, J. E. Technology Acceptance Model for Wireless Internet. *Internet Res.* **2003,** *13*(3), 206–222.

Melas, C.; Zampetakis, L.; Dimopoulou, A.; Moustakis, V. Modeling the Acceptance of Clinical Information Systems Among Hospital Medical Staff: An Extended TAM Model. *J. Biomed. Inform.* **2011,** *44*, 553–564.

Mohamed, A. H. H.; Tawfik, H.; Al-Jumeily, D.; Norton, L. MoHTAM: A Technology Acceptance Model for Mobile Health Applications. In 2011 Developments in E-systems Engineering; IEEE, 2011; pp 13–18.

Pai, F. Y.; Huang, K. I. Applying the Technology Acceptance Model to the introduction of Healthcare Information Systems. *Technol. Forecast. Social Change* **2011,** *78*, 650–660.

Rahimi, B.; Nadri, H.; Lotfnezhad Afshar, H.; Timpka, T. A Systematic Review of the Technology Acceptance Model in Health Informatics. *Appl. Clin. Inform.* **2018,** *9*(3), 604–634.

Rasmi, M.; Alazzam, M. B.; Alsmadi, M. K.; Almarashdeh, I. A.; Alkhasawneh, R. A.; Alsmadi, S. Healthcare Professionals' Acceptance Electronic Health Records system: Critical Literature Review (Jordan Case Study). *Int. J. Healthcare Manag.* **2018,** (Online), 1–13.

Rawstorne, P; Jayasuriya, R.; Caputi, P. In *Issues in Predicting and Explaining Usage Behaviors with the Technology Acceptance Model and the Theory of Planned Behavior When Usage is Mandatory,* Proceedings of the 21st International Conference on Information Systems, 2000; pp 35–44.

Saare, M. A.; Hussain, A.; Yue, W. S. Conceptualizing Mobile Health Application Use Intention and Adoption Among Iraqian Older Adults: From the Perspective of Expanded Technology Acceptance Model. *Int. J. Interact. Mobile Technol.* **2019,** *13*(10), 28–41.

Sekaran, U. *Research Methods for Business: A Skill Building Approach,* 4th ed.; John Wiley & Sons Inc.: New York, NY, 2003.

Statista. Internet Usage in India-Statistics & Facts. [Online] 2020. https://www.statista.com/ topics/2157/internet-usage-in-india/ (accessed November 2020).

Vaithianathan, R.; Ryan, M.; Anchugina, N.; Selvey, L.; Dare, T.; Brown, A. Digital Contact Tracing for COVID-19: A Primer for Policymakers. Google. Aarogya Setu; 2020. https://play.google.com/ /apps/details?i d=nic.goi.aarogyasetu and hl=en_IN and showAllReviews=true (accessed Oct 13, 2020).

Wu, J. H.; Wang, S. C.; Lin, L. M. Mobile Computing Acceptance Factors in the Healthcare Industry: A Structural Equation Model. *Int. J. Med. Inform.* **2007,** *76*(1), 66–77.

Xue, L.; Yen, C. C.; Chang, L.; Chan, H. C.; Tai, B. C.; Tan, S. B.; Choolani, M. An Exploratory Study of Ageing Women's Perception on Access to Health Informatics via a Mobile Phone-Based Intervention. *Int. J. Med. Inform.* **2012,** *81*(9), 637–648.

Zhao, Y.; Ni, Q.; Zhou, R. What Factors Influence the Mobile Health Service Adoption? A Meta-Analysis and the Moderating Role of Age. *Int. J. Inform. Manag.* **2018,** *43*, 342–350.

APPENDIX I

Construct	Construct code	Questions
Perceived ease of use (PEoU) (Davis, 1989; Hu, et al., 1999)	PEoU1	Aarogya Setu m-health app is easy to install.
	PEoU2	Aarogya Setu m-health app is clear to understand.
	PEoU3	It is easy to become skillful with the Aarogya Setu m-health app.
	PEoU4	It is easy to learn and operate the Aarogya Setu m-health app.
Perceived usefulness (PU) (Davis, 1989; |Hu et al., 1999)	PU1	Aarogya Setu m-health app is a useful means for contact tracing.
	PU2	Aarogya Setu m-health app enhances the COVID-19 contact tracing management.
	PU3	Aarogya Setu m-health app increases my awareness about the spread of COVID-19 virus around me.
	PU4	Aarogya Setu m-health app improves quality of my precautionary measures for the pandemic.
	PU5	Aarogya Setu m-health app is a useful for government in the fight against COVID-19 pandemic.
Intention to use mobile application (IUMA) (Rawstorne, 2000)	IUMA1	I intent to use Aarogya Setu m-health app.
	IUMA2	I will continue to use Aarogya Setu m-health app till the end of pandemic.
	IUMA3	I can recommend Aarogya Setu m-health app to my family and friends.
	IUMA4	I will adopt Aarogya Setu m-health app for my own safety.
Actual use (AU)	AU1	I check for information on Aarogya Setu m-health app in a day:
		1: Never 2: Rarely 3: Sometimes 4: Often 5: Frequently
	AU2	I use Aarogya Setu m-health app for updates:
		1: Never 2: Rarely 3: Sometimes 4: Often 5: Frequently
	AU3	I use Aarogya Setu m-health app for knowing my risk status:
		1: Never 2: Rarely 3: Sometimes 4: Often 5: Frequently
	AU4	I use Aarogya Setu m-health app for my contact tracing:
		1: Never 2: Rarely 3: Sometimes 4: Often 5: Frequently

CoReS-Respiratory Strength Predicting Framework Using Noninvasive Technology for Remote Monitoring During Heath Disasters

ADARSH GARG*

GL Bajaj Institute of Management and Research, Greater Noida, India

E-mail: adarsh.15@hotmail.com

ABSTRACT

Infection and spread of viral diseases is undesirably not easy to regulate. The speed and scope of virus continues to grow due to multiple factors, be it social or environmental leading to sometimes the endemic or pandemic as is the case of SARS-CoV-2, which has appeared as a grave pandemic with a high mortality rate and post-recovery complications. One of the major complications of SARS-CoV-2 is pulmonary deterioration followed by pneumonia and even death. The noncritical patients also developed the potential risk of reducing respiratory strength (RS) even after successful recovery from this virus attack. It has become essential to evolve new and safe techniques to monitor the RS of patients rapidly so as to detect any potential complication and report to the healthcare providers for timely management. This pandemic COVID-19 caused by SARS-CoV-2 has sited new hassles on the health systems worldwide. Despite the terrific efforts of the governments and the healthcare providers across the world to combat this disease and its spread, develop the vaccine using technology, it is also vital to detect, track, and monitor the patients for their RS using internet of things (IoT) sensors. The chapter walks around the probability of monitoring the RS of the patients (also non-patients) from inside as well as outside the homes to report to the healthcare providers for quick action. A framework, CoReS is proposed as a life-saving technology to monitor and manage the RS of patients to detect any sign of potential complication. This technology will support patient satisfaction and decrease the mortality rate in health disaster.

7.1 INTRODUCTION

The COVID-19 infection is caused by SARS-CoV-2. SARS-CoV-2 belongs to a group of viruses like SARS-CoV, MERS-CoV. They have a wide spread among humans and show different symptoms in humans when infected with. These viruses attack the respiratory system (RS) hindering the normal respiratory functions (RF). The symptoms include from mild cough, fever to reduced RS to pneumonia to respiratory distress (RD) to even death (Zhou et al., 2020). The person infected with SARS-CoV-2 virus may sometimes remain asymptomatic also. The extent of impact of COVID-19 can be measured by knowing the RS of the patient. RS depends upon the rate of respiration (RoR) and the respiration curve (RC) gives the status of RS. The RC portrays the RoR which is measured when the person is not doing any physical activity. RoR may show an increase or decrease from a normal value in case of illness. In patients infected with COVID-19, abnormal RoR may indicate reduced RS and some complication (Tenhunen et. al., 2013). Also, the patients with abnormal RoR may increase the spread of the disease. Sometimes the patients recovered successfully from COVID-19 may also show the symptoms of deteriorating RS over a period of time leading to death. The healthcare providers have the proficiency to measure the RoR with the required equipment deployed usually in hospitals or occasionally at home. But the dilemma of healthcare providers to send the recovered patients is quite apparent as symptoms may worsen in second week in comparison to the first week (Huang, 2019). Lack of healthcare expertise and negligence of recovered patients to monitor themselves carefully after they are discharged from hospitals may lead to increased mortality rate and transmittable rate.

Here, technology comes to play a significant role when it becomes essential to monitor the hospitalized or nonhospitalized COVID-19 patients, indoor or outdoor or self-isolation scenarios, by healthcare experts remotely in real-time manner. Recovered or unrecovered patients are at a high risk of deteriorating RS and need real-time monitoring of their RS.

The use of internet of things (IoT) sensors/devices are used to monitor the RoR through Wi-Fi technologies 24*7. So far, many devices are available to monitor RS but they have their own limitations making it problematic to the patients. Table 7.1 shows the available tools and technologies used for monitoring the RS along with their features.

TABLE 7.1 Tools for Monitoring RS.

Tool and technologies	Requirement	Ease of use	Features
Cuff, watch, camera	Invasive	Wearable	Disruptive
Sensors (IR,PR,VB, FS,LC) ratio frequency (RF) (Brser, 2012; Ni et al., 2010; Clemente, 2020; Chen et al., 2017; Alaziz et al., 2016; Adami et al., 2006), Wi-Fi, cloud	Noninvasive	Non-wearable	Nondisruptive, 24*7

*IR, infrared; PR, pressure; VB, vibrations; LC, load cell; FS, force.
Source: Created by author

Due to the disadvantages of invasive technologies, noninvasive technologies are preferred and proposed in the framework. Noninvasive technologies have the advantage of hassle-free monitoring vitals of a patient without hindering any routine activity of the patient. Though all noninvasive technologies are real time but there is no such framework which can be applied to monitor the patient's vitals remotely with holistic approach.

Since COVID-19 has posed a massive threat to the healthcare system worldwide with countries like the United States, Italy, France, Spain, Brazil, Mexico, China, India have observed that the pandemic engulfs their healthcare management system. It posted a critical problem of defining priority criteria for healthcare given to the patients based on the severity of their symptoms. The rapid upsurge of infected people has left the healthcare system almost deserted in countries like Italy, and the United States with finely honed medical assistance. It was challenging to support thousands of the patients at the same time. The patients are given healthcare only when hospitalized on deterioration of their RS and other complications in vitals while the asymptomatic patients are isolated and aided at home (WHO), increasing the burden on healthcare providers.

In this pandemic situation, the world is still fighting with COVID-19 and looking for some real-world and economical solution to face the difficulties to reduce the loss of lives apart from creating vaccines. Industry 4.0

provides telemedicine services for proper prevention and control of this pandemic. Also the IoT-based technologies have significantly contributed to fight COVID-19 (significant applications of IoT during COVID-19 has been shown in Table 7.2), yet a more holistic approach of application of emerging technologies is needed for real-time management of indoor and outdoor patients remotely.

TABLE 7.2 Key Applications of IoT During COVID-19 Outbreak.

S. No.	IoT applications
1	Hospitals connected through internet
2	Healthcare providers connected through internet
3	Smart Healthcare network to identify COVID-19 infected patients
4	Medical tools and devices connected through internet
5	Telehealth and telemedicine
6	Real-time update on COVID-19
7	Forecasting of the virus status based on available data

Source: Created by author on review of literature

Here, CoReS is the proposed framework with more holistic approach to detect, analyze, and transfer the information on patients vital remotely to healthcare provider using noninvasive technology, that is, Wi-Fi for immediate action. This framework can be used for monitoring health during pandemics like COVID-19. This technology will support patient satisfaction and decrease the mortality rate in health disasters. The chapter is organized as discussion on the noninvasive technology approaches vis-à-vis Wi-Fi to monitor vitals of the patient remotely to acquire health-related information followed by the overview of the proposed CoReS framework with its potential usage in detection of early symptom of RS and conclusion with some future directions.

7.2 NONINVASIVE TECHNOLOGY FOR HEALTHCARE

Health monitoring systems (HMS) can detect the abnormality in vitals and generate an alarm in case of complications. HMS are advantageous to the patients as well as healthcare providers. Majority of the HMS need dedicated devices set up at healthcare centers and are controlled by some technical persons. A few sensor-equipped wearable devices are used by the patients themselves which may be quite inconvenient. Also, such HMS are not useful at the time of health disasters like COVID-19 due to the need to handle multiple patients together and that also remotely.

Amongst the various health monitoring techniques, Wi-Fi-enabled detecting techniques have been largely used for monitoring the vitals of the patients. The widespread use of Wi-Fi-enabled detecting is attributed to its global use due to noninvasive, cost-effective, and convenient deployment feature. The Wi-Fi-enabled detecting techniques usually include Wi-Fi module board, Wi-Fi signals, and application programming interface (API) software (Gringoli et al., 2019). The Wi-Fi signals are penetrating adequately to sense and collect changes in the surroundings, thus can be used for the sensing. Due to its noninvasive feature, it is best suited and used in healthcare systems to monitor the vitals of the patient for detecting any complication, besides its use in gesture recognition, circumstantial information acquisition, and validation. Table 7.3 portrays the Wi-Fi-enabled detecting applications. Noninvasive means, Wi-Fi-enabled detecting, either active or passive, uses the radio signals to sense the surroundings removing the direct contact with the user and thus do away with the uneasiness.

TABLE 7.3 Wi-Fi-Enabled Detecting Applications.

Type of application	Applications
Gesture recognition	Sign language (Yang et al., 2016), lip movement (Wang et al., 2014), human activity recognition (Abdelnasser et. al., 2015)
Circumstantial information acquisition	Direction (Kumar et al., 2014; Kotaru et al., 2015; Wang et al., 2016), location (Sen et al., 2012; Bahl and Padmanabhan, 2000; Youssef and Agrawala, 2005), range sensing (Vasisht et al., 2016)
Validation	Intrusion and abnormality detection (Li et al., 2014; Shi et al., 2017)
Health monitoring	RoR monitoring (Kaltiokallio et al., 2014)
	Heartbeat sensing (Liu et al., 2015; Adib et al., 2015)
	Respiratory irregularities sensing during sleep (Abdelnasser et al., 2015)

Source: Created by author on review of literature

Wi-Fi-enabled detecting is an emergent technology that uses Wi-Fi radio signals as sensors (Yang et al., 2018). The rational for RoR detection is small chest movement can modify the radio signal. The respiration cycle is captured by Wi-Fi signal through inhalation and exhalation. This technology usually uses radio signal strength indicator (RSSI) and channel state information (CSI). RSSI defines the relative power strength at the received end reflecting the link quality (Vlavianos et al., 2008). However, due to multipath effect (Numerous replicas of the same radio signal with different delays reach the receiver (Sen et al., 2013).), these RSSI systems distort the location inference in indoor surroundings resulting in limited accuracy in detecting indoor activities (Xu et al., 2019).

CSI is preferred over RSSI and widely adopted in Wi-Fi sensing. CSI estimates the properties of propagation channel and signal power attenuation is quantified after multipath effect (Xu et al., 2019). It is well suited for indoor activity detection.

Here, we aim to propose a framework to monitor and estimate RS by detecting RoR signals in healthcare system using best-fit noninvasive technology for real-time detection of deteriorating condition of COVID-19 patients, remotely. Table 7.4 reflects the use of Wi-Fi-enabled technology studied so far with their limitations to detect RoR and then the RS.

TABLE 7.4   Wi-Fi-Enabled Technology to Detect RoR.

Authors	Wi-Fi-enabled technology		Limitations
	Radio signal strength indicator (RSSI)	Channel state information (CSI)	
Wang et al., 2020	√		Unable to detect immediate RoR changes
Zhang et al., 2019	√		Not able to distinguish RoR of multiple patients
Yang et al., 2018	√		Sleeping RoR of multiple patients needs to have different rating to be detected
Chen et al., 2017		√	Detected only periodic vibrations
Liu et al., 2015		√	Environmental noise interference
Abdelnasser et al., 2015		√	Multipath effect
Patwari et al., 2014		√	Motion interference
Kaltiokallio et al., 2014		√	Not reliable to detect minute respiratory changes

Source: Created by author on review of literature

RSSI and CSI approaches of Wi-Fi-enabled technology to detect the RS using respiratory pattern of the patient have their own limitation as studied and reflected in Table 7.4. These approaches are briefly explained here along with the limitations to understand the proposed framework.

7.2.1 RSSI-BASED APPROACH

Multiple applications have been developed in the healthcare area using RSSI. RSSI values are used to locate and estimate RoR of a patient irrespective of his position but should be nearer to the Wi-Fi link in noise-free environment for the measurements to be accurate. This measurement is further improved by placing a change detector to detect occasional movements of the patient using change-pint detection methods (Wilcoxon, Welch's t-test (Kay, 1993)). Usually transmitter-receiver pair is used to detect RoR. RSSI-based approach is further improved by implementing fast Fourier transformation (FFT) to limit the RoR frequency filtering between the ranges of 0.1–0.5 Hz, which is the range of normal human respiration frequency. The filtered frequency with highest frequency for estimation of RoR is extracted by combining overlapping respiratory frequency spectrum for continuous results.

This method has a little precision due to the limitations due to multipath effect, required close proximity with the links, interference of large noise from surroundings, and inability to detect sudden and small respiratory changes. Thus, RSSI approach is not suitable for detecting RS remotely in case of global health disasters.

7.2.2 CSI-BASED APPROACH

CSI-based approach of Wi-Fi-enabled technologies is preferred over RSSI-approach. It can be phase-based or spectrum-based. While phased approach assume single patient, spectrum approach detects RoR signals for multiple patients. In phased approach, presence of respiration is detected by using radio signals, followed by measuring the highest frequency and amplitude of the signal along with movement interference. Any distortion is removed by taking the difference between two periodic radio signals as phase of CSI on different antennas is affected by respiration but this does not signify the actual change in respiration.

Spectrum-based approach is the most common noninvasive approach to detect RoR remotely, for multiple patients at a given time without assuming the fixed number of patients. First, periodic respiratory signals are extracted by applying short FT on CSI values. Signals are made stronger by using adaptive subcarrier method for estimated RoR. But this method requires a large delay of more than 30 s for improving frequency resolution which might skip instant RoR changes.

Looking at the limitations of the abovementioned approached, we propose a little advanced noninvasive Wi-Fi-enabled approach of detecting human vitals remotely especially RoR as in the case of global health disaster, COVID-19.

7.3   THEORETICAL OVERVIEW OF CORES FRAMEWORK

The frameworks if given keeping in view the huge loss to the human lives during worst ever global health disaster—COVID-19 where the number of patients is so large that it is difficult to provide them an appropriate health-care in the healthcare centers. It has actually raised a massive challenge to the healthcare system. The need is to establish a remote HMS system which has the capability to detect instant changes in RS, generate an alert to the healthcare provider to provide the care to the multiple patients indoor as well as outdoor at the same time without any face-to-face interaction. The structure of CoReS is depicted in Figure 7.1. The framework has three-tier architecture.

1.   Physical sensing tier
2.   Processing tier
3.   Monitoring tier

The physical sensing tier consists of a Wi-Fi device and Wi-Fi access point (Raspberry Pi/Laptop). The patient has to be within Wi-Fi covering area which may include the wall as well. Hampel filter (Davies and Gather, 1993) is applied to remove the outliers due to some hindrances caused by physical obstruction or a large movement (as they are nonperiodic in comparison to the RoR). Small movements of the body, as RoR with exhalation and inhalation, are extracted when patient is lying relaxed without any physical movement. The CSI of multiple-input multiple-output orthogonal-frequency-division-multiplexing (MIMO-*OFDM*)-modulated

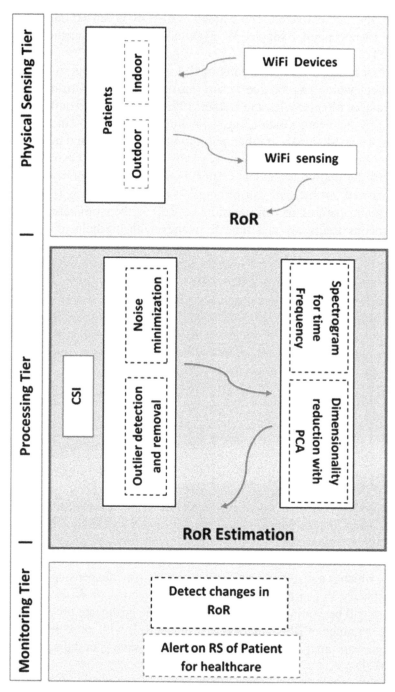

FIGURE 7.1 CoReS-proposed model for healthcare monitoring by detecting RS

Wi-Fi frames are extracted. The extraction of RoR is carried out within the Wi-Fi access point. Extracted Wi-Fi signals are then put together using some API (Gringoli et al., 2019).

In processing tier, preprocessing of CSI is first carried out to remove the outliers which can be due to any movement in the surroundings, using Hampel filter (Davies and Gather, 1993). The removed outliers are replaced by the nearest data using their moving average to smooth out the data. The CSI signals are then put into the frequency band matching with the human RoR frequency, typically 0.2–0.4 Hz (Clemente et al., 2020), by applying bandpass filter. Further, dimensionality reduction is carried out by applying principal component analysis (PCA) to extract main features of respiration. The RoR is then estimated using instantaneous frequency and time frequency with the help of Fourier transformations. Both frequencies will estimate the shortness of respiration and thus RS to evaluate criticality of COVID-19. RoR is extracted in real-time manner and evaluated value is sent to cloud for storage and visualization. This supports storage and visualization of data of multiple patients at the same time.

The healthcare provider accesses the data from cloud in real-time using monitoring tier. Visualization tool helps the healthcare provider to get the alarm on out of range RoR values and current health status is visualized.

7.4 FUTURE WORK

CoReS, a framework to detect RS of the patients remotely using noninvasive Wi-Fi-enabled CSI technologies are presented here. The potential of the proposed theoretical framework to detect RoR is broad but needs testing with real-time data as it is based on the comprehensive review of available noninvasive approaches. The hardware and software specifications need to be decided to setup the HMS for its remote operation on multiple patients, which is cost-effective as well. Some simple, inexpensive devices like Raspberry Pi can be used for desirable extraction of Wi-Fi signals. The work will be continued in association with the healthcare providers to enhance the range of RS symptoms to estimate RoR with more precision. The framework after implementation can be life-saving in the scenarios like COVID-19.

7.5 CONCLUSION

The chapter presents the theoretical framework to monitor RoR for COVID-19 patients or any other global disaster with impact on RS, using noninvasive, real-time, technology. The noninvasive technology here can be used for indoor as well as outdoor patients. Using the Wi-Fi signals, RoR of the monitored patient/patients is communicated to the healthcare provider sitting remotely, after processing. The signal is preprocessed to remove the outliers for smoothening of the signal. The processing is done on smooth signal and RoR is extracted. The extracted RoR is stored in cloud storage and communicated through API to generate an alert whenever some instant change is detected in RoR through PCA. This is a theoretical framework which is in the process of testing in small setup using inexpensive tools and will be evaluated empirically.

KEYWORDS

- IoT
- sensors
- respiratory strength
- COVID-19

REFERENCES

Abdelnasser, H.; Harras, K. A; Youssef, M. Ubibreathe: A Ubiquitous Non-Invasive WiFi-Based Breathing Estimator. *In Proceeding of the 16th ACM International Symposium Mobile Ad Hoc Networking Computing (MobiHoc)*, 2015; pp 277–286.

Adib, F.; Mao, H.; Kabelac, Z.; Katabi, D.; Miller, R. C. Smart Homes that Monitor Breathing and Heart Rate. In *Proceedings of the 33rd Annual ACM Conference on Human Factors in Computing System (CHI)*, 2015; pp 837–846.

Bahl, P.; Padmanabhan, V. N. RADAR: An In-Building RF-Based User Location and Tracking System. *In Proceedings of the 19th Annual Joint Conference of the IEEE Computer and Communications Societies (INFOCOM)*, 2000; pp 775–784.

CDC, Coronavirus Disease 2019 (COVID-19) Situation Summary, Library Catalog: www.cdc.gov. https://www.cdc.gov/coronavirus/2019-ncov/casesupdates/summary.html (accessed Apr 2020).

Clemente, J.; Valero, M.; Li, F.; Wang, C.; Song, W. Helena: Real-time Contact-free Monitoring of Sleep Activities and Events around the Bed. In *IEEE International Conference on Pervasive Computing and Communications*, 2020.

Davies, L.; Gather, U. The Identification of Multiple Outliers. *J. Am. Stat. Assoc.* **1993,** *88*(423), 782–792.

Gringoli, F.; Schulz, M.; Link, J.; Hollick, M. Free Your CSI: A Channel State Information Extraction Platform for Modern Wi-Fi Chipsets. In *Proceedings of the 13th International Workshop on Wireless Network Testbeds, Experimental Evaluation & Characterization*, 2019; pp 21–28.

Home Care for Patients with COVID-19 Presenting with Mild Symptoms and Management of Their Contacts, Library Catalog: www.who.int., shorturl.at/asAM7.

Huang, C.; Wang, Y.; Li, X.; Ren, L.; Zhao, J.; Hu, Y.; Zhang, L.; Fan, G.; Xu, J.; Gu, X.; et al. Clinical Features of Patients Infected with 2019 Novel Coronavirus in Wuhan, China. *Lancet* **2020,** *395*(10223), 497–506.

Kaltiokallio, O.; Yigitler, H.; Jäntti, R.; Patwari, N. Non-Invasive Respiration Rate Monitoring Using a Single COTS TX-RX Pair. In *Proceedings of the* 13th *International Symposium on* Information Processing in Sensor Network (IPSN), 2014; pp 59–69.

Kay, S. M. *Fundamentals of Statistical Signal Processing*, Prentice Hall PTR, 1993.

Kotaru, M.; Joshi, K.; Bharadia, D.; Katti, S. Spotfi: Decimeter Level Localization Using WiFi. In *Proceedings of the ACM Conference on Special Interest Group on Data Communication (SIGCOMM)*, 2015; pp 269–282.

Kumar, S.; Gil, S.; Katabi, D.; Rus, D. Accurate Indoor Localization with Zero Start-Up Cost. In *Proceedings of the 20th Annual International Conference on Mobile Computing and Networking (MobiCom)*, 2014; pp 483–494.

Li, F.; Clemente, J.; Song, W. Non-Intrusive and Non-Contact Sleep Monitoring with Seismometer. In *2018 IEEE Global Conference on Signal and Information Processing* (Global SIP), IEEE, 2018; pp 449–453.

Li, H.; Yang, W.; Wang, J.; Xu, Y.; Huang, L. WiFinger: Talk to Your Smart Devices with Finger-Grained Gesture. In *Proceedings of the ACM International Joint Conference on Pervasive Ubiquitous Computing* (UbiComp), 2016; pp 250–261.

Liu, H.; Wang, Y.; Liu, J.; Yang, J.; Chen Y. Practical User Authentication Leveraging Channel State Information (CSI). In *Proceedings of the 9th ACM Symposium on Information, Computer and Communications Security (CCS)*, 2014; pp 389–400.

Liu, J.; Wang, Y.; Chen, Y.; Yang, J.; Chen, X.; Cheng, J. Tracking Vital Signs During Sleep Leveraging off-the-Shelf WiFi. In *Proceedings of the 16th ACM International Symposium on Mobile Ad Hoc Networking and Computing (MobiHoc)*, 2015; pp 267–276.

Sen, S.; Radunovic, B.; Choudhury, R. R.; Minka, T. You are Facing the Mona Lisa: Spot Localization Using PHY Layer Information. In *Proceedings of the 10th International Conference on Mobile System, Applications, and Services* (MobiSys), 2012; pp 183–196.

Sen, S.; Lee, J.; Kim, K. H.; Congdon, P. Avoiding Multipath to Revive in building Wifi Localization. In *Proceeding of the 11th Annual International Conference on Mobile Systems, Applications, and Services*, 2013; pp 249–262.

Shi, C.; Liu, J.; Liu, H.; Chen, Y. Smart User Authentication Through Actuation of Daily Activities Leveraging WiFi-Enabled IoT. In *Proceedings of the 18th ACM International Symposium on Mobile Ad Hoc Networking and Computing (Mobihoc)*, 2017, Art. no. 5.

Singh, R. P.; Javaid, M.; Haleem, A.; Suman, R. Internet of Things (IoT) Applications to Fight Against COVID-19 Pandemic. *Diabetes Metab Syndr.* **2020,** *14*, 521–524.

Tenhunen, M.; Elomaa, E.; Sistonen, H.; Rauhala, E.; Himanen, S. L. Emfit Movement Sensor in Evaluating Nocturnal Breathing. *Respir. Physiol. Neurobiol.* **2013,** *187*(2), 183–189.

Vlavianos, A.; Law, L. K.; Broustis, I.; Krishnamurthy, S. V.; Faloutsos, M. Assessing Link Quality in IEEE 802.11 Wireless Networks: Which is the right Metric? In *Proceedings of the IEEE 19th International Symposium on Personal, Indoor Mobile Radio Communication. (PIMRC),* 2008; pp 1–6.

Vasisht, D.; Kumar, S.; Katabi, D. Decimeter-Level Localization with a Single WiFi Access Point. In *Proceedings of the 13th USENIX Conference on Networked Systems Design and Implementation (NSDI),* 2016; pp 165–178.

Wang, X.; Yang, C.; Mao, S. Phasebeat: Exploiting CSI Phase Data for Vital Sign Monitoring with Commodity Wifi Devices. In *2017 IEEE 37th International Conference on Distributed Computing Systems (ICDCS), IEEE,* 2017; pp 1230–1239.

Wang, Y.; Wu, K.; Ni, L. M. WiFall: Device-Free Fall Detection by Wireless Networks. *IEEE Trans. Mobile Comput.* **2016,** *16*(2), 581–594.

Wang, Y.; Liu, J.; Chen, Y.; Gruteser, M.; Yang, J.; Liu, H. E-Eyes: Device-Free Location-Oriented Activity Identification Using Fine-Grained WiFi Signatures. In *Proceedings Of the 20th Annual International Conference on Mobile Computing Networking (MobiCom),* 2014; pp 617–628.

Wang, G.; Zou, Y.; Zhou, Z.; Wu, K.; Ni, L. M. We can Hear you with Wi-Fi! In *Proceedings of the 20th Annual International Conference on Mobile Computing and Networking (MobiCom),* 2014; pp 593–604.

Wilcoxon, F. Individual Comparisons by Ranking Methods. In *Breakthroughs in Statistics;* Springer, 1992; pp 196–202.

Xu, Q.; Han, Y.; Wang, B.; Wu, M.; Liu, K. R. Indoor Events Monitoring Using Channel State Information Time Series. *IEEE Internet Things J.* **2019,** *6*(3), 4977–4990.

Yang, W.; Wang, X.; Song, A.; Mao, S.; Wi-Wheat: Contact-Free Wheat Moisture Detection With commodity Wifi. In *2018 IEEE International Conference on Communications (ICC), IEEE,* 2018; pp 1–6.

Youssef, M.; Agrawala, A. The Horus WLAN Location Determination System. In *Proceedings of the 3rd International Conference on Mobile Systems, Applications, and Services (MobiSys),* 2005; pp 205–218.

Zhou. F.; Yu, T.; Du, R.; Fan, G.; Liu, Y.; Liu, Z.; Xiang, J.; Wang, Y.; Song, B.; Gu, X. Clinical Course and Risk Factors for Mortality of Adult In patients with COVID-19 in Wuhan, China: A Retrospective Cohort Study. *Lancet* **2020,** 1054–1062.

CHAPTER 8

Exploring the Scope of Policy Issues Influencing IoT Health and Big Data: A Structured Review

ANTHONY MAINA[1*] and UPASANA SINGH[2]

[1]School of Computer Science and IT,
Dedan Kimathi University of Technology, Nyeri, Kenya

[2]School of Management, IT, and Governance,
University of KwaZulu-Natal, Durban, South Africa

*Corresponding author. E-mail: anthony.maina@dkut.ac.ke

ABSTRACT

IoT-health and big data technologies are transforming healthcare. By unlocking the value of massive biomedical data sets, novel technologies' capacity improves individual and public health outcomes and drives health policy. Whilst a host of ethical and privacy concerns threaten the assimilation of health big data, there is limited attention to the myriad of other social and technical issues that hinder the progress of data-driven innovations. Using a structured review of the literature, we explore the range of policy matters influencing big data technologies in the health. Results identified the following themes: (1) data sharing, utilization, and governance, (2) security and privacy, (3) standards and interoperability, (4) stakeholders, (5) human capital, (6) technology and innovation, (7) funding and partnerships, and (8) legal and regulatory issues. By uncovering the policy landscape, this work provides a framework to understand and address the IoT-health and big data integration concerns in health systems. Moreover, it assimilates the often disjoint and isolated accounts of policy narratives.

8.1 INTRODUCTION

Over the years, digital tools have emerged as integral components of health systems. More recently, health communities have acknowledged the potential of emergent digital health technologies—notably the Internet of things (IoT), artificial intelligence, and big data analytics—to transform healthcare (Laplante and Laplante, 2016; Raghupathi and Raghupathi, 2014; Wahl et al., 2018). By tapping the potential of health data sets, novel technologies improve individual and population health outcomes (Vayena et al., 2018). In particular, big data technologies are being used to, among other applications, automate the analysis of medical images (Esteva et al., 2017), support clinical decisions (Liu et al., 2014), introduce learning health systems (Beane et al., 2019), model the trajectory of disease outbreaks (Al-qaness et al., 2021), and drive health policy (Mählmann et al., 2017).

Policy action influences the digital technologies' capacity to function in the health sector (Scott et al., 2002). It is understood to mean statements, guidelines, regulations, and statutes that govern information technology initiatives (Scott et al., 2002). Guidelines and standards lead to more robust health systems through the practical application of information technologies (WHO, 2020). In particular, they clarify the need, validate expenditure, and promote eHealth development (Scott and Mars, 2013). Yet, as data-driven applications explode and IoT-health devices proliferate, evidence shows that policy oversight and regulation lags behind (Bates et al., 2018). For instance, in the last global survey, tracking digital health applications diffusion, less than 20% of countries had policy regulations and guidelines on big data (WHO, 2016).

This research is an attempt to explore the range of policy issues impacting health big data technologies. Although studies have examined emergent privacy and security issues, (Vayena et al., 2015, 2018; Wyber et al., 2015), there is a need to consider the broader scope of policy concerns collectively. Based on a comprehensive review of extant literature, the chapter investigates the variety of policy themes influencing IoT-health and big data assimilation. By demarcating significant action points, we establish a reference point for governments and health administrators as they consider how to introduce or revamp policy and practices surrounding intelligent health devices and data-driven innovations. By extension, practical digital strategies will be fundamental to leveraging big data's tremendous opportunities while also mitigating risks and challenges.

8.1.1   REVIEW PROTOCOL

8.1.1.1   SEARCH STRATEGY

The search of peer-reviewed and gray literature was performed based on the following databases: EBSCO Academic Search Complete, PubMed, MEDLINE, ScienceDirect, IEEE, and Google Scholar. Search terms were based on the concepts of big data, IoT, healthcare, and policy, with appropriate synonyms in each case (Table 8.1).

TABLE 8.1   Included Words.

Variable	Search words
Big data	Big data, data science
Internet of things	Internet of things (IoT), smart devices, connected devices
Healthcare policy	Health, medical, medicine
	policy, policies, regulation, rules, guidelines

There was no regard to methodological choices such as surveys, experimental studies, or reviews. Additional documents were retrieved by checking the reference lists of included studies.

8.1.1.2   STUDY SELECTION

Study selection was limited to the English language literature and work published between January 2009 and December 2019. A total of 593 results were screened via title and 126 results retrieved. After review by title and abstract and removal of duplicates, 37 articles were excluded. Full text evaluation was carried out on the remaining papers, and 43 publications were retained for detailed analysis. Figure 8.1 illustrates the selection process. Inclusion criteria included: (1) empirical or nonempirical research into the use and/or impact of big data and/or IoT; and (2) raises security, privacy, ethical, or other regulatory concerns that pertain or affect healthcare. Further, articles considered had the full text available and references. Publications were excluded for the following reasons:

- Does not meet the study's context of big data technologies (specifically, IoT-health, big data analytical techniques/artificial intelligence);

- Reviews on digital health technologies (e.g., mHealth, her, etc.) but the issues raised do not directly interact with big data/IoT paradigms;
- Discourse on definitions, history, enabling technologies, implementation architectures, or applications but limited or no clear importance to health policy;
- Discusses how big data/IoT innovations (e.g., RFID, multi-agents, etc.) facilitate effective and efficient delivery of services but lacking immediate significance to the health sector;
- Presents the business value of the technologies (e.g., business analytical capabilities);
- Focuses on design or architecture of big data/IoT applications in healthcare;
- Describes the experiences of patients or health workers but not concerning health big data projects/programs.   ·

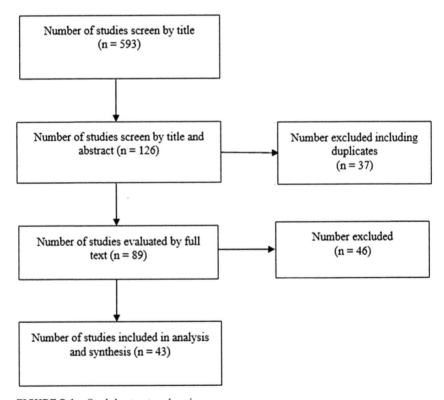

FIGURE 8.1   Study's structured review process.

Out of the studies profiled, 38 (88%) were peer-reviewed while the rest were gray literature. More than 45% of the documents were published after 2017, while less than 10% were available in 2012 or earlier. This observation corresponds to the growth in interest in introducing digital health technologies over the last decade. The majority of the studies (72%) had general context or did not specify their regional settings. A significantly higher number of reports (16%) featured advanced economies of Europe or North America compared to those (12%) which addressed the context of low and middle-income economies. Though predictable, the trend shows that interest in advanced digital health technologies is widespread (Table 8.2).

TABLE 8.2 Included Studies.

Year of publication	Publication number	Publication %
2009–2010	1	2%
2011–2012	2	5%
2013–2014	6	14%
2015–2016	14	33%
2017–2018	15	35%
2019	5	12%
Peer-review/Gray literature		
Peer-reviewed	38	88%
Gray literature	5	12%
Regional context		
High income	7	16%
General/not specified	31	72%
Middle income/low income	5	12%

8.1.2 RESULTS

The study identified varied policy concerns about IoT-health and big data and organized them under key themes based on their application similarities. Key themes are summarized in Figure 8.2.

FIGURE 8.2   Policy action for big data applications.

8.1.2.1   *DATA SHARING, UTILIZATION, AND GOVERNANCE*

Data governance and collaboration are critical pillars in promoting big data applications (Dutton, 2014; KPMG, 2018; Wang et al., 2016). Data management and access, including collaboration, data ownership, public trust, data quality, and data integration, has two-fold advantages: (1) clinical and research benefits and (2) citizen benefits (Kostkova et al., 2016). Clinical and research benefits include adding to available data on symptoms, diseases, diagnosis, treatment, and prescriptions; linking data sets to generate new evidence or information on unfamiliar symptoms; and supporting evidence-based policymaking. Benefits to the public include improving care for chronic diseases; new opportunities for home-based care services via telemedicine; and a better understanding of specific ailments.

Conventional approaches to data ownership and control hamper the ability to use predictive analytical techniques on a large scale (Sánchez and Sarría-Santamera, 2019; Dhindsa et al., 2018). For instance, health data is usually scattered across multiple facilities, each with its data handling guidelines (Olaronke and Oluwaseun, 2016), while stringent consent requirements for the reuse of EHR data generate prohibitive time and costs overheads (Mbuthia et al., 2019). Redundancies and resource underutilization precipitated by data fragmentation, by extension, leads to high healthcare costs (Austin and Kusumoto, 2016). Thus, current practices on data collection and dissemination need to be complemented by revamped consent protocols (Bublitz et al., 2019; Roski et al., 2014). Health institutions also require policy and regulatory guidelines to open big data to scientific communities (Kayaalp, 2018).

However, there are concerns about open data initiatives, principally on the constant tension between data sharing and appropriate use (Wyber et al., 2015). The right balance between privacy and the benefits of sharing data remains a contentious issue (Sánchez and Sarría-Santamera, 2019; Vayena et al., 2015). At the crux of the ethical debate is, how do you use data for the public good while also protecting individual rights? One proposal is a cost-benefit analysis to evaluate if the benefits of data access outweigh the possible risks (Weber et al., 2014). According to this view, the benchmark should be the extent to which a project proposal serves the interest of the public. This perspective assumes that data collected through public funding should be equally available to accommodate public interest (Wahl et al., 2018). While privacy and security threats are not new to health research, big data approaches significantly magnifies their profile. In particular, because health data is materially different from other forms of personal data, its unintended release can result in serious psychological harm (Bates et al., 2018; Price and Cohen, 2019). Though experience shows that individuals may be ready to share their medical records to enhance healthcare, this is dependent on the level of trust placed in institutions (Auffray et al., 2016; Pastorino et al., 2019). Mistrust, ineffective communication, and lack of accountability often erode public goodwill on sharing health data (Kostkova et al., 2016). In this regard, defining boundaries vis-à-vis expectations on data acquisition and personal data usage is essential to supporting big data initiatives (Bates et al., 2018).

Another significant data management challenge is access to health-related data of sufficiently high quality (Auffray et al., 2016; Dhindsa et al., 2018). Problems arise directly from inaccuracies and errors in the data itself, or indirectly from data sources, aggregation tools, and analytical techniques (Sukumar et al., 2015). Such deficiencies hinder health data application for secondary purposes (Auffray et al., 2016). Technology, on its own, cannot surmount the challenges introduced bogus or spurious data. For instance, erroneous, incomplete, or inaccurate raw data distort machine learning algorithms' ability to detect subtle patterns or trends (Dhindsa et al., 2018). As more health data is amassed, the questions about data veracity become more significant. As a result, action supporting revamped health standards is necessary to guarantee the quality of biomedical data and data sets' compatibility for pooling (Dhindsa et al., 2018). Further, information systems handling health data need to evolve to meet the requirements of quality and safety. Policies can either mandate or offer incentives for compliance (Vayena et al., 2018).

Data fragmentation is the other governance problem (Sánchez and Sarría-Santamera, 2019; Dhindsa et al., 2018). Aggregation becomes difficult because of different schemas, formats, metadata, and standards (Olaronke and Oluwaseun, 2016). Without data pooling, the potential of predictive analytical algorithms, which work by recognizing patterns in large data sets, is moderated (Dhindsa et al., 2018). Accordingly, the support for efficient data gathering and aggregation requires interoperable systems based on common standards (Wyber et al., 2015). Table 8.3 lists the policy issues under the theme of data sharing, utilization, and governance.

TABLE 8.3   Data Sharing, Utilization, and Governance.

Policy category	Issues
Government-level (national, provincial/ subnational) policies	Promotion of an information sharing culture Guidelines for inter-facility and organizational data sharing Clear communication on the benefits of data sharing Boundaries on data acquisition and use of personal data Standards on health data
Institutional-level (facility, organization) policies	Sharing of health data Technology use Quality and integrity of data Reformed consent protocols

8.1.2.2   SECURITY AND PRIVACY

Security and privacy issues are arguably the most significant factors influencing health big data programmes (Abouelmehdi et al., 2018; Bublitz et al., 2019; Vayena et al., 2018). Security tackles three critical issues: confidentiality (preventing unauthorized access), integrity (protection against irregular data modification), and availability (measures to guarantee access to data by authorized personnel) (Blobel et al., 2016; Riazul Islam et al., 2015). Privacy is seen as "the ability to protect sensitive information about personally identifiable healthcare information" (Abouelmehdi et al., 2018). It has the notion of "concealment of personal information" as well as controls as to what happens to that information (Weber, 2010). Additionally, the law delimits the concept of privacy (Kayaalp, 2018). For instance, neither can individuals withhold information from the government about their income on privacy grounds, nor can a government agency reveal personal information to other parties without their permission or legal order. (Kayaalp, 2018).

In principle, IoT-big data health security requirements are similar to provisions of standard eHealth applications (Abouelmehdi et al., 2018; Blobel et al., 2016). Big data settings, however, compound the security dangers posed to health information. First, private, user-generated health data via social media, wearable technologies, and personal fitness gadgets exist mostly unregulated and in the hands of big technology companies (Kostkova et al., 2016). Second, IoT-health devices extend the attack surface of cybersecurity threats (Baldini et al., 2018). Third, powerful analytical techniques and machine learning algorithms increase the likelihood of privacy leaks by reidentifying previously de-identified data (Rumbold and Pierscionek, 2017).

Individual privacy rights need to be protected not only as a legal issue but also as a fundamental human rights issue (Coetzee and Eksteen, 2011; Weber, 2010). Privacy challenges emerge directly from the nature and scope of data itself (Vayena et al., 2018). Indirectly, privacy concerns arise from the way information is integrated, the technology and platforms handling the data, and the data usage (Vayena et al., 2018). Admittedly, privacy protection is critical. Yet, it has implications for health research and big data initiatives (Olumide et al., 2013). On the one hand, limited access and sharing of health information inhibit big data projects' integration into mainstream eHealth solutions (Mählmann et al., 2017). On the one hand, privacy violations have a damaging effect on personal and professional life (Mounia and Habiba, 2015). Specifically, misuse of data may lead to discrimination of vulnerable and minority groups while commercial exploitation of data by corporations can run contrary to expectations of the people providing the data (Pastorino et al., 2019; Vayena et al., 2018). Policy oversight, therefore, should advocate balanced approaches that safeguard privacy objectives and at the same time foster the responsible use of medical data to drive healthcare (Auffray et al., 2016; Kostkova et al., 2016; Vayena et al., 2015).

Privacy protection requires collective effort among key stakeholders, such as patients, health providers, consumers of health information, developers of de-identification tools, and legal and regulatory agencies (Kayaalp, 2018). Each group bears different roles and responsibilities. For instance, the general public needs to be more aware of their rights on usage and control of user-generated health data, typically controlled by technology and social media companies (Kostkova et al., 2016). Health providers are accountable for selecting the right tools, evaluating their efficacy over time and ensuring the validity of de-identifying data (Kayaalp, 2018). Providers and technology companies handling personal data need to establish mechanisms to secure health IoT applications against hackers and Internet attacks (Laplante and Laplante, 2016; Roman et al., 2011). Governments must align policies and legal protections to balance big data approaches' societal benefits and protections for patients' privacy (Roski et al., 2014; Vayena et al., 2018). Table 8.4 lists policy issues under the theme of security and privacy.

TABLE 8.4 Security and Privacy.

Policy category	Issues
Government-level (national, provincial/ subnational) policies	Rights of consumers over private, user-generated health data
	Adequate data protection and privacy legislation
	Guidelines for collection and usage of personal data
Institutional-level (facility, organization) policies	Compliance with data protection and regulation laws
	Technology tools to secure health data
	Technical tools to safeguard privacy (de-identification)
	Guidelines for collection and usage of personal data

8.1.2.3 STANDARDS AND INTEROPERABILITY

Big data analytics' power is its capacity to tap the potential of integrated health-related information data sets (Austin and Kusumoto, 2016; Bates et al., 2018). However, there are no widely accepted approaches on how to link the data. To develop health big data applications, there two essential considerations. First, the need for common protocols to facilitate device interoperability (Baker et al., 2017) and, second the need to move toward widely accepted standards that streamline information exchange (Dhindsa et al., 2018). As the number health-based smart devices, wearable technologies, tracking devices, and wireless sensors increases, there are concerns about limited guidelines for compatible interfaces and communication protocols (Riazul Islam et al., 2015). Accordingly, there is a need for cooperation in establishing international technical standards to tackle interoperability problems and level the playing field for industry players (Coetzee and Eksteen, 2011). As crucial as device interoperability is, however, it is not sufficient to guarantee big data integration. In particular, gadgets may communicate with each other from a technical angle, but vendors may lock data behind proprietary algorithms (Bublitz et al., 2019). HL/7/FHIR standard and other protocols exist that facilitate structured and comprehensible data exchange. Health data standards support streamlined assimilation data sets from different sources and safeguard data quality and promote timely data access to research communities (Sánchez and Sarría-Santamera, 2019; Dhindsa et al., 2018). Thus, the opportunity to advance healthcare using big data should motivate the adoption of new data sharing policies, and the need for collaboration among government agencies, clinicians, data scientists, and developers on common standards to govern the exchange of health data (Dhindsa et al., 2018; Pastorino et al., 2019). Table 8.5 lists the policy issues under the theme standards and interoperability.

TABLE 8.5 Standards and Interoperability.

Policy category	Issues
Government-level (national, provincial/subnational) policies	Collaboration on technical standards Health data standards Data sharing policies
Institutional-level (facility, organization) policies	Health data standards Common device protocols Data sharing policies

8.1.2.4 STAKEHOLDERS

The health sector has a diverse range of stakeholders. Its actors comprise government, health providers, health workers, workers unions, professional associations, universities, research bodies, pharmaceutical companies, insurance companies, software developers, and not least the general public

(Bublitz et al., 2019; Vayena et al., 2018). While players' plurality is boon because it contributes to the abundance of data, it is also a setback because it complicates access and use of such data. In particular, big data settings introduce competing interests beyond the traditional players—health providers and health practitioners—on questions of control and use of health data (Salas-Vega et al., 2015).

The success in deploying predictive analytical tools has influenced interactions between physicians and patients because such novel tools also capture nonmedical parameters (e.g., patient preferences) (Austin and Kusumoto, 2016). While novel analytical techniques may improve patient satisfaction and the likelihood of medication adherence, other concerns vis-à-vis patient data privacy and security risks require attention. Patients should not be left vulnerable to security breaches and privacy-infringing surveillance (Banaan, 2016). As consumers of eHealth services and products, they should demand greater data protection and security. Although the public tends to approve data sharing and personalized services, reservations emerge over the possible loss of data control to commercial enterprises such as insurers, leading to negative consequences (for instance, exorbitant premiums). Thus, the public's role should extend providing informed consent and include other considerations such as data ownership, data commercialization, and benefits sharing (Auffray et al., 2016; Vayena et al., 2018).

At the same time, scientific communities also need access to relevant, accurate data to foster big data projects. National governments on their part should provide health services, infrastructure support (such as access to power, network connectivity, and so on), implementation of standards, and promote the protection of privacy and security rights (Maksimović and Vujović, 2017; Vayena et al., 2018). Overall, competing interests among different stakeholders draw implications for quality of care and the development of clinical trials (Salas-Vega et al., 2015). Future policies should foster cooperation between government and other stakeholders to address emergent issues and close digital health gaps. Table 8.6 lists the policy issues under the theme of stakeholders.

8.1.2.5 HUMAN CAPITAL

The limited capacity of health professionals and researchers to use intelligent analytical tools and technologies presents a significant bottleneck to advancing big data in health, particularly in resource-constrained settings (Auffray et al., 2016). Countries poised for big data success are those that possess a workforce competent in relevant ICT skills (Auffray et al., 2016). For example, in India, there is an increased focus to strengthen its workforce in data science, programming, and artificial intelligence (Chatterjee and Kar, 2018).

TABLE 8.6 Stakeholders.

Policy category	Issues
Government-level (national, provincial/subnational) policies	Guidelines for stakeholder engagement Policy reforms on ethics review boards
Institutional-level (facility, organization) policies	Reevaluate the mandate of ethics review boards Citizen/public participation in healthcare services/research

Compared to businesses in other sectors, health organizations lag in their ability to transform data into actionable information to a large extent because of the unavailability of qualified talent (Bates et al., 2018). Primary skill sets revolve around the four stages of deploying a typical big data analytics model—data acquisition, building and validating models, testing models, and deploying models in real-life settings (Cohen et al., 2014). Thus, there is a growing need for data experts and clinicians skilled in automated data collection and the use of artificial intelligence tools (Dhindsa et al., 2018).

Organizations should also ensure that their staff can utilize the outputs of big data analytics effectively. Mistakes in the interpretation of reports could lead to questionable decisions, or even serious harm to patients (Wang et al., 2016). Consequently, health professionals' training and educational programmes should integrate topics on data handling to facilitate the development of relevant skills and data management competencies (Pastorino et al., 2019). Areas of focus should include but not limited to basic statistics, data mining, and business intelligence, and research in big data technologies. These disciplines are essential for building professionals with appropriate skills for working in data-centric, knowledge-driven environments (Wang et al., 2016). Table 8.7 lists the policy issues under the theme of human capital.

TABLE 8.7   Human Capital.

Policy category	Issues
Government-level (national, provincial/subnational) policies	Policy action on the training of health professionals Funding training and research Research culture
Institutional-level (facility, organization) policies	Capacity building Research culture

8.1.2.6   *TECHNOLOGY AND INNOVATION*

IoT devices, cloud computing, and machine learning are among the most prominent technologies intertwined with health big data applications (Riazul Islam et al., 2015). The deployment of these technologies has implications for data capture, storage, analytics, and reporting, including quality and accessibility of health information (Auffray et al., 2016). Technology is equally pivotal to ensure security and privacy of health data using authentication, encryption, data masking, access control, and monitoring and auditing techniques (Abouelmehdi et al., 2018).

IoT-wearable technologies and connected medical devices impact the quantity and quality of health data (Banerjee et al., 2018). These technologies capture the pulse and respiratory rate, body temperature, and other vital signs used to detect a wide range of clinical problems from heart conditions, hypothermia, and heatstroke to fevers (Baker et al., 2017). But wearables and IoT-based medical devices pose privacy and security risks. Data gleaned can be commercially exploited and used without the informed consent of those affected and without proper checks from government authorities (Banerjee et al., 2018). As such, there is need for overarching policy oversight and control on the handling of health-related data. Technologies such as blockchain—a novel type of database or "blockchain" that relies on cryptographic algorithms—can also be used to establish trust among communicating entities, thus improving data security (Bublitz et al., 2019).

Cloud computing involves the remote use of servers, computing platforms, and software systems over the Internet. In resource-constrained settings, cloud technologies can be an effective way of lowering infrastructure cost while also facilitating technical robustness (Wang et al., 2016). Nevertheless, there are concerns about using public clouds to host health data, including technical setbacks such as Internet bandwidth limitations (Auffray et al., 2016; Wahl et al., 2018).

Machine learning algorithms are cutting edge in predictive big data analytics (Dhindsa et al., 2018). These approaches build more accurate models for multiple clinical settings, thus, supporting quicker medical interventions (Raghupathi and Raghupathi, 2014). They recognize trends, associations, or patterns by exploiting instances of variance in medical data sets (Dhindsa et al., 2018). However, the algorithms are not infallible. The techniques are vulnerable misdirection by spurious, unpredictable patterns. The introduction of national language processing and other sophisticated forms of artificial intelligence is projected to lead to novel clinical insights (Auffray et al., 2016). Table 8.8 lists the policy issues under the theme of technology and innovation.

TABLE 8.8 Technology and Innovation.

Policy category	Issues
Government-level (national, provincial/subnational) policies	Mobile network technology and infrastructure Guidelines for the use of public/private clouds Policy guidelines for the use of private, user-generated health data
Institutional-level (facility, organization) policies	Quality control for AI/machine learning algorithms Data quality Policies on data access Deployment of novel technologies to strengthen data security

8.1.2.7 FUNDING AND PARTNERSHIPS

Big data initiatives have implications for resources and funding. Some are direct costs, such as the initial capital costs of setting up the relevant technology infrastructure. In India, for example, the government set aside a budget of USD 1.5 billion for the first phase of the creation of 100 smart cities (Chatterjee and Kar, 2018). Others are indirect, for instance, the cost of compliance with new guidelines of data protection. After the General Data Protection Regulation (GDPR) in Europe came to effect in 2018, countries and institutions incurred costs to rerig their privacy policies and strengthen their IT systems (Bates et al., 2018).

Though the benefits of big data technologies are widely acknowledged, the uptake of these innovations is slow in the health sector. While the general trend points to declining infrastructure and technology costs, the overall costs after factoring installation and staff training make big data applications economically challenging for low and middle-income countries (Roski et al., 2014). African countries can scale up IoT-enabled eHealth services through partnerships and collaborations with technology giants and service providers (Coetzee and Eksteen, 2011). In Europe, collaborations and partnerships on technical standards, funding, data security, and privacy protection are instrumental to health data programmes (Pastorino et al., 2019). Table 8.9 lists the policy issues under the theme of funding and partnerships.

TABLE 8.9   Funding and Partnerships.

Policy category	Issues
Government-level (national, provincial/subnational) policies	Collaboration with international partners Guidelines on financing health technology projects Resource allocation for health projects Public–private partnerships
Institutional-level (facility, organization) policies	Retrain staff Partnerships collaboration Invest in digital technologies Compliance with policy regulations and controls

8.1.2.8   LEGAL AND REGULATORY ISSUES

Big data initiatives raise novel legal and regulatory challenges because of the personal nature of the information involved (Pastorino et al., 2019). For instance, legal issues emerge when a consumer device becomes a smart diagnostic device. In this case, it is arguable that quality assurance and regulatory approval should be more stringent (Auffray et al., 2016). Moreover, though new data streams for health big data unlock opportunities for research and commercial exploitation, challenges emerge surrounding ownership and responsibility of user-generated personal data (Kostkova et al., 2016). In general, the legal and regulatory oversight for these forms of health data is not adequately covered.

Statutory control is an integral pillar in protecting health information and safeguarding individual privacy, especially in the age of big data. Data protection laws include provisions that address "privacy, individual consent, transparency in data governance, liability for data and accountability for harm" (WHO, 2018). Data protection laws apply to personal data. Personal data denotes information that can directly or indirectly identify an individual (Rumbold and Pierscionek, 2017). Data laws define responsibilities for data controllers and set penalties for violations. But there is also the danger of privacy overprotection. Here, the concern is that far-reaching controls hamper data-driven innovation and curtail data integration, either in pooling data from different sources, creating longitudinal records, or using data for new causes (Price and Cohen, 2019). So far, many countries lag in adoption of legal frameworks that take into account big data for health (WHO, 2018).

Legal guidelines entail provisions on different aspects of personal data. First, they define the meaning of what counts as personal data. A new act in Europe has classified DNA and RNA as personal data (Auffray et al., 2016). Next, statutes express how health data is treated or handled. For instance, HIPAA (US privacy law) treats health data differently based on how it was created and who is handling it—that is, its custodian. GDPR (EU privacy law), on the other hand, has a broad categorization of health data, independent of who is the custodian or how the data were collected (Price and Cohen, 2019). Finally, data laws give clarity on anonymization or the removal of markers that can be used to link data to an individual. Table 8.10 lists the policy issues under the theme of legal and policy issues.

TABLE 8.10 Legal and Regulatory Issues.

Policy category	Issues
Government-level (national, provincial/subnational) policies	Regulatory approval of medical devices
	Legal guidelines on ownership and responsibility for private, user-generated data
	Data protection and privacy laws
	Guidelines for personal data handling
Institutional-level (facility, organization) policies	Data anonymization guidelines
	Guidelines for data protection and privacy
	Compliance with data protection laws

8.2 DISCUSSION

This chapter provides a range of health policy issues that require action to promote sustainable IoT-health and big data applications. The principal themes present the vast array of health big data concerns, including the policy reforms necessary to account for privacy and security concerns, data management transparency, and legal and regulatory oversight.

Further, we identify the need to strengthen collaboration on data access, stakeholder engagement, standards and interoperability, and technology and innovations. Lastly, the research highlights the importance of human capital and funding in advancing health big data and IoT interests. The topics discussed collectively underlie the significant considerations during the planning and implementing of health big data projects.

Policy themes' distinctions should not be seen as precise because there are potential overlaps (Laschkolnig et al., 2016). For instance, data access and availability are identified as critical areas of policy reform, yet the topics have to be counterbalanced by privacy protections and appropriate use. The duty to protect data has to be seen along with the obligation to share data (Caldicott, 2013). Simultaneously, attempts to assimilate data are hindered by device interoperability and lack of data standards (Riazul Islam et al., 2015). Next, the legal and regulatory issues incorporate most of the other central topics. Notably, legal and regulatory matters govern security and privacy, standards and interoperability, data sharing, and stakeholder engagement. Funding is also significant because it influences that capacity to achieve policy goals. In particular, organizations need to set aside funds to rerig their operations to comply with legislative guidelines, invest in technology tools, and retrain their staff (Rumbold and Pierscionek, 2017).

8.3 CONCLUSION

To advance IoT-health and big data, leaders and administrators need to understand the scope of policy ideas and their significance. Based on the findings, we recommend a framework of policy actions at government and institutional levels for developing health big data policies and guidelines. This work's main contribution lies in assimilating the often disjoint and isolated accounts of policy matters that impact data-driven innovations in healthcare.

This research was not without limitations. In the literature review, 43 articles formed the basis for analyzing and synthesizing IoT-health and big data policies. Although we attempted to achieve diversity and theoretical saturation according to the selection criteria, we cannot assume that we covered all the relevant literature. Further, it was not possible to review literature in languages other than English because of limitations on time and resources.

As a follow-up to this work, studies should be conducted to identify and evaluate the extent of coverage of issues raised in existing digital health strategies. Policymakers can identify the gaps and propose appropriate action based on the context. Further investigations should be conducted on the relationships among the key policy areas. Outcomes of how policy issues interact can offer additional insights about policy action.

KEYWORDS

- **big data**
- **Internet of things**
- **digital health**
- **digital strategies**
- **policy**
- **eHealth**

REFERENCES

Abouelmehdi, K.; Beni-Hessane, A.; Khaloufi, H. Big Healthcare Data: Preserving Security and Privacy. *J. Big Data* **2018,** *5*(1), 1. https://doi.org/10.1186/s40537-017-0110-7

Al-qaness, M. A. A.; Saba, A. I.; Elsheikh, A. H.; Elaziz, M. A.; Ibrahim, R. A.; Lu, S.; Hemedan, A. A.; Shanmugan, S.; Ewees, A. A. Efficient Artificial Intelligence Forecasting Models for COVID-19 Outbreak in Russia and Brazil. *Process Safety Environ. Protect.* **2021,** *149*, 399–409. https://doi.org/10.1016/j.psep.2020.11.007

Auffray, C.; Balling, R.; Barroso, I.; Bencze, L.; Benson, M.; Bergeron, J.; Bernal-Delgado, E.; Blomberg, N.; Bock, C.; Conesa, A.; Del Signore, S.; Delogne, C.; Devilee, P.; Di Meglio, A.; Eijkemans, M.; Flicek, P.; Graf, N.; Grimm, V.; Guchelaar, H. J.; Zanetti, G. Making Sense of Big Data in Health Research: Towards an EU Action Plan. *Genome Med.* **2016,** *8*(1), 71. https://doi.org/10.1186/s13073-016-0323-y

Austin, C.; Kusumoto, F. The Application of Big Data in Medicine: Current Implications and Future Directions. *J. Interv. Cardiac Electrophysiol.* **2016,** *47*(1), 51–59. https://doi.org/10.1007/s10840-016-0104-y

Baker, S. B.; Xiang, W.; Atkinson, I. Internet of Things for Smart Healthcare: Technologies, Challenges, and Opportunities. *IEEE Access* **2017,** *5*, 26521–26544. https://doi.org/10.1109/ACCESS.2017.2775180

Baldini, G.; Botterman, M.; Neisse, R.; Tallacchini, M. Ethical Design in the Internet of Things. *Sci. Eng. Ethics* **2018,** *24*(3), 905–925. https://doi.org/10.1007/s11948-016-9754-5

Banaan, C. The IoT Threat to Privacy. *Tech. Crunch.* **2016**. https://social.techcrunch.com/2016/08/14/the-iot-threat-to-privacy/

Banerjee, S. (Sy); Hemphill, T.; Longstreet, P. Wearable Devices and Healthcare: Data Sharing and Privacy. *Inform. Soc.* **2018**, *34*(1), 49–57. https://doi.org/10.1080/01972243.2017.1391912

Bates, D. W.; Heitmueller, A.; Kakad, M.; Saria, S. Why Policymakers Should Care About "Big Data" in healthcare. *Health Policy Technol.* **2018**, *7*(2), 211–216. https://doi.org/10.1016/j.hlpt.2018.04.006

Beane, A.; Wagstaff, D.; Abayadeera, A.; Wijeyaratne, M.; Ranasinghe, G.; Mirando, S.; Dondorp, A. M.; Walker, D.; Haniffa, R. A Learning Health Systems Approach to Improving the Quality of Care for Patients in South Asia. *Global Health Action* **2019**, *12*(1), 1587893. https://doi.org/10.1080/16549716.2019.1587893

Blobel, B.; Lopez, D. M.; Gonzalez, C. Patient Privacy and Security Concerns on Big Data for Personalised Medicine. *Health Technol.* **2016**, *6*(1), 75–81. https://doi.org/10.1007/s12553-016-0127-5

Bublitz, F. M.; Oetomo, A.; S. Sahu, K.; Kuang, A.; X. Fadrique, L.; E. Velmovitsky, P.; M. Nobrega, R.; P. Morita, P. Disruptive Technologies for Environment and Health Research: An Overview of Artificial Intelligence, Blockchain, and Internet of Things. *Int. J. Environ. Res. Public Health* **2019**, *16*(20), 3847. https://doi.org/10.3390/ijerph16203847

Caldicott, F. *To Share or Not to Share? The Information Governance Review.* Department of Health, 2013. https://assets.publishing.service.gov.uk/government/uploads/system/uploads/attachment_data/file/192572/2900774_InfoGovernance_accv2.pdf

Chatterjee, S.; Kar, A. K. Regulation and Governance of the Internet of Things in India. *Digital Policy Regul. Gov.* **2018**, *20*(5), 399–412. https://doi.org/10.1108/DPRG-04-2018-0017

Coetzee, L.; Eksteen, J. The Internet of Things – Promise for the Future? An Introduction. *2011 IST-Africa Conference Proceedings*, 2011; pp 1–9. https://ieeexplore.ieee.org/abstract/document/6107386/

Cohen, I. G.; Amarasingham, R.; Shah, A.; Xie, B.; Lo, B. The Legal And Ethical Concerns That Arise From Using Complex Predictive Analytics In Health Care. *Health Affairs* **2014**, *33*(7), 1139–1147. https://doi.org/10.1377/hlthaff.2014.0048

Dhindsa, K.; Bhandari, M.; Sonnadara, R. R. What's Holding up the Big Data Revolution in Healthcare? *BMJ* **2018**, k5357. https://doi.org/10.1136/bmj.k5357

Dutton, W. H. Putting Things to Work: Social and Policy Challenges for the Internet of Things. *Info* **2014**, *16*(3), 1–21. https://doi.org/10.1108/info-09-2013-0047

Esteva, A.; Kuprel, B.; Novoa, R. A.; Ko, J.; Swetter, S. M.; Blau, H. M.; Thrun, S. Dermatologist-Level Classification of Skin Cancer with Deep Neural Networks. *Nature* **2017**, *542*(7639), 115–118. https://doi.org/10.1038/nature21056

Kayaalp, M. Patient Privacy in the Era of Big Data. *Balkan Med. J.* **2018**, *35*(1), 8–17. https://doi.org/10.4274/balkanmedj.2017.0966

Kostkova, P.; Brewer, H.; de Lusignan, S.; Fottrell, E.; Goldacre, B.; Hart, G.; Koczan, P.; Knight, P.; Marsolier, C.; McKendry, R. A.; Ross, E.; Sasse, A.; Sullivan, R.; Chaytor, S.; Stevenson, O.; Velho, R.; Tooke, J. Who Owns the Data? Open Data for Healthcare. *Front. Public Health* **2016**, *4*. https://doi.org/10.3389/fpubh.2016.00007

KPMG. *Data Governance: Driving Value in Healthcare,* 2018. https://assets.kpmg/content/dam/kpmg/pl/pdf/2018/10/pl-Raport-KPMG-International-pt-Data-governance-driving-value-in-health.pdf

Laplante, P. A.; Laplante, N. The Internet of Things in Healthcare: Potential Applications and Challenges. *IT Prof.* **2016**, *18*(3), 2–4. https://doi.org/10.1109/MITP.2016.42

Laschkolnig, A.; Habl, C.; Renner, A. T.; Bobek, J. European Commission, Directorate-General for Health and Food Safety, Sogeti, & Gesundheit Österreich Forschungs- und Planungs GmbH. *Study on Big Data in Public Health, Telemedicine and Healthcare: Final Report.* Publications Office, 2016. http://dx.publications.europa.eu/10.2875/734795

Liu, N. T.; Holcomb, J. B.; Wade, C. E.; Batchinsky, A. I.; Cancio, L. C.; Darrah, M. I.; Salinas, J. Development and Validation of a Machine Learning Algorithm and Hybrid System to Predict the Need for Life-Saving Interventions in Trauma Patients. *Med. Biol. Eng. Comput.* **2014,** *52*(2), 193–203. https://doi.org/10.1007/s11517-013-1130-x

Mählmann, L.; Reumann, M.; Evangelatos, N.; Brand, A. Big Data for Public Health Policy-Making: Policy Empowerment. *Public Health Genom.* **2017,** *20*(6), 312–320. https://doi.org/10.1159/000486587

Maksimović, M.; Vujović, V. Internet of Things Based E-health Systems: Ideas, Expectations and Concerns. In *Handbook of Large-Scale Distributed Computing in Smart Healthcare;* Khan, S. U., Zomaya, A. Y., Abbas, A., Eds.; Springer International Publishing, 2017; pp 241–280. https://doi.org/10.1007/978-3-319-58280-1_10

Mbuthia, D.; Molyneux, S.; Njue, M.; Mwalukore, S.; Marsh, V. Kenyan Health Stakeholder Views on Individual Consent, General Notification and Governance Processes for the Re-Use of Hospital Inpatient Data to Support Learning on Healthcare Systems. *BMC Med. Ethics* **2019,** *20*(1), 3. https://doi.org/10.1186/s12910-018-0343-9

Mounia, B.; Habiba, C. Big Data Privacy in Healthcare Moroccan Context. *Procedia Comput. Sci.* **2015,** *63*, 575–580. https://doi.org/10.1016/j.procs.2015.08.387

Olaronke, I.; Oluwaseun, O. Big Data in Healthcare: Prospects, Challenges and Resolutions. *2016 Future Technologies Conference (FTC)*, 2016; pp 1152–1157. https://doi.org/10.1109/FTC.2016.7821747

Olumide, A.; Uju, I.; Oparadike, C.; Oyeyemi, I.; Uyanwa, E. *Patient Privacy in a Mobile World*. Thomas Reuters Foundation and Trust Law Connect, 2013. https://www.trust.org/contentAsset/raw-data/03172beb-0f11-438e-94be-e02978de3036/file

Pastorino, R.; De Vito, C.; Migliara, G.; Glocker, K.; Binenbaum, I.; Ricciardi, W.; Boccia, S. Benefits and Challenges of Big Data in Healthcare: An Overview of the European Initiatives. *Europ. J. Public Health* **2019,** *29*(Supplement_3), 23–27. https://doi.org/10.1093/eurpub/ckz168

Price, W. N.; Cohen, I. G. Privacy in the Age of Medical Big Data. *Nature Med.* **2019,** *25*(1), 37–43. https://doi.org/10.1038/s41591-018-0272-7

Raghupathi, W.; Raghupathi, V. Big Data Analytics in Healthcare: Promise and Potential. *Health Inform. Sci. Syst.* **2014,** *2*(1), 3.

Riazul Islam, S. M.; Kwak, D.; Humaun Kabir, M.; Hossain, M.; Kwak, K. S. The Internet of Things for Health Care: A Comprehensive Survey. *IEEE Access* **2015,** *3*, 678–708. https://doi.org/10.1109/ACCESS.2015.2437951

Roman, R.; Najera, P.; Lopez, J. Securing the Internet of Things. *Computer* **2011,** *44*(9), 51–58. https://doi.org/10.1109/MC.2011.291

Roski, J.; Bo-Linn, G. W.; Andrews, T. A. Creating Value In Health Care Through Big Data: Opportunities And Policy Implications. *Health Affairs* **2014,** *33*(7), 1115–1122. https://doi.org/10.1377/hlthaff.2014.0147

Rumbold, J. M. M.; Pierscionek, B. The Effect of the General Data Protection Regulation on Medical Research. *J. Med. Internet Res.* **2017,** *19*(2), e47. https://doi.org/10.2196/jmir.7108

Salas-Vega, S.; Haimann, A.; Mossialos, E. Big Data and Health Care: Challenges and Opportunities for Coordinated Policy Development in the EU. *Health Syst. Reform* **2015,** *1*(4), 285–300. https://doi.org/10.1080/23288604.2015.1091538

Sánchez, M. C.; Sarría-Santamera, A. Unlocking Data: Where is the Key? *Bioethics* **2019,** *33*(3), 367–376. https://doi.org/10.1111/bioe.12565

Scott, R. E.; Chowdhury, M. F. U.; Varghese, S. Telehealth Policy: Looking for Global Complementarity. *J. Telemed. Telecare* **2002,** *8*(3_suppl), 55–57. https://doi.org/10.1258/13576330260440871

Scott, R. E.; Mars, M. Principles and Framework for eHealth Strategy Development. *J. Med. Internet Res.* **2013,** *15*(7), e155. https://doi.org/10.2196/jmir.2250

Sukumar, S. R.; Natarajan, R.; Ferrell, R. K. Quality of Big Data in Health Care. *Int. J. Health Care Quality Assur.* **2015,** *28*(6), 621–634. https://doi.org/10.1108/IJHCQA-07-2014-0080

Vayena, E.; Dzenowagis, J.; Brownstein, J. S.; Sheikh, A. Policy Implications of Big Data in the Health Sector. *Bull. World Health Organ.* **2018,** *96*(1), 66–68. https://doi.org/10.2471/BLT.17.197426

Vayena, E.; Salathé, M.; Madoff, L. C.; Brownstein, J. S. Ethical Challenges of Big Data in Public Health. *PLOS Comput. Biol.* **2015,** *11*(2), e1003904. https://doi.org/10.1371/journal.pcbi.1003904

Wahl, B.; Cossy-Gantner, A.; Germann, S.; Schwalbe, N. R. Artificial Intelligence (AI) and Global Health: How can AI Contribute to Health in Resource-Poor Settings? *BMJ Global Health* **2018,** *3*(4), e000798. https://doi.org/10.1136/bmjgh-2018-000798

Wang, Y.; Kung, L.; Byrd, T. A. Big Data Analytics: Understanding its Capabilities and Potential Benefits for Healthcare Organisations. *Technol. Forecast. Social Change* **2016,** *126*, 3–13. https://doi.org/10.1016/j.techfore.2015.12.019

Weber, G. M., Mandl, K. D., Kohane, I. S. Finding the Missing Link for Big Biomedical Data. *JAMA,* **2014.** https://doi.org/10.1001/jama.2014.4228

Weber, R. H. Internet of Things – New Security and privacy Challenges. *Comput. Law Security Rev.* **2010,** *26*(1), 23–30. https://doi.org/10.1016/j.clsr.2009.11.008

WHO. *Global Diffusion of eHealth: Making Universal Health Coverage Achievable: Report of the Third Global Survey on eHealth,* 3rd ed.; World Health Organisation, 2016. http://www.who.int/goe/publications/global_diffusion/en/

WHO. *Big Data and Artificial Intelligence for Achieving Universal Health Coverage: An International Consultation on Ethics: Meeting Report, 12–13 October 2017, Miami, Florida, USA.* World Health Organization, 2018.

WHO. *Draft Global Strategy on Digital Health.pdf.* World Health Organisation, 2020. https://www.who.int/docs/default-source/documents/gs4dhdaa2a9f352b0445bafbc79ca799dce4d.pdf?sfvrsn=f112ede5_38

Wyber, R.; Vaillancourt, S.; Perry, W.; Mannava, P.; Folaranmi, T.; Celi, L. A. Big Data in Global Health: Improving Health in Low- and Middle-Income Countries. *Bull. World Health Organ.* **2015,** *93*(3), 203–208. https://doi.org/10.2471/BLT.14.139022

CHAPTER 9

COVID-19 Disaster Healthcare Management System in Rural Areas

M. BHUVANA[1] and S. VASANTHA[2*]

[1]*ICSSR Post-Doctoral Research Scholar, School of Management Studies, Vels Institute of Science, Technology & Advanced Studies (VISTAS), Chennai, India*

[2]*Professor, School of Management Studies, Vels Institute of Science, Technology & Advanced Studies (VISTAS), Chennai, India*

[*]*Corresponding author. E-mail: vasantha.sms@velsuniv.ac.in*

ABSTRACT

The coronavirus disease outbreak has stunned the entire world through its rapid spread between the countries, and at last, it has become a deadly virus that results in millions of patients, increased the occurrence of deaths, and has created a destructive impact on the world economics. People who reside in metropolitan cities have sufficient knowledge related to this disaster virus and they have gained enough experience to fight against this virus. But, 70% of the entire population has been surrounded by the rural population in developing countries like India. This chapter is an endeavor to address the current situation of the pandemic infection of COVID-19 that impacts the rural areas in our country. The authors have developed a model called "Hierarchy of COVID-19 Disaster Healthcare Management System" based on the National Emergency Management System to fight against the coronavirus in rural areas.

9.1 INTRODUCTION

The World Health Organization (WHO, 2020) has declared an International concern of emergency for public health on January 30th, 2020 with a new virus "coronavirus" disease also called COVID-19. This pandemic virus was first identified in December 2019 in the Wuhan City of China and it widely spread all over the country. There exists a huge amount of deaths and millions of people were highly infected. It has pushed million hundreds of people all over the world into the state of wider regional and national instabilities, food insecurities, worldwide disrupting the supply chain, and so on (Sly, 2020). This virus has been named as "Human Crisis" (United Nations, 2020) by Secretary-General Antonio Guterres of United Nations; they pointed out that "it is an unprecedented scale that demands an unprecedented response." Mohammad (2020) has stated that the global community should approach these "new uncertainties" of economic and social disruption collaboratively and collectively. The scope for addressing the impact of this deadly virus over communities, countries, regional, and at global levels are found to be insufficient.

Through examining the information about past global or regional disease outbreaks several best practices for recovery have been followed and maintained by the people in the countries. This unusual nature of the present disaster of COVID-19 directs the recommendation of the world to take up various novel approaches to overcome it effectively. Even though the response to the crisis for COVID-19 remains to be dynamic and active, it is the time every individual especially rural areas to get initiated for its recovery. Figure 9.1 displays the active distribution of cases across the world till January 21st, 2021. The United States occupies the majority of the population (25,569,883 cases) affected by COVID 19. India is the second-largest country reported 10,658,889 cases infected by the coronavirus. Hence, this research study is an endeavor to design a hierarchy of the COVID-19 Disaster Healthcare Management System to overcome the emergencies caused by the epidemic disease of coronavirus, particularly in rural areas.

9.1.1 PRINCIPLES OF EMERGENCY MANAGEMENT SYSTEM

The term "emergency management" is historically collaborative in various fields from the 20th century (Kapucu, 2008; Rubin, 2007). Collective public

organizations from various levels of government, community organizations, individuals, nonprofits, and private sector organizations are the major
elements of the emergency management system. However, several variations
exist between the environment of rural and urban areas in setting multiple
resources such as education, knowledge, infrastructure, and awareness to
handle emergencies (Comfort and Kapucu, 2006; Petak, 1985). Comfort
(2002) has examined the system of emergency management through the
lens of complex robust systems. She states that information networks and
infrastructure are considered to be the important dimensions for timely decisions. Complex systems are defined as the self-organizing and emergent
groups that involve nonprofits and individual responders. Effective information and knowledge sharing have been done by the complex system during
times of disasters (Weick, 1993). Citizen' initiatives and engagements are
the factors that have a predominant role in handling emergencies (Stallings
and Quarantelli, 1985).

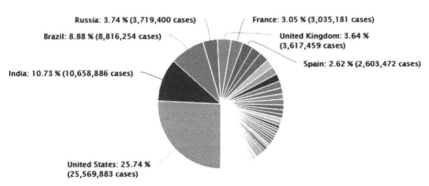

FIGURE 9.1   Distribution of COVID-19 cases across the countries.
Source: Worldometer, 2020.

In 1985, the federal government has developed the department of
Homeland security to facilitate the two important presidential directives
that make national emergency management standards for state, local,
and federal governments (HSDL, 2020). This agency assists the four
important emergency planning strategies namely "Mitigation," "Preparation," "Response," and "Recovery." It also provides technical, funding

resources, equipment, and direct federal assistance. Figure 9.1 describes the principles of the emergency management system developed by the federal government.

FIGURE 9.2   National Emergency Management System.
Source: Homeland Security Digital Library.

The private and government organizations are utilizing this management system with a common module structure and regular terminologies. The basic principles of this emergency management system consist of four different phrases and it has been discussed below:

9.1.1.1   PHASE 1: MITIGATION

Mitigation is defined as the phase of pre-disaster risk reduction. In this phase, risk assessment on the annual threat, alleviation has been conducted to analyze the most critical areas where the country has to be focused on the upcoming year. This phase helps the countries to narrow down the areas that are to be more concentrated; thereby the country could easily reduce the risk to the wider space.

9.1.1.2   PHASE 2: PREPAREDNESS

Preparation is defined as the capacity-building phase of pre-disaster preparation. In this phase, action teams have been developed for facing the crisis. Members of the action team have been well trained about the procedures of emergency management, executing the emergency response, and following the operations plans that are framed earlier.

9.1.1.3   PHASE 2: RESPONSE

The response is defined as the phase of "intra-disaster emergence reaction." It is the phase of combating and confronting the risk directly by the people in the country. The guidelines of this phase are directed by the members of the countries' facility planning and management, public safety departments, environmental safety, and health departments.

9.1.1.4   PHASE 4: RECOVERY

Recovery is defined as the phase of "post-disaster reconstruction" phase. The objective of this phase is to bring the emergency condition to normal as early as possible. This phase is highly recommended by the emergency recovery members of snowstorms, fire, or flood accidents.

9.2   METHODS

In India, a national wide lockdown was announced by the government on March 24th, 2020 to terminate the spread of COVID-19 within the country. The Government of India has taken multiple initiatives to protect the people from this deadly pandemic disease. The majority of the institutions of various fields like education institutions, IT, and manufacturing industries have been temporarily closed. The Indian government has appointed several medical practitioners and healthcare workers to create awareness of the deadly infection. People are directed to wear masks and take sufficient precautionary measures of maintaining social distancing among the people. The spreading of the virus has infected nearly millions of rural people in our country. The primary reason is mainly due to the migrant workers who enter their villages since they face several challenges like lack of jobs, financial loss, and closure of hostels, etc. The World Health Organization (WHOb) has recommended appointing one trained doctor for attending 1000 COVID-19 patients. While countries like India are concerned, two-third of the entire population resides in rural areas that require four times as many healthcare workers to attend the COVID-19 patients and it seems to be quite challenging. The majority of the rural communities have relied on untrained healthcare workers and the government officially has faced several obstacles in reaching the rural people for creating awareness on protecting them from this epidemic infection.

9.2.1   CONCEPTUAL MODEL

The researchers have constructed the framework based on the principles of the National Emergency Disaster Management System developed by the federal government in 1985. The present research study has added the features in the existing model by associating the phases with the parameters of COVID-19 for developing a new model named "Hierarchy of COVID-19 Disaster Healthcare Management System" (Fig. 9.1) for rural communities. The present model facilitates the set of policies that directs the citizens as well the government that is to be executed during each phase of the COVID-19 disaster.

At each phase, the model describes the significant measures that are to be taken care of by the individual as well as the government officials to overcome the deadly infection of COVID-19.

9.3   COMPARISION OF NATIONAL EMERGENCY MANAGEMENT SYSTEM WITH COVID-19 DISASTER HEALTHCARE MANAGEMENT SYSTEM

9.3.1   MITIGATION

Mitigation is stated as the risk reduction phase of pre-disaster. In this phase, the number of rural patients infected or deaths has to be reduced by developing an effective healthcare management system. The epidemic disease risk can be terminated in the villages by adopting precautionary measures through proper education, resource planning, and encouraging the rural citizens' to take medical insurance for satisfying financial needs.

FIGURE 9.3   Hierarchy of COVID-19 Disaster Healthcare Management System.
Source: Authors' Model.

9.3.1.1   RURAL HEALTH EMERGENCY RESPONSE SYSTEM

The rural areas of the countries are still lacking behind to have an emergency response system. Even though they have such type of system, the rural citizens face multiple obstacles with untrained staff members and timely needs of healthcare services (Kruk, 2015). Hence, the new rural health emergency response system has to be developed with properly trained medical staff and healthcare workers to treat the COVID-19 patients in rural areas.

9.3.1.2   MANPOWER AND RESOURCE PLANNING

In the preliminary phase of COVID-19, it has been noted that even in many developed countries, there exists inadequate and insufficient healthcare providers and staff members to treat the COVID-19 patients (Mitchell, 2020). Several challenges like lack of medicines, medical equipment, and isolation centers have been faced by the countries to overcome the spread of the deadly virus. In India, 70% of the entire population is occupied by the communities of rural people (Nandi, 2020). Hence, proper manpower and sufficient resources have to be effectively planned by the authorities of rural areas to safeguard and to meet the needs of the rural poor.

9.3.1.3   PROMOTING RURAL EDUCATION

Organizing medical campaigns for sharing information about corona-virus increases the awareness among rural people to face the pandemic situation. These initiatives help the rural people to change their existing healthcare behavior and understand the current epidemic condition of the entire world (Siddique, et al., 2020). Through proper healthcare education, people in rural communities could safeguard their health as well as the members of their families.

9.3.1.4   ENCOURAGING RURAL CITIZENS TO PURSUE MEDICAL INSURANCE

Other than the challenges of COVID-19, the people in rural areas face multiple obstacles daily for meeting their basic needs and requirements. Lack of infrastructure, distance from financial institutions, low-income level, etc. are the challenges faced by the rural people for accessing any kind of services facilitated by the government (David, 2020). Hence, pursuing medical insurance at a very low affordable cost by the government to the rural people decreases their burden for meeting the emergency needs and medical expenses of COVID-19.

9.3.2   PREPAREDNESS

Preparation is defined as the capacity-building phase of pre-disaster preparation. In this phase, the government officials should direct both the members involved in the existing healthcare system and the rural people to perform anti-epidemic activities to overcome the deadly virus of COVID-19. State preparedness, individual preparedness, anti-epidemic training, and enough food supplies are the preparedness measures to be considered as the major dimensions to meet the pandemic of COVID-19 among the rural people.

9.3.2.1 STATE PREPAREDNESS

The preparedness of the authorized members of the state plays a predominant role in focusing on the rural areas to protect and recover the people who are infected by the epidemic disease (Vladimir, et al, 2020). The legal officials of the state should direct the local government officials to take preparatory measures like restricting the crowd, entering migrants to the villages, frequent monitoring of rural peoples' health, and taking sanitary measures to limit the spread of the virus in rural areas.

9.3.2.2 INDIVIDUAL PREPAREDNESS

Once the proper training and awareness have been cultivated among the rural people, the level of preparedness among each individual belongs to rural communities could be increased automatically (Vladimir, et al., 2020). Through individual preparedness, the members get a thorough knowledge to safeguard themselves from the infected people; this helps to decrease the spread of the pandemic disease of COVID-19 in villages.

9.3.2.3 ANTI-EPIDEMIC TRAINING

The individual and state preparedness in rural areas helps in controlling the spread of COVID-19 only at a restricted period. The complete termination of the coronavirus is not yet found in any countries or states of the entire world (Weintraub, 2020). Hence, the medical practitioners and the healthcare workers from the rural areas should be given adequate training about the epidemic virus to make the rural people understand the current scenario of COVID-19 daily with its health symptoms such as breathing difficulties, rise in body temperature, and respiratory infections such as wheezing, cold or cough, etc.

9.3.2.4   ENOUGH FOOD SUPPLIES

As stated by World Health Organization (WHOa, 2020), epidemic disease of COVID-19 infects the people who have a low immune system; rural people belonging to the age group of above 60 years and below 10 years have to be focused and taken care with supplying health food supplements to increase their efficiency of the immune system and protect themselves from the global infection (Vladimir, et al., 2020). The healthcare workers in rural areas should target the age group category people of above 60 years and below 10 years for facilitating frequent medical advice to monitor their existing health issues like diabetics, blood pressure, and respiratory problems, etc.

9.3.3   RESPONSE

The response is defined as the phase of "intra-disaster emergence reaction." It is time for the local government to dispatch the team members of the rural healthcare management system to combat the pandemic infection in rural areas. Life safety, increasing the medical capacities, sharing the medical health services, and strengthening the international collaboration are the response measures that have to be made by the members of the rural communities as well as the government officials to fight against COVID-19.

9.3.3.1   LIFE SAFETY

It is the duty and responsibility of each rural citizen to protect themselves and stop the widespread of COVID-19 from their localities. In this phase, the rural citizens' have been thoroughly trained by the medical practitioners and healthcare workers about the information related to COVID-19 (Morton, 2020). If any symptoms of coronavirus have been incurred by the rural people such as breathing difficulties, rise in body temperature, respiratory infections such as wheezing, cold, or cough, or any kind of health disturbances, the members of the family should report the problem directly to the nearby healthcare centers to protect their life from this deadly virus.

9.3.3.2 INCREASING MEDICAL CAPACITY

It has been noted that lakhs of cases infected by COVID-19 have been reported per day at several places all over the countries. It has become another great challenge for healthcare workers and doctors to treat infected people (Department of Global Communications, 2020). It is time for the local government members to increase the medical capacity by recruiting more healthcare workers and medical practitioners, increase the medical accessories and instruments, increasing the healthcare and isolation centers, etc. to treat and save the infected people in rural areas.

9.3.3.3 SHARING MENTAL HEALTH SERVICES

The healthcare workers, medical practitioners, and doctors are supposed to face multiple obstacles and stress in treating thousands and lakhs of COVID-19 patients (Sturm, 2020). This situation disturbs their mental health since they work under pressure and panic condition. Hence, the government must give regular counseling and encourage them with proper wages and rewards.

9.3.3.4 STRENGTHENING INTERNATIONAL COLLABORATION

The pandemic virus of COVID-19 has been widely spread across the globe. About 99,771,343 active cases have been found all over the world (till January 21st, 2020); hence, it is time for strengthening the international collaboration for availing medical support between the countries for protecting the public health of the people residing in their respective countries (Sumbal and Vijay, 2020). It is time to acknowledge the medical requirements and needs by considering the security of all the countries as part of world health security.

9.3.4 RECOVERY

Recovery is defined as the phase of "post-disaster reconstruction" phase. At this stage, the members' local healthcare system in rural areas helps the COVID-19 patients to get completely recovered from the deadly infection. Psychological support, addressing the social problems, recruiting a rehabilitation team, and vaccination are important measures that have to be followed by the members of the local healthcare system toward COVID-19 patients in rural areas.

9.3.4.1 PSYCHOLOGICAL SUPPORT

It has been well known that low-income group people face several challenges daily to meet their fundamental requirements; saving their lives from COVID-19 seems to be the most highly difficult condition for them to survive in society (WHOa, 2020). Hence, it is required to give them proper psychological guidance and support by the healthcare team members to fight against COVID-19 and recover them completely.

9.3.4.2 ADDRESSING SOCIAL PROBLEMS

Several COVID-19 patients have lost their jobs and most of the people in rural areas are financially affected since the entire world has entered into the state of lockdown to stop the widespread of the virus (WHOa, 2020). These issues should be considered as a social problem by the local government bodies to address the challenges of the rural people and support them financially for satisfying their minimum requirement to survive in this society.

9.3.4.3 RECRUITING REHABILITATION TEAM

Even though the members of the healthcare teams and the medical practitioners support the rural people to recover from COVID-19 (David, 2020), it is time to construct a rehabilitation team in rural areas to monitor the health of people who have recovered from COVID-19. Since the complete termination of the virus is not yet seen in many countries, there are many chances of getting the infection again by those category people.

9.3.4.4 VACCINATION

Scientists across the globe are working relentlessly to produce vaccines to stop the spread of coronavirus (David, 2020). They face multiple challenges in administrating the vaccines since the response of COVID-19 measures varies on daily basis. Globally, several vaccine trials have been made by the medical institutes to wipe out the virus completely from the world. At this phase, vaccination is the only solution for terminating the virus. Once it has been successfully launched, it would be facilitated at the rural population at an affordable cost since they occupy a wider space throughout the world.

9.4 CONCLUSION

Coronavirus pandemic is said to be a biological disaster. Such kind of disasters, are found to be more powerful and seems to be challenging to resist especially rural people from infection and deaths. Creating awareness towards people, developing health care teams, and training health care team members, are the significant measures for recovering the people socially psychologically, and physically from the deadly pandemic disease of COVID-19. The authors would like to conclude that the government of India should mobilize the resources effectively, screen the health condition of rural people, strengthen and increase the rural healthcare system, and address their problems to combat the coronavirus in this present world condition till the vaccine for the deadly virus has been launched successfully and distributed all around the world.

KEYWORDS

- **COVID-19**
- **Disaster Healthcare Management System**
- **rural people**
- **mitigation**
- **preparedness**

REFERENCES

Chan, D. W. K. A Reflection on the Anti-Epidemic Response of COVID-19 from the Perspective of Disaster Management. *Int. J. Nursing Sci.* **2020,** *7,* 382–385.

Claire B. Rubin. Long Term Recovery from Disasters–The Neglected Component of Emergency Management. *J. Homeland Security Emerg. Manag.* **2009,** *6*(1), 1–18.

Comfort, L. K. Rethinking Security: Organizational Fragility in Extreme Events. *Public Admin. Rev.* **2002,** *62*(s1), 98–107.

Comfort, L. K.; Kapucu, N. Inter-Organizational Coordination in Extreme Events: The World Trade Center Attack, September 11, 2001. *Nat. Hazards J. Int. Soc. Prev. Mitig. Nat. Hazards* **2006,** *39*(2), 309–327.

Department of Global Communications. Funding the Fight Against COVID-19 in the World's Poorest Countries. United Nations COVID-19 Response [Internet]. 2020 March [cited 2020 May 28]. https://www.un.org/en/uncoronavirus-communications-team/funding-fight-against-COVID-19-world%E2%80%99s-poorest-countries

Homeland Security Digital Library. National Emergency Management System, 2020. https://www.hsdl.org/c/

J. Lack of PPE, Poor Infection Control put Medical Staff at risk of COVID-19. Hindustan Times [Internet]. 2020 April [cited 2020 May 28]. https://www.hindustantimes.com/india-news/lack-of-ppe-poorinfection-control-put-medical-staff-at-risk-of-COVID-19/story-5jmeJgwUAaFuu4wfiCu8XN.html.

Javed, S.; Kumar, V. Strengthening the COVID-19 Pandemic Response, Global Leadership, and International Cooperation Through Global Health Diplomacy. *Health Promot. Perspect.* **2020,** *10*(4), 300–305.

Kapucu, N. Collaborative Emergency Management: Better Community Organising, Better Public Preparedness and Response. *Disaster Prev. Manag.* **2008,** *7*(4), 526–535.

Kruk, M. E. Emergency Preparedness and Public Health Systems Lessons for Developing Countries [Internet]. *Am. J. Prev. Med.* **2008,** *34*(6), 529–534. https://pubmed.ncbi.nlm.nih.gov/18471591/.

Kruks-Wisner, G. Navigating the State: Citizenship Practice and the Pursuit of Services in Rural India. Present at the Harvard South Asia Institute, 2015. http://southasiainstitute.harvard.edu/website/wpcontent/uploads/2013/ 07/GKW_SAI-working-paper_2015. Pdf

Mitchell, G. Not Enough Intensive Care Nurses for Coronavirus Outbreak. Nursing Times [Internet]. 2020 March [cited 2020 May 28]. https://www.nursingtimes.net/news/hospital/not-enough-intensive-carenurses-for-coronavirus- outbreak-12-03-2020/.

Mohammad, Amina J. A New Normal: UN Lays Out Roadmap to Lift Economies and Save Jobs After COVID-19. United Nations, April 27, 2020. https://bit.ly/2SL11OR

Morton, M. J. Pandemic Influenza and Major Disease Outbreak Preparedness in US Emergency Departments: A Selected Survey of Emergency Health Professionals [Internet]. *Am. J. Disaster Med.* **2011,** *6*(3), 187–195. https://pubmed.ncbi.nlm.nih.gov/21870667/.

Nandi, J. Lack of PPE, Poor Infection Control put Medical Staff at Risk of COVID-19. Hindustan times [Internet]. 2020 April [cited 2020 May 28]. https://www.hindustantimes.com/india-news/lack-of-ppe-poorinfection-control-put-medical-staff-at-risk-of-COVID-19/story-5jmeJgwUAaFuu4wfiCu8XN.html.

Siddique, A., et al. Raising COVID-19 Awareness in Rural Communities: A Randomized Experiment in Bangladesh and India, Munich Papers in Political Economy Working Paper No. 9/2020, TUM School of Management.

Sly, L. Hunger Could Be More Deadly Than Coronavirus in Poorer Countries. The Washington Post. May 14, 2020. https://wapo.st/3dXcPWr.

Stallings, R. A.; Quarantelli, E. L. [Special issue]. Emergent Citizen Groups and Emergency Management. *Public Admin. Rev.* **1985,** 93–100.

Sturm, A. Mental Health Stress and Resilience in Times of COVID-19. Physiopedia [Internet]. May 2020 [cited 2020 May 28]. https://www.physio-pedia.com/Mental_Health_Stress_and_Resilience_in_Times_of_COVID-19.

United Nations. Remarks by UN Secretary General Antonio Gutierrez to the ECOSEC Forum on Financing Sustainable Development in the Context of COVID-19. Press Release. April 23, 2020. https://bit.ly/3dsR1l8.

Vladimir, M.; et al. Public Health. *Int. J. Environ. Res.* **2020,** *17*(4124), 1–23.

Weick, K. E. The Collapse of Sensemaking in Organizations: The Mann Gulch Disaster. *Admin. Sci. Quart.* **1993,** *38*(4), 628–652.

Weintraub, K. Not Just Ventilators: Staff Trained to Run them are in Short Supply. Scientific American [Internet]. 2020. April [cited 2020 May 28]. https://www.scientificamerican.com/article/not-justventilators-staff-trained-to-run-them-are-in-short-supply/

World Health Organization (WHOa). Mental Health and Psychosocial Considerations During the COVID-19 Outbreak [Internet]. World Health Organization; 2020 March [cited 2020 May 28]. https://www.who.int/docs/default-source/coronaviruse/mental-health-considerations.pdf?sfvrsn¼6d3578af_2

World Health Organization (WHOb) Publications, Rural Population, 2018. https://www.who.int/publications

Worldometers. Country Wise Number of Active Cases of COVID-19, 2020. https://www.worldometers.info/coronavirus/worldwide-graphs/#total-deaths

CHAPTER 10

Sentiment Analysis for Sustainable Healthcare During Pandemic Outbreak: Lessons Learned from COVID-19

ARCHANA SINGH[1*], SARIKA SHARMA[2], and SANDEEP SINHA[3]

[1]*Associate Professor, Faculty of Commerce & Management, Vishwakarma University, Pune, India*

[2]*Professor, Symbiosis Institute of Computer Studies and Research, Pune, India*

[3]*Head Healthcare Consulting, JLL MENA, Dubai, UAE*

Corresponding author. E-mail: archume02@gmail.com

ABSTRACT

The pandemic outbreak of COVID-19 in March 2020 has been a nightmare for each and every human being globally. To be prepared for such outbreaks in the future is the need of the hour. The study imbibes the role of sentiment analysis with the introduction of what it means and how it can help in such outbreaks through the contribution of information in social media by general public worldwide. Various authors from different parts of the world have contributed toward the study on sentiment analysis used for social media comments through Facebook, Twitter, Pinterest, etc during COVID-19. Two cases from India and UAE have been presented to provide better insight on the usage of sentiment analysis for sustainable healthcare and thereby to enhance the decision-making skills at real time as and when needed.

10.1   INTRODUCTION

Sentiment analysis, also called opinion mining, is the field of study that analyses people's opinions, sentiments, evaluations, appraisals, attitudes, and emotions toward entities such as products, services, organizations, individuals, issues, events, topics, and their attributes (Mäntylä et al., 2018). The roots emerge from public opinion analysis in the era of 20th century. Natural language processing gives rise to sentiment analysis, which is the way toward AI-based text analysis. Today, the buzz word is data analysis and data scientist, who looks for extraction of meaning from unstructured data; sentiment analysis is the first step to provide additional information with lesser cost and time thereby improving the ROI of the company. The area of implementation rises from product reviews like and continues in the fields of stock markets, elections, disasters, medicine, software engineering and cyberbullying, etc. (Yaakub et al., 2019). Due to explosion of data especially in the form of text in digital format, the dire need of sentiment analysis and other NLP techniques can be felt for analyzing the data for better decision-making in today's business scenario. Prabowo and Thelwall (2009) describes the newly introduced sentiment analysis which combines rule-based classification, supervised learning, and machine learning into a new combined method known as hybrid classification, which was tested on reviews of movies, products, and comments of myspace. The authors also proposed a semiautomatic complementary approach for achieving the good level of effectiveness wherein each classifier is contributing to the other classifier. The researchers after lots of models and techniques used have made the sentiment analysis effortless and simple to work on today. Zhang et al. (2009) depict that there is an extensive research on sentiment analysis and opinion mining as it's the need of hour for sustainability in the flattened world digital era connecting all the geographical boundaries. The study also shows major studies have appeared after 2004 making sentiment analysis available and getting attention of general public. Thus, the objective of sentiment analysis is to define instinctive tools which are able to extract subjective information from texts in natural language such as opinions and sentiments so as to create structured as well as actionable knowledge which are used for better decision-making in diverse field of study and to sustain in the volatile market of the digital era.

10.1.1 VARIOUS LEVELS OF SENTIMENT ANALYSIS

Sentiment analysis is the task of classification of target document into positive or negative (Ray and Chakrabarti, 2019). It can be classified into three main classifications as follows (Fig. 10.1).

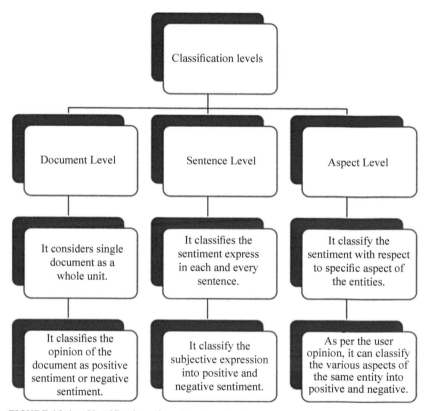

FIGURE 10.1   Classification of sentiment analysis.

Fang and Zhan (2015) explain categorization of sentiment polarity; it is the matter of concern in terms of positive or negative sentiments. The given piece of text can be divided into three levels of sentiment polarity categorization, that is, document level, sentence level, and entity and aspect level. The document level represents about the whole document expressing positive or negative sentiment whereas the sentence level categorizes the sentiments of each sentence, and lastly the entity level categorizes the sentiments on entity and level, for example, what exactly likes and dislikes of people's opinion are on a particular aspect.

10.1.2   PROCESS FOR CARRYING SENTIMENT ANALYSIS

The complex process of sentiment analysis can be divided into five steps as shown in Figure 10.2

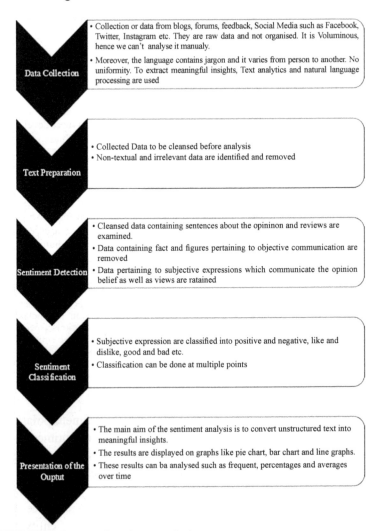

Data Collection
- Collection or data from blogs, forums, feedback, Social Media such as Facebook, Twitter, Instagram etc. They are raw data and not organised. It is Voluminous, hence we can't analyse it manualy.
- Moreover, the language contains jargon and it varies from person to another. No uniformity. To extract meaningful insights, Text analytics and natural language processing are used

Text Preparation
- Collected Data to be cleansed before analysis
- Non-textual and irrelevant data are identified and removed

Sentiment Detection
- Cleansed data containing sentences about the opininon and reviews are examined.
- Data containing fact and figures pertaining to objective communication are removed
- Data pertaining to subjective expressions which communicate the opinion belief as well as views are ratained

Sentiment Classification
- Subjective expression are classified into positive and negative, like and dislike, good and bad etc.
- Classification can be done at multiple points

Presentation of the Ouptut
- The main aim of the sentiment analysis is to convert unstructured text into meaningful insights.
- The results are displayed on graphs like pie chart, bar chart and line graphs.
- These results can ba analysed such as frequent, percentages and averages over time

FIGURE 10.2   Process of sentiment analysis.

10.1.2.1 APPROACHES OF SENTIMENT ANALYSIS

As described by authors for analysis of Twitter data there are two main techniques used for sentiment analysis viz machine learning approaches and Lexicon-based approaches (Kharade and Sonawane, 2016).

10.1.2.1.1 Machine Learning

The machine learning approach is widely applied to forecast the polarity of sentiments based on training datasets and tested the model with testing datasets. In machine learning, further there are two approaches unsupervised and supervised learning. The unsupervised learning rely on clustering whereas supervised depends on labeled datasets which gives meaningful outputs for decision-making. It was also found that in machine learning techniques involves Naive Bayes (NB), Support vector machines (SVM), and maximum entropy (ME). There are two main approaches for sentiment analysis, one is rule based or lexicon method and other is machine learning-based system also known as supervised technique.

10.1.2.1.2 Sentiment Lexicons

Sentiment analysis for social web has become a recent buzz word for identifying the role of emotions during online and offline communication in almost all varied fields using tools like R and Python (Liu, 2013; Kharade and Sonawane, 2016). The mood setting and lexicon extensions are two methods used lately for enhancing the accuracy on specific topic lexical sentiments for social media which is of immense help in improvising the sentiment analysis performance for industry (Liu, n.d.). The sentiment words or opinion words are very important indicators of sentiment analysis. At times phrases or words like good, amazing, awesome for positive sentiment and words, terrible, bad are negative sentiments along with idiom or phrases like, for example, "cost me an arm and leg." These words and phrases are called sentimental lexicon. Lots of algorithms have been made for compiling such lexicons. Rule based or lexicon not only deals with positive, negative, and neutral words but also with emotional, cognitive, and structural component of the texts or phrases based on the dictionary of classified categories (Liu, n.d.). Further sentiment words are further classified into base type and comparative type. Base types are positive or negative sentiments and comparative types includes comparative and superlative opinions like better, worse, best, etc. Example also includes "Pepsi tastes better than Coke." This expression doesn't give an opinion on good or bad but compares Coke and Pepsi. The manual approach, dictionary-based approach, and corpus-based approach are to compile sentiment words.

10.1.2.1.3   Hybrid Technique

The study by Ahmad et al. (2018) study focuses on the literature present through a decade on sentimental analysis using SVM, which is a text-based classification using machine learning techniques. The research trend includes proposal of new techniques including polarity detection and sentiment analysis, usage of hybrid techniques, and classification techniques for sentence and document level sentiment analysis (Figs. 10.3–10.6).

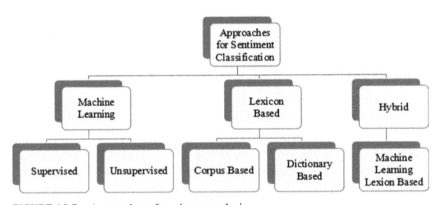

FIGURE 10.3   Approaches of sentiment analysis.

10.1.3   TOOLS USED FOR SENTIMENT ANALYSIS

Some of the popular tools used for sentiment analysis are SentiStrength, Chatterbox, Sentiment140, Textalytics, Intridea, AiApplied, ViralHeat, Lightside, FRN, and BPEF etc and for text analysis popular tools are Discover Text, IBM Watson Natural Language Understanding, Google Cloud Natural Language API, or Microsoft Text Analytics API.

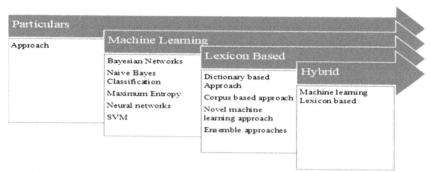

FIGURE 10.4   Comparative analysis of approaches of sentiment classification.

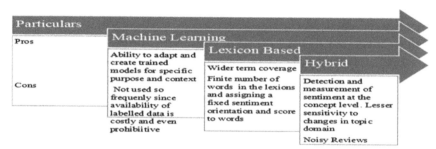

FIGURE 10.5   Pros and cons of sentiment analysis.

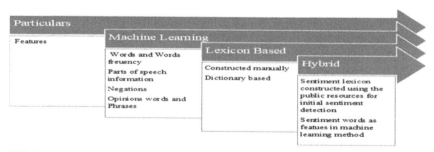

FIGURE 10.6   Features of sentiment analysis.

10.1.4   APPLICATION OF SENTIMENT ANALYSIS IN VARIOUS FIELDS

Under the umbrella of sentiment analysis, with minute demarcation, it can be classified as opinion mining, opinion extraction, sentiment mining, subjectivity analysis, affect analysis, emotion analysis, and review meeting. Earlier the collection of data was a cumbersome process. But nowadays, by the click of the button, enormous unstructured opinion is available online. Let us take the example of Amazon; each and every day, millions of customers voluntarily share their views about the quality of products, service, and feedback about their experience. Fang and Zhan (2015) have done online product review using sentiment analysis of amazon.com which depicts business organizations can reap the benefit to improvise their brand by analyzing these opinions. As the name suggests, it is mining of the public sentiment using the science of text analytics and derive meaningful insights. Usually, individual opinion reflects a broader view. Let us consider Jio has launched a new plan. As soon one customer posts their issues, immediately many people start liking and disliking the post. Moreover, they add their comments as well. Hence, individual opinion is reflective in nature. After collecting the opinions from various sources, analyzing it correctly will result to judge the feelings of many customers. Business organizations should not stop at what they feel; they will be probing in-depth why they feel so. Saad and Yang (2019) in their study revealed the usage of Twitter analysis based on ordinal regression framework using machine learning. The framework included Softmax (multinomial logistic regression), support vector regression, decision tree (DT), and random forest algorithm, wherein DT obtained the best result out of all. Ahmad et al. (2018) has presented a systematic literature review on sentiment analysis by using SVM which is supervised machine learning techniques for text classification which gives an insight of not only the work done in sentiment analysis but also the application in varied field from the year 2012–2017. Kechaou et al. (2013), Zhang et al. (2012), Badjatiya et al. (2019), Abualigah et al., (2020), Palomino et al. (2016) and many more authors have applied sentiment analysis ranging from the product reviews, hate speech detection in Twitter, video news analysis, healthcare, political analysis through different social media platforms. These applications have genuinely helped to predict the outcomes and have taken the corrective measures at the right time and the right place so as to attain the blue ocean market or else to survive in the red ocean market with the competitors.

10.1.4.1   SENTIMENT ANALYSIS APPLICATION FOR SUSTAINABLE DEVELOPMENT GOAL 3

"Sustainability" is the study to balance the ecology by maintaining its natural resources aptly. It also depicts how the modern world without destroying the natural resources can live in harmony with mankind. UNESCO came up with 17 sustainable goals which is the need of the hour to protect today's society. Out of 17 sustainable goals, SDG 3 focuses on health (ensure healthy lives and promote well-being for all at all ages) which was the vital concern during the COVID-19 worldwide as well as the World Health Organization (Fig. 10.7).

Since the last three decades, sustainable global goals has been devised for elimination of poverty, hunger, and improvement of health worldwide which extended toward the 17 goals made in 2015 during the United Nations General Assembly where 193 countries discussed the concerns about the population explosion, loss in biodiversity, spread of diseases, pollution of air and water, terrorism, climate extremities, and depletion of ozone layer (Rica, n.d.). The SDG faced an important challenge to understand which countries faced the above given factors most and how much progress have they made till date. The data for advancement of SDG is mandatory and social media is playing a vital role in information sourcing, wherein the peoples opinion are provided thereby making SDG goals measurable. Further, the authors extends the usage of sentiment analysis is one of the best technique which not only extracts the information from texts and social media but also helps in the implementation of SDG. AlKhatib et al. (2020) in their study depict about sustainable urban development in the form of smart cities to provide high quality life to the residents of Dubai. The sentiment analysis has helped the Dubai government to analyze the sentiments of residents so as to avoid any violence and formulate any laws which are acceptable to the residents and also overall public monitoring is done. Kumar and Joshi (2017) discussed about application of sentiment analysis on governance in India which is linked to all SDG. They deployed ontology-based technique for mining the sentiments of people on the subjects topics discussed in tweets related to ministries of India which included policies, rules, schemes, and thereafter analyzing the citizen's sentiment through a tool SentIndiGov-O using Naïve Bayesian classification of machine learning. Palomino et al. (2016) proposes a nature deficit disorder and nature- health model based on sentiment analysis wherein a dataset was built for analyzing the tweets linked to NDD and made recommendation thereafter on how to disseminate the public health messages which has contributed toward the third goal of SDG on promoting healthy lives. Rica (n.d.) discusses that sentiment analysis has played a vital role in the implementation of SDG for the health benefit of worldwide society.

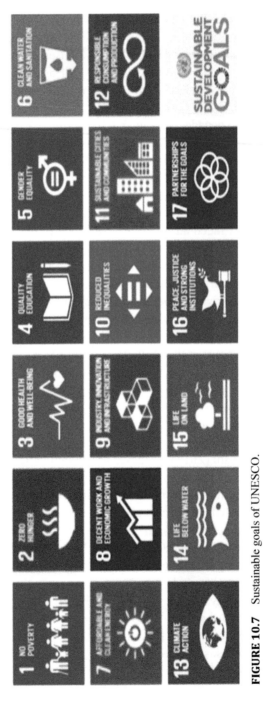

FIGURE 10.7 Sustainable goals of UNESCO.

Reprinted Source: https://en.unesco.org/sustainabledevelopmentgoals

The authors explored the use case on immigration in Columbia and Costa Rica. The issue still persists and is a major concern in the SDG areas of human rights, poverty, unemployment, and security wherein intervention of international organization are much required for the benefit of both the countries. Other than the UNESCO sustainability goals, it is getting tougher day by day for the companies of global stature to compete in the digital world (Pavaloaia et al., 2019). Companies like Pepsi and Coke are using sentiment analysis by analyzing the customers reaction by the types of posts put on social media viz: Instagram, Pinterest, Google, Twitter, Facebook, YouTube, etc. Through the big set of data, sentiment analysis and various statistical tools give a clear picture on the decision-making for marketing strategies to be applied for engaging the millennial. Nowadays not only business organizations are relying upon sentimental analysis to improve the quality of the product as well as service, but also has versatile use wherein it is beneficial for the health sector. It can be used to classify the polarity of sentiment expressed as positive, negative, and neutral. Similarly, it can be applied to evaluate the polarity of outcome of the experiment to understand the enhancement of quality of the outcome. In case of political debate, sentiment analysis can be applied to vote for or against the proposal. It can also be applied for classifying the news as good or bad. Liu (2013) explains about Twitter which is the popular microblogging service for short message writing on any topic across the world in not more than 140 characters. Granger causality analysis of tweets by popular users to understand their genuine popularity through their followers were the one depicting that positive—negative influence were on real-time basis and in the real world.

10.1.4.2 SOCIAL MEDIA ASSISTING SENTIMENT ANALYSIS IN HEALTHCARE

In this digital era where most of the industry are benefitting from the social media feedback, healthcare industry are also part of it wherein the patients seek and share the medical/health information on the internet which gets stored and is analyzed to benefit the healthcare and pharmaceutical industry in terms of meaningful insights. Abualigah et al. (2020) depict that humongous data on healthcare is available online in form of blogs, websites, social media about the medical issues rating not present in a methodological manner, which portrays the dire need of sentiment analysis to improve the quality of healthcare. To get a deeper insight of healthcare industry in terms of requirement of treatment for a particular patient, which hospital is preferred by each patient, quality of services provided, and satisfaction of patients are the queries answered through opinion mining or sentiment analysis. Khan and Khalid (2015) provide insight on the usage of aspect-based sentiment analysis toward initial self-diagnosis by the patients, which are the perspectives for making policies to address their problems in right direction and in right time. The authors also depicts that supervised techniques of machine learning are more accurate than unsupervised but lack in extension toward unknown domain.

10.1.4.3   SENTIMENT ANALYSIS FOR SDG 3 DURING COVID-19

In times of crisis or pandemic like COVID-19, sentiment analysis has played a pivotal role in terms of providing true insights of human emotions toward not only the outbreak of COVID-19 but it also continued for months as and when the phases of lockdown started and people were forced to be at home. This not only impacted the economy of various countries but the physical and mental health was the main concern. Social media post have been a catalyst toward capturing and understanding the human thoughts and feelings during the wee hours of COVID crisis. Myriad posts were put on social media platforms ranging from Facebook, Instagram, Twitter, and many more platforms wherein highlights of people's stories of positive and negative emotions were captured in terms of undergoing preventive measures or recovering from the dreaded disease. Few lost their loved ones and the same emotions were depicted on social media. The sentiment analysis has common parameters to identify the frequency of an emotion. The higher the frequency or appearance of words increases number of times in a set of sample data, this depicts the stronger emotion on that particular topic or agenda. In general, the positive sentiments with huge frequency were words like frontline workers, lockdown, immunity, work from home, social distancing, hope, cure, testing, kits, vaccine, etc. whereas the negative high frequency words included isolation, anger, sadness, depression, symptoms of COVID, travel restriction, borders closed, hospital, death, crisis, economy, unemployment, etc. Out of these, most words were addressed in perspective of healthcare which also included masks, sanitizers, covering face, self-care, immunity booster foods, yoga, etc. Yigitcanlar et al. (2020) analyzed during the outbreak of COVID-19, the mobility of people were restricted due to lockdown in most of the countries and people were left with the usage of digital media to communicate and work. The concerned authorities worldwide had to also rely on the public perception put on social media. The usage of social media analytics was the need of hour for the pandemic-related policy decisions which was done through systematic geo Twitter analysis for Australian states. The study gave valuable insight to the concerned authorities toward understanding the public perception for identifying the needs and demands. Pokharel's (2020) research work has done sentiment analysis of tweets of 12 countries related to COVID-19 to understand the methods at which the public of these 12 countries were handling COVID-19. The analysis depicted that majority of countries took positive approach countries like the United States, the Netherlands, France, and Switzerland showed anger and distrust. The study by de las Heras-Pedrosa's et al. (2020) examined the effect of social media toward communication risk in uncertain contexts which had impact on emotions and sentiment which was done through semantic analysis during the COVID-19 period in Spain. The techniques used were web scrapping and usage of API's. Gohil et al. (2018) represents that there exists number of methods for sentiment analysis of tweets in healthcare which ranges from basic to complex categorization along with expensive commercial software. These methods haven't been tested and accuracy isn't checked which reveals there is a dire need for an accurate and tested tool for analysis of healthcare tweets. Lamsal (2020) in his paper has presented the details of work done by various authors on sentiment analysis during COVID-19 through Twitter analysis. Abd-Alrazaq et al. (2020) studied and analyzed 2.8 million tweets on COVID-19 from February to March 2020, using frequencies of unigrams and bigrams through sentiment analysis and topic modeling to identify the interaction rate of Twitter users in this period. Lwin et al. (2020) further studied the public emotional trends in terms of joy, anger, sadness, and fear during the outbreak of dreaded disease and also the storylines following the same during the time period of January to April 2020. The study depicted that the emotions showed rapid shift from fear to anger also surfacing the anger and joy within few weeks.

10.2 COVID-19: CASE STUDIES FROM INDIA AND UAE

Barkur et al. (2020) showered light on India during COVID-19 outbreak about the one day Janta curfew and also about the 21 days initial lockdown and the sentiments were analyzed through the tweets comprising words like India lockdown and India fights corona. The study depicted amidst of negative sentiments of fear, negativity, and sadness. Due to quarantine, the positive sentiment won in the scenario was trust toward the government so as to flatten the curve which assisted the healthcare sector to take the grip of spread of COVID-19 where the whole world was struggling. Aljameel et al. (2020) reported in their study during COVID-19, that sentiment analysis used on public of UAE contributed valuable information for the safety and health issues and all were addressed in a proper manner. A plan to imbibe precautionary procedure by inculcating the awareness among the residents of UAE was developed. The study collected the Arabic tweets of COVID-19 by utilizing machine learning predictive models like Naïve Bayes, K-nearest neighbor and SVM and the result depicted lowest awareness was in middle region and highest in south regarding the containment measures to be implied. The model also supported the government officials and health officials to deliver appropriate procedure for each region based on the resident's attitude.

10.3 CONCLUSION

The study analyses brief about the usage and importance of sentiment analysis mainly for SDG-Goal 3 during outbreak of pandemics. The study reveals the importance of social media analytics for not only capturing the sentiments of people but also to take appropriate steps to control such outbreaks in the real-time situations. Global organizations like UNESCO, WHO, and government or concerned authorities world-wide have benefitted from the sentiment analysis during the pandemic and have taken appropriate measures and decisions from time to time. In future if some pandemic prevails, the public data can be analyzed on real-time basis and through sentiment analysis for appropriate planning and control to avoid the mortality rate in each country which suffices the third goal of SDG.

KEYWORDS

- **sentiment analysis**
- **sustainable development**
- **COVID-19**
- **machine learning**

REFERENCES

Abd-Alrazaq, A.; Alhuwail, D.; Househ, M.; Hai, M.; Shah, Z. Top Concerns of Tweeters During the COVID-19 Pandemic: A Surveillance Study. *J. Med. Internet Res.* **2020,** *22*(4), 1–9. https://doi.org/10.2196/19016

Abualigah, L.; Alfar, H. E.; Shehab, M.; Hussein, A. M. A. Sentiment Analysis in Healthcare: A Brief Review. *Studies Comput. Intell.* **2020,** *874*(January), 129–141. https://doi.org/10.1007/978-3-030-34614-0_7

Aggarwal, A.; Mehta, S.; Gupta, D.; Sheikh, S.; Pallagatti, S.; Singh, R.; Singla, I. Clinical & Immunological Erythematosus Patients Characteristics in Systemic lupus Maryam. *J. Dent. Educ.* **2012,** *76*(11), 1532–1539. https://doi.org/10.4103/ijmr.IJMR

Ahmad, M.; Aftab, S.; Bashir, M. S.; Hameed, N. Sentiment Analysis Using SVM: A Systematic Literature Review. *Int. J. Adv. Comput. Sci. Appl.* **2018,** 9(2), 182–188. https://doi.org/10.14569/IJACSA.2018.090226

Aljameel, S. S.; Alabbad, D. A.; Alzahrani, N. A.; Alqarni, S. M.; Alamoudi, F. A.; Babili, L. M.; Aljaafary, S. K.; Alshamrani, F. M. A Sentiment Analysis Approach to Predict an Individual's Awareness of the Precautionary Procedures to Prevent COVID-19 Outbreaks in Saudi Arabia. *Int. J. Environ. Res. Public Health* **2020,** *18*(1), 218. https://doi.org/10.3390/ijerph18010218

AlKhatib, M.; El Barachi, M.; AleAhmad, A.; Oroumchian, F.; Shaalan, K. A Sentiment Reporting Framework for major City Events: Case Study on the China-United States Trade War. *J. Clean. Prod.* **2020,** *264*, 121426. https://doi.org/10.1016/j.jclepro.2020.121426

Badjatiya, P.; Gupta, S.; Gupta, M.; Varma, V. Deep Learning for hate Speech Detection in Tweets. 26th International World Wide Web Conference 2017, WWW 2017 Companion, 2019, 2, 759–760. https://doi.org/10.1145/3041021.3054223

Barkur, G.; Vibha; Kamath, G. B. Sentiment Analysis of Nationwide Lockdown Due to COVID-19 Outbreak: Evidence From India. *Asian J. Psychiatry* **2020,** *51*, 102089. https://doi.org/10.1016/j.ajp.2020.102089

de las Heras-Pedrosa, C.; Sánchez-Núñez, P.; Peláez, J. I. Sentiment Analysis and Emotion Understanding During the COVID-19 Pandemic in Spain and its Impact on Digital Ecosystems. *Int. J. Environ. Res. Public Health* **2020,** *17*(15), 1–22. https://doi.org/10.3390/ijerph17155542

Fang, X.; Zhan, J. Sentiment Analysis Using Product Review Data. *J. Big Data* **2015**, *2*(1). https://doi.org/10.1186/s40537-015-0015-2

Gohil, S.; Vuik, S.; Darzi, A. Sentiment Analysis of Health Care Tweets: Review of the Methods Used. *JMIR Public Health Surveill.* **2018**, *4*(2), e43. https://doi.org/10.2196/publichealth.5789

Khan, M. T.; Khalid, S. Sentiment Analysis for Health Care. *Int. J. Privacy Health Inform. Manag.* **2015**, *3*(2), 78–91. https://doi.org/10.4018/ijphim.2015070105

Kharade, V.; Sonawane, S. S. Sentiment Analysis of Twitter Data: A Survey of Techniques. *Int. J. Comput. Appl.* **2016**, *139*(11), 5–15. https://doi.org/10.5120/ijca2016908625

Kumar, A.; Joshi, A. SentIndiGov-O: An Ontology-Based Tool for Sentiment Analysis to Empower Digital Governance, 2017; pp 576–577. 10.1145/3047273.3047340.

Kechaou, Z.; Wali, A.; Ammar, M. B.; Karray, H.; Alimi, A. M. A Novel System for Video News' Sentiment Analysis. *J. Syst. Inform. Technol.* **2013**, *15*(1), 24–44. https://doi.org/10.1108/13287261311322576

Lamsal, R. Design and Analysis of a Large-Scale COVID-19 Tweets Dataset. *Appl. Intell.* **2020**, *October*. https://doi.org/10.1007/s10489-020-02029-z

Liu, X. Full-Text Citation Analysis : A New Method to Enhance. *J. Am. Soc. Inform. Sci. Technol.* **2013**, *64*(July), 1852–1863. https://doi.org/10.1002/asi

Lwin, M. O.; Lu, J.; Sheldenkar, A.; Schulz, P. J.; Shin, W.; Gupta, R.; Yang, Y. Global Sentiments Surrounding the COVID-19 Pandemic on Twitter: Analysis of Twitter Trends. *JMIR Public Health Surveill.* **2020**, *6*(2), 1–4. https://doi.org/10.2196/19447

Mäntylä, M. V; Graziotin, D.; Kuutila, M. The Evolution of Sentiment Analysis. *Comput. Rev.* **2018**, *27*(February), 16–32. https://doi.org/10.1016/j.cosrev.2017.10.002.

Nasukawa, T.; Yi, J. Sentiment Analysis: Capturing Favorability Using Natural Language Processing. Proceedings of the 2nd International Conference on Knowledge Capture, K-CAP 2003, January 2003, 70–77. https://doi.org/10.1145/945645.945658

Palomino, M.; Taylor, T.; Göker, A.; Isaacs, J.; Warber, S. The Online Dissemination of Nature–Health Concepts: Lessons from Sentiment Analysis of Social Media Relating to "Nature-Deficit Disorder." *Int. J. Environ. Res. Public Health* **2016**, *13*(1). https://doi.org/10.3390/ijerph13010142

Pavaloaia, V. D.; Teodor, E. M.; Fotache, D.; Danileţ, M. Opinion Mining on Social Media Data: Sentiment Analysis of User Preferences. *Sustain. (Switzerland)* **2019**, *11*(16). https://doi.org/10.3390/su11164459

Pokharel, B. P. Twitter Sentiment Analysis During COVID-19 Outbreak in Nepal. *SSRN Electron. J.* **2020**, *March*, 1–9. https://doi.org/10.2139/ssrn.3624719

Prabowo, R.; Thelwall, M. Sentiment Analysis: A Combined Approach. *J. Inform.* **2009**, *3*(2), 143–157. https://doi.org/10.1016/j.joi.2009.01.003

Rica, C. (n.d.). Sentiment Analysis to Inform SDGs: Immigration in Colombia and Costa Rica.

Ray, P.; Chakrabarti, A. A Mixed approach of Deep Learning Method and Rule-Based Method to Improve Aspect Level Sentiment Analysis. *Appl. Comput. Inform.* **2019**, xxxx. https://doi.org/10.1016/j.aci.2019.02.002

Ridzwan Yaakub, M.; Iqbal Abu Latiffi, M.; Safra Zaabar, L. A Review on Sentiment Analysis Techniques and Applications. *IOP Conf. Series Mater. Sci. Eng.* **2019**, *551*(1). https://doi.org/10.1088/1757-899X/551/1/012070

Saad, S. E.; Yang, J. Twitter Sentiment Analysis Based on Ordinal Regression. *IEEE Access* **2019**, *7*, 163677–163685. https://doi.org/10.1109/ACCESS.2019.2952127

Yigitcanlar, T.; Kankanamge, N.; Preston, A.; Gill, P. S.; Rezayee, M.; Ostadnia, M.; Xia, B.; Ioppolo, G. How can Social Media Analytics Assist Authorities in Pandemic-Related Policy Decisions? Insights from Australian States and Territories. *Health Inform. Sci. Syst.* **2020,** *8*(1), 1–21. https://doi.org/10.1007/s13755-020-00121-9

Zhang, C.; Zeng, D.; Li, J.; Wang, F. Y.; Zuo, W. Sentiment Analysis of Chinese Documents: From Sentence to Document Level. *J. Am. Soc. Inform. Sci. Technol.* **2009,** *60*(12), 2474–2487. https://doi.org/10.1002/asi.21206

Zhang, W.; Xu, H.; Wan, W. Weakness Finder: Find Product Weakness from Chinese Reviews by Using Aspects Based Sentiment Analysis. *Expert Syst. Appl.* **2012,** *39*(11), 10283–10291. https://doi.org/10.1016/j.eswa.2012.02.166

CHAPTER 11

Design Schema to Offer Security and Confidentiality to Healthcare Data in Cloud Environment

N. THILLAIARASU[1*], RAJU SHANMUGAM[2], K. THIRUNAVUKKARASU[2], and SHAHNAWZ KHAN[3]

[1]School of Computing & Information Technology, Reva University, Bengaluru, India

[2]USCI, Karnavati University, Gandhinagar, India

[3]Department of Information Technology, University College of Bahrain, Bahrain

*Corresponding author. E-mail: thillai888@gmail.com

ABSTRACT

The cloud environment is an emerging technology due to its broad utilization nowadays because of the availability of the internet for processing and storing the information. It offers abundant support such as availability since it eliminates the necessity to provide expensive applications, software, or intricate software. Alternatively, it carries out the operations by making use of cloud-based services, applications, and communications that can be employed based on the need. The cloud environment provides the possibility to store abundant data in terms of inexpensive manner. Overcloud users can make use of the services or applications regardless of their position or devices required for accomplishing analysis. Furthermore, spaced out from gains accumulated from the cloud environment there emerge several threats like safety and confidentiality which lingers to the greatest threat to the system. The confidentiality-related threats might emerge because of the trouble-free access to the cloud resources, protecting the privacy of the data prevailing over the cloud, and examining the cloud routines. Some threat model believes that the service providers of the cloud are intricate to believe since trust is essential for carrying out the encoding of data within the cloud environment but some again believe that the service suppliers of the cloud could be considered while the threats arise from the outer illicit users and the users of the cloud. Various public cloud-related services are currently being implemented over massively consistent companies such as Google and IBM. Furthermore, these firms can design their private clouds in term of their open-source software which is overall the entrusted service supplier model matching the conditions. Consequently, the belief model can trigger the modeling of confidential and safe frameworks that are reliant on the belief-based cloud service providers for accomplishing executable modules within the framework. It pays attention to constructing enormous aggregated confidential and privacy offering framework with trouble-free access to the users.

11.1 INTRODUCTION

Various schemes were modeled by scholars for assessing the prevailing confidentiality safeguarding mechanisms in the cloud environment. It is to be noted that not all schemes offer the fullest secrecy to the data present within the cloud environment. The focus is to perform an analysis of other schemes to model a fresh and novel mechanism for addressing the prevailing disputes.

Nhuong et al. (2018) described that cloud computing is monitored as the increasing techniques modifying the information technology. The information subcontracting is an interesting depiction with the focus of belief storage and talented query implementation to the users. The information is stored in the cloud with increased consideration. Moreover, the safety disputes related to storage over the cloud is a great intimidating reason for the probable consumers. Therefore, the intention is to locate schemes that provide increased safety. Several ailment aggressive firms are focused on planning cloud as information sharing medium. It is mandatory to create interesting solutions with the focus of merging several schemes for creating scalable and adjustable system precisely for accomplishing increased levels of using improved schemes. Here, the focus is on recommending an interesting scheme based on the segmentation, secure scattering, and encoding for medical repositories which will further segment the information over diverse cloud service suppliers. The goal is to design a methodological framework using the vulnerable nature of the data and offers improved levels of safety. The repository for medical system portrays an element link and relational representation. The cloud-based scheme is designed for providing safe patient focused on gaining access to public healthcare documents in an interesting manner. The outcomes are executed using NetBeans Java for assessing the performance based on the conventional cryptography-based schemes for depiction. The designed safety schemes are estimated using CrypTool 1.4 based on the entropy of schemes. The forthcoming system comprises the creation of automated system retrieval, storing, and preservation of information effectively and rapidly.

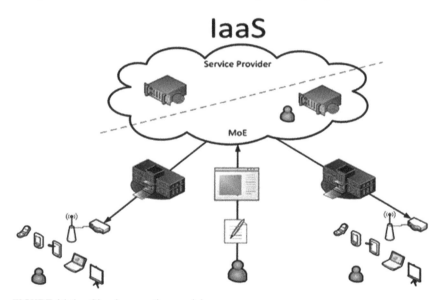

FIGURE 11.1   Cloud computing model.

Banothu et al. (2018) described a fresh methodology for information subcontracting which liberates the information supervision permitting the information creator to effortlessly distribute their information with the besieged users. It also creates fresh disputes in terms of confidentiality and privacy. For safeguarding the safety of the information based on the truthful but interesting service suppliers several assessments are designed to aid the information access governance with accuracy rules.

Moreover, the system is capable to aid both rough access governance and periodicity of time-dependent information. Here, combining the time-based cryptosystem based on the cybertext cryptographic encoding allows designing of fresh governance of time access and elements based on time-dependent information for combining over the public cloud. Here, the designed scheme is based on designing an effective scheme for proposing strategies to gain access to several access prerequisites for time-dependent information. The deep assessment of privacy and performance reveals that the designed scheme is extremely effective and fulfills the privacy prerequisites for information storage over the public cloud.

Gao et al. (2019) portrayed cloud computing is a budding technology and the role of cloud safety becomes more and more crucial in terms of cloud analyses. For enhancing the multiuser information distribution over the hybrid cloud and to improve the safety of hybrid cloud, the intention is to design a fresh safety storage model of hybrid cloud that aggregates the public cloud cost savings and elasticity with the safety and alterations of the private cloud. Moreover, the investigations of safeguarding the information storage and interoperability of the hybrid cloud, the paper makes use of a forward safety key update encoding scheme to assure the safety of confidential information over the hybrid clouds.

Gunavathy and Meena (2019) described that over the present years cloud computing is gaining attention and offers services to the users based on the internet connection. Cloud is a cluster of the information center and servers that are positioned at various locations and these applications are employed by the users on pay peruse with the aid of the internet. The user will pay based on the volume of storage space used by him. The main reason for making use of the cloud is that the user can store and access the stored information into the cloud remotely. The users of the cloud need to bother about safeguarding the software, hardware, and storage space. The key benefits of cloud computing are that all these services are offered at minimal cost for the users. Due to this reason, all the users shift their information on to the cloud. The key risk in cloud computing is safety since the data stored into the cloud is not straightforwardly preserved by the users. While forwarding the information through the internet, any illicit user can alter the information and gain access to it. For addressing the safety risks, several cryptographic and stenography schemes are designed. Here, the intention is on the fundamentals of cloud computing and discussed several cryptographies and stenography schemes prevailing in the traditional methods.

Marwaha and Singh (2019) described that cloud computing is an increasing technology over the prevailing technological age. It is internet-based technology where the user needs to pay based on the usage. Therefore, the great disputes for broad recognition of the cloud are confidentiality and safety over the cloud. The numerical framework of the information sanitization for offering fake look too vulnerable information before communicating the information to the cloud and MAC address are based on the advanced encryption standard for communication the non-vulnerable and sanitized information for the modeled scheme.

Kibiwott et al. (2019) described that mobile technology offers exceptional benefits by offering increased and effective communication and access to healthcare-related services. Hence, the mobile devices are resource-limited. It remains a great drawback for storing and assessing the needed electronic healthcare-related information. To lessen these setbacks, the mobile computing combines expandable cloud computing which remains a great benefit for the mobile users by expanding the restricted device resources which also gives rise to safety and confidentiality risks. To address these disputes, there prevail disputes linked with safety and confidentiality where the creator of the information encodes the information based on the element-based encoding primordial to the finely grained access governance-based benefits as it transfers ciphertext to the cloud. For visualizing the rapid information access, the resource-limited device safely migrates high-level assessments to these resource-rich cloud servers representing with an assurance that the cloud server cannot understand about the plaintext. Here, the goal is to perform a study on element-based encoding with migrated decoded conventional works that are suitable to the resource-limited devices for gaining access to the electronic health big data.

Marwen et al. (2019) portrayed that the volume of records generated on an everyday basis over the healthcare domain is anticipated to grow strongly. For sure the medical image holds essential data to acquire untimely and precise prediction and treatment. Furthermore, the utilization of an electronic medical record system is the most effective way to increase association among healthcare experts to enhance the quality of care and patient results. Based on the usage, complicated software and platforms are needed to effectively store and process these digital documents. Despite their significance creation and preservation under a local information center for hosting these, IT-based services will unavoidably improve the expenses of the healthcare-related services. Promisingly cloud computing has offered healthcare organizations with reasonable and flexible services to address these disputes. Indeed the design system permits these healthcare organizations to gain merits of the remote computational resources provided by external sources. On this regard, the healthcare practitioners could gain control to the stored information of the individuals. These services are priced based on the original utilization of cloud resources. However, the approval of cloud storage over the healthcare domain faces various disputes precisely those linked to safety and confidentiality. Though there prevail various solutions to safeguard the information which are mostly dependant on conventional cryptographic techniques like AES (Advanced Encryption Standard), RSA (Rivest, Shamir, Adleman), and DSA (Digital Signature Algorithm). Therefore, the schemes are often time exhausting and are not suited for medical domain and due to which the designed solution makes use of Shamir's Private share for resolving the issues prevailing on safety in cloud storage. The selection of the scheme needs intricate mathematical operations to encode the information as estimated against the prevailing schemes. It remains an effective solution for assuring error lenience in the cloud environment. Here, the intention is to accurately address information privacy in cloud storage which experimentally assesses the designed scheme to demonstrate its precision. The outcomes of simulation reveal that the designed solution effectively minimizes the safety threats while storing the medical records on remote cloud storage.

11.2 DESIGN INTENTION

The intention is to design an autonomous internet-based trade framework employing encoding based on security and influenced model helping in addressing the prevailing setbacks over the internet-based businesses. These setbacks could be easily addressed using encoding (cyber secutity protection certificate, CSPC) and fuzzy-based keyword (fKE) inquiry to provide data safely stored into the cloud environment. Diverse safety aware applications like healthcare services over the cloud are created with several cheap and diving out benefits with the necessity of enhancing confidentiality. Alongside the design of fresh anonymization scheme for gathering enhanced safety requirements with enhanced usage over the distributed and iterative data sets over the cloud environment. The capability of protecting the data secrecy and improved confidentiality needs are assessed to measure the performance.

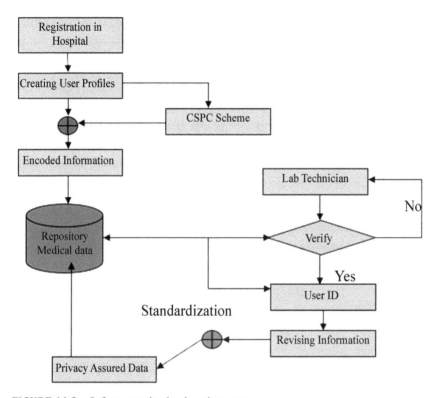

FIGURE 11.2 Safe storage in cloud environment.

11.3 PROPOSED SYSTEMS

The prevailing models do not offer the fullest for implementing internet-based firms effortlessly over the cloud environment. Furthermore, the user falls short in differentiating the bigger online business where the drawbacks are dejected users and businesses to accomplish within the cloud environment. The prevailing confidentiality mechanisms offered to the data hoarded into the cloud environment is demanding and important. For addressing the safety requirements, various mechanisms are designed which greatly disputes in terms of elevated costs, time, and deprived safety features. The goal is to design a fresh scheme for gathering enhanced safety requirements with enhanced usage over the distributed and iterative data sets over the cloud environment. The capability of protecting the data secrecy and improved confidentiality needs are assessed to measure the performance.

11.3.1   AGENT-BASED CONFIDENTIALITY EXPLORATION IN CLOUD

The cycle of the agent-based catchphrase investigation is portrayed in Figure 11.3 where the doctor, influenced individual, and related clients access their profiles. During the presence of a checked profile of the doctor, the required ID of the influenced individual and their related medical services information will be resuscitated to get the normalized data. Because of the checked profile of the influenced individual, the normalized data will be acquired by resuscitating the ID of the influenced individual from the archives. On the off chance that it has a place with different clients an enquiry is requested to the archive dependent on their position. Followed by which, the connected results are shipped off the clients and the code enquiry will be made dependent on coordinating with investigation. Finally, the screened results are restored dependent on the agent-based investigation schedule.

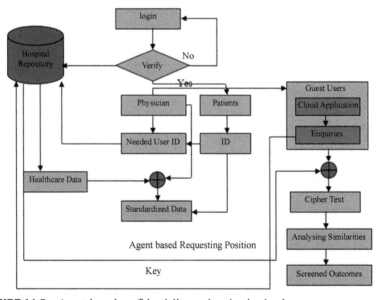

FIGURE 11.3   Agent-based confidentiality exploration in cloud.

11.3.2   DESIGNED SCHEMES

Preliminarily, the association among the trust and safety is needed for assuring a Bayesian-based technique was chosen as it provides a manner of attaining unique probabilities from the gathered safety and earlier information. The modeling of illustrating the trusts is essential to believe for which the trust is characterized. Three parameters are employed over precise logics such as vagueness "*v*" representing the level of average score. "*p*" representing the trust possibilities, and average score "*r*" represents rendered by the earlier analysis.

The below equations represent the parameters:

$$\text{Average scoring, } r = \begin{cases} \dfrac{0.5}{o_p/(o_p+n_p)else} & ifo_p+n_p=0. \end{cases} \tag{11.1}$$

Hence, "*op*" represents the count of positive proofs and "*np*" represents the count of negative proofs.

$$\text{Vagueness, } v = \frac{m_p(o_p+n_p)}{2.d(m_p(o_p+n_p)+m_p(o_p+n_p))} \tag{11.2}$$

Here, "*d*" represents dislocated trust, "*mp*" represents the highest number of proofs. The parameters are used to acquire the highest value of the chosen a(r,v,p) as:

$$a(r, v, p) = p * v + (1-v) * p. \tag{11.3}$$

The trust "*b*" is represented based on the vagueness "*v*" and average scoring "*a*" as:

$$\text{Trust, } b = \frac{v*p}{utmostvalueforanking}*100 \tag{11.4}$$

11.3.2.1 SAFEGUARDING INFORMATION REPOSITORY AND COMMUNICATION SYSTEM

For the modeled confidentiality framework, a onetime password is used for authenticating the users. Passwords are used to comprise the user profile confidentially from illicit users. But the user-created passwords can be negotiated clearly. To resolve these conflicts, a one-time password is greatly used for confidentiality modeling.

Safeguarding Privacy

The goal is to provide a clear insight of the modeled CSPC confidentiality safeguarding in public cloud for safeguarding the privacy. The aim is to upload the data into the cloud for safeguarding them. Here, the assessments were carried out for offering confidential storage and safe search into the cloud environment.

Algorithm

User creation (ci–cn)

For each ci create profile into cloud repository cr

Tree-based characteristics = {Hospital_ID, Physician_ID, User_ID, User_position}

key ← characteristics

information (User_Data, Encoded_key)

cr←upload (information)

for any user (physician, user, lab technician) encode

key elements ← = {Hospital_ID, Physician_ID, User_ID, User_position}

perform encoding of information ie and acquire key sk

if (physician|| lab technician)

perceive information from the cr

if (user)

perceive required information

endif

endif

end for

11.3.2.2 FUZZY-BASED CONFIDENTIALITY ANALYSIS

The mechanism of location-based keyword search comprises the physician, patients, and all associated users desiring to gain access to the profiles. Here, the authorized profile is the physician based on his approval, the ID of the patient and his healthcare-related data are fetched to acquire standard data.

For every user gaining access to cr

Generate (User_guestID, up)

Load inquiry (e)

Categorize (k from e)

Match (k, ie)

If directory matches

Create sk

sk (User_guestID, up)

outcomes (o) ← operate (e, User_guestID)

decode (o, skUser_guestID)

if (o ← revival (cr))

verify (precision (o))

verify (totality (o))

verify (newness (o))

perceive ci ← Generate (User_guestID, up)

endif

if (ci ←cr) && (up actual_position)

assure precision

else

carry out verification

if (ci ←cr) && (up actual_position)

match (e, ci)

if (biased (ci))

reiterate exploration with more precise inquiry

else

assure totality

endif

mine ci ← cr

set up in terms of ti

if (ci within up)

assure evidence of newness

else

reiterate inquiry search

Iterative Anonymization Scheme

The data are divided into categories of rational data segments that are stored in the cloud. The concrete data sets are divided based on the anonymized levels of "k." Based on the combination of fresh data, the modifications can be possibly controlled after commencing the precise anonymized data sets.

Algorithm

Input: o_i, i_f, k_e,

Result: (if + oi)*\

$i_f^* =$ simplify (i_f, k_e)

$o_i = (i_f^* + o_i^*)$

$k_n =$ verify $(k_n > k_e)$

while $(k_n > k_e)$

$(i_f^* + o_i^*) =$ specialization $(i_f^* + o_i^*)$

$k_n =$ verify $(k_n > k_e)$

end

if $(k_n > k_e)$

export (if)

return

end

$(i_f + o_i^*)^* = k -$ closeness $(i_f + o_i)$

export (if)

return

Here, o_f^* represents the anonymized data sets of "k" anonymized levels, i_f^* represents fresh data, "kn" represents the order of oversimplified anonymized data sets.

11.4   PERFORMANCE ANALYSIS

The analyses are performed at undesirable times with various users and their cost-effective transactions that are not distinctive to one another in terms of size, contents, conservatory, and cost involved as in Figure 11.1. Depending on the size of the information, the program execution time varies from user to user as in Figures 11.1 and 11.2.

A few of the cryptography examinations have been moved for making frameworks containing capacity to bear both regular and quantum dangers. At last, they are fundamentally of four key classes of the public key cryptography as involved beneath.

Code-based cryptography

Hash-based cryptography

Lattice-based cryptography

Multivariable-based cryptography

Speed

The multivariable plans (Fig. 11.1) are fast, especially for marks. There win different tips where the multivariable plans are quick than conventional public-key plans, for example, RSA and ECC (eliptic curve cryptography).

TABLE 11.1 Speed Evaluation.

Data size in bits (x-axis)	Speed (y-axis)	RSA	ECC	New scheme
05	50	60	45	70
25	90	80	65	100
32	100	100	70	120
70	110	105	85	145
110	250	120	100	165
155	300	140	120	185
180	375	170	140	200

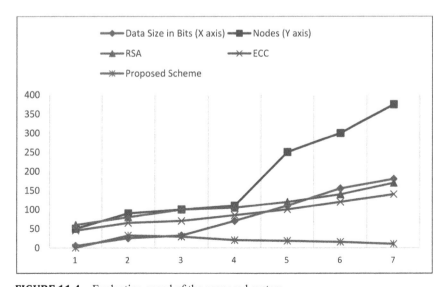

FIGURE 11.4 Evaluating speed of the proposed system.

Saved Computational Needs

The scientific cycles are completed by the multivariable plans that are typically basic enough where a large portion of them need just adding and augmentation over insignificantly limited areas. Henceforth, the multivariable plan need just saved computational assets that make them intriguing for the use over the financially savvy gadgets like RFID chips and shrewd chips without the requirement for the cryptographic coprocessor.

TABLE 11.2 Computation Node Assessment.

Data size in bits (x-axis)	Nodes (y-axis)	RSA	ECC	New scheme
05	50	60	45	0
25	90	80	65	32
32	100	100	70	29
70	110	105	85	20
110	250	120	100	18
155	300	140	120	15
180	375	170	140	10

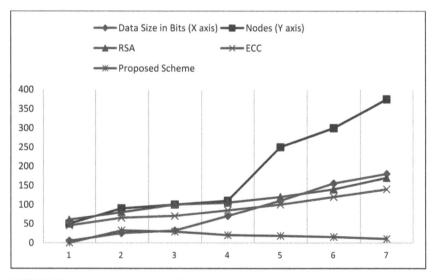

FIGURE 11.5 Assessing computation nodes in the proposed system.

11.5 CONCLUSIONS

The cloud environment is a budding technological advancement that is striking and used by almost all the information technology business platforms. It offers unlimited storage facilities with abundant analysis features. These cheap characteristics without expensive models allow users to employ big data-based applications. The prevailing technologies and interests for cloud computing induce various big data associated applications for migrating them into the cloud for processing and storing them. The key intention is to offer enhanced privacy to the data stored in the cloud environment. The outcomes of the modeling schemes are evaluated in terms of the cost required for evaluation, the cost for transmission, query redressal, encoding time, decoding time, and time for replying to the queries.

KEYWORDS

- **cloud computing**
- **confidentiality**
- **healthcare**
- **record**

REFERENCES

Aldeen Yousra, S.; Mazleena, S. A New Heuristic Anonymization Technique for Privacy-Preserving Datasets Publication on Cloud Computing. *J. Phys.* **2018**.

Banothu, N.; Dayaker, P.; Reddy, B. A Novel Approach for Efficient Data Sharing and Revocation with Data Access Control. *Int. J. Comput. Sci. Eng.* **2018**, *6*(11).

Dhamodaran, V.; Napa, K. K.; Ravulapalli, L. T. A Privacy-Preserving Technique for Incremental Dataset on Cloud by Synthetic Data Perbutation. *Int. J. Eng. Technol.* **2018**, *7*(3), 331–334.

Gao, G.; Wu, L.; Yan, Y. A Secure Storage Scheme with Key Updating in Hybrid Cloud. *Int. J. High Perform. Comput. Netw.* **2019**, *13*(2), 175–183.

Grassi, M.; Rouleaux, N.; Caldirola, D.; Lowenstein, D.; Schruers, K.; Perna, G.; Dumontier, M. A Novel Ensemble Based Machine Learning Algorithm to Predict the Conversion from Mild Cognitive Impairment to Alzheimer's Disease Using Socio-Demographic

Characteristics, Clinical Information and Neuropsychological Measures. *Front Neurol.* **2019,** arXiv.

Gunavathi; Meena. A Survey: Data Security in Cloud Using Cryptography and Stenography. *Int. Res. J. Eng. Technol.* **2019,** *6*(5).

Kibiwott, K. P.; Fengli, Z.; Victor, K.; Anyembe, O. A.; Opoku-Mensah, E. Privacy Preservation for eHealth Big Data in Cloud Accessed Using Resource-Constrained Devices: Survey. *Int. J. Netw. Secur.* **2019,** *21*(2), 321–325.

Kumar, A. S.; Anbarasi, M, S. A Privacy Preservation Framework in Cross-Cloudud Services for Big Data Applications. *Int. J. Curr. Eng. Sci. Res.* **2018,** *5*(2).

Li, Y.; Li, H.; Yao, H. Analysis and Study of Diabetes Follow Up Data Using a Data Mining Based Approach in New Urban Area of Urumqi, Xinjiang, China, 2016–2017. *J. Comput. Math. Methods Med.* **2018.**

Lo-Ciganic, W. H.; Huang, J. L.; Zhang, H. H.; Weiss, J. C.; Wu, Y.; Kwoh, K.; Donohue, J. M.; Cochran, G.; Gordon, A. J.; Malone, D. C.; Kuza, C. C.; Gellad, W. F. Evaluation of Machine Learning Algorithms for Predicting Opioid Overdose Risk Among Medicare Beneficiaries with Opioid Prescriptions. *JAMA Netw. Open* **2019,** *2*, 3.

Marwaha, H.; Singh, R. The Secure Migration of Data to Cloud Using Data Sanitization and MAC Address Based AES. *Int. J. Recent Technol. Eng.* **2019,** *7*(6).

Marwan, M.; Alshahwan, F.; Sifou, F.; Kartit, A.; Ouahmane, H. Improving the Security of Cloud-Based Medical Image Storage. *Eng. Lett.* **2019,** *27*(1).

Nhuong, D.; Shen, J.; Li, T. A Novel Security Scheme based on Instant Encrypted Transmission for Cloud Computing. *J. Secur. Commun. Netw.* **2018.**

Palanisamy, B.; Liu, L.; Zhou, Y.; Wang, Q. Privacy-Preserving Publishing for Multilevel Utility Controlled Graph Datasets. *J. ACM Transac. Internet Technol.* **2018,** *18*(2).

Ram Mohan Rao, P.; Murali Krishna, S; Siva Kumar, A. P. Privacy Preservation Techniques in Big Data Analytics: A Review. *J. Big Data* **2018,** Vol. 5, No. 33.

Ranjithkumar, S.; Thillaiarasu, N. A Survey of Secure Routing Protocols of Mobile Adhoc Network. *SSRG Int. J. Comput. Sci. Eng.* (SSRG-IJCSE) **2015,** *2*.

Shyamambika, N.; Thillaiarasu, N. *A Survey on Acquiring Integrity of Shared Data with Effective User Termination in the Cloud.* 10th International Conference on Intelligent Systems and Control (ISCO), Coimbatore, 2016; pp 1–5. DOI: 10.1109/ISCO.2016.7726893.

Thillaiarasu, N.; Chenthur Pandian, S. *Enforcing Security and Privacy Over Multi-Cloud Framework Using Assessment Techniques.* 10th International Conference on Intelligent Systems and Control (ISCO), Coimbatore, 2016; pp 1–5. DOI: 10.1109/ISCO.2016.7727001.

Thillaiarasu, N., Chenthur Pandian, S. A Novel Scheme for Safeguarding Confidentiality in Public Clouds for Service Users of Cloud Computing. *Cluster Comput.* **2019,** *22*, 1179–1188 https://doi.org/10.1007/s10586-017-1178-8

Thillaiarasu, N.; Pandian, S. C.; Vijayakumar, V.; et al. Designing a Trivial Information Relaying Scheme for Assuring Safety in Mobile Cloud Computing Environment. *Wireless Netw.* **2019.** https://doi.org/10.1007/s11276-019-02113-4

Thillaiarasu, N.; Pandian, S. C.; Naveen Balaji, G.; Benitha Shierly, R. M.; Divya, A.; Divya Prabha, G. Enforcing Confidentiality and Authentication over Public Cloud Using Hybrid Cryptosystems. In *International Conference on Intelligent Data Communication Technologies and Internet of Things (ICICI) 2018. ICICI 2018. Lecture Notes on Data*

Engineering and Communications Technologies; Hemanth, J., Fernando, X., Lafata, P., Baig, Z., Eds.; Springer: Cham, 2019, Vol. 26. https://doi.org/10.1007/978-3-030-03146-6_175

Thillaiarasu, N.; Susmitha, M.; Devadharshini, D.; Anantharaj, T. *Solar Powered Fire Extirpation Robot with Night Vision Camera.* 5th International Conference on Advanced Computing & Communication Systems (ICACCS), Coimbatore, India, 2019; pp 741–744. DOI: 10.1109/ICACCS.2019.8728438.

Triantafyllidis, A. K; Tsanas, A. Applications of Machine Learning in Real – Life Digital Health Interventions: Review of Literature. *J. Med. Internet Res.* **2019,** *21*(4).

Wolff, P.; Grana, M.; Rios, S. A.; Yarza, M. B. Machine Learning Readmissions Risk Modeling: A Pediatric Case Study. *Biomed Res. Int.* **2019**.

Index

Milton Keynes UK
Ingram Content Group UK Ltd.
UKHW051533141024
449569UK00001B/6